CHASING OCTOBER

CHASING OCTOBER
The Dodgers-Giants
Pennant Race of 1962

David Plaut

Diamond Communications
South Bend, Indiana
1994

CHASING OCTOBER

Copyright © 1994 by David Plaut

10 9 8 7 6 5 4 3 2

Manufactured in the United States of America

DIAMOND COMMUNICATIONS, INC.
POST OFFICE BOX 88
SOUTH BEND, INDIANA 46624
(219) 299-9278 or FAX (219) 299-9296

Excerpts from "The D-O-D-G-E-R-S Song" (Oh Really? No, O'Malley), written by Sylvia Fine and Herbert Baker, Dena Music, Inc., Reprise #20105, 1962, have been reprinted with the kind permission of Dena Kaye.

"The D-O-D-G-E-R-S Song" is available on *Baseball's Greatest Hits* (1989), released through Rhino Records, Inc.

Library of Congress Cataloging-in-Publication Data

Plaut, David.
    Chasing October : the Dodgers-Giants pennant race of 1962 / by
David Plaut.
        p.   cm.
    Includes bibliographical references and index.
    ISBN 0-912083-69-7 : $22.95
    1. Los Angeles Dodgers (Baseball team)--History.   2. San Francisco
Giants (Baseball team)--History.   I. Title.
GV878.L6P53 1994
7966.357'64'0979494--dc20   94-9008
                                                             CIP

TABLE OF CONTENTS

To Jonathan
My Artful Dodger...
My Say Hey Kid.

ACKNOWLEDGMENTS

Writing the story of the 1962 National League pennant race has been a longtime goal, but I must frankly confess that I am not and never have been a Dodger or Giant fan. Truth be told, I was a nine-year-old Reds rooter living in Cincinnati back in '62, with far greater interest in *TV Guide*'s fall preview issue than the October playoffs between two traditional rivals.

My zeal for *The Beverly Hillbillies*, *Ben Casey*, and *Bonanza* has waned considerably, but the personalities and events of the '62 season still hold fascination. As both a writer and filmmaker, all I have ever asked is to be given a good story. I believe the saga of this pennant race is a compelling one, and I am indebted to those who have helped me bring it to fruition. I would like to thank my agent, David Black, and his valued associate, Lev Fruchter, for their tireless efforts, and I'm very appreciative of the many editorial contributions of Jill Ann Langford and the staff of Diamond Communications.

Numerous subjects in this book were extremely gracious with their time during lengthy interview sessions. Their recollections are the soul of this story. My thanks to Felipe Alou, Ed Bailey, Red Barber, Buzzie Bavasi, Carl Boles, Doug Camilli, Al Campanis, Andy Carey, Orlando Cepeda, Alvin Dark, Jerry Doggett, Charles Einstein, Ron Fairly, Chub Feeney, Tom Haller, Chuck Hiller, Larry Jansen, Joe Moeller, Mike McCormick, Stu Miller, Billy O'Dell, Billy Pierce, Ron Perranoski, Johnny Podres, Ed Roebuck, Vin Scully, Norm Sherry, Duke Snider, Daryl Spencer, Bob Stevens, Stan Williams, and Maury Wills.

Those who were instrumental in helping me arrange these interviews include Jon Braude with the Cincinnati Reds, Ron Colangelo with the West Palm Beach Expos, Katy Feeney with the National League office, Matt Fischer with the San Francisco Giants, Duke Snider biographer Bill Gilbert, Jay Horwitz with the New York Mets, Steve McCormick with the Winter Haven Red Sox, Craig Pletenik with the Phoenix Firebirds, Larry Shenk with the Philadelphia Phillies, and Mike Williams with the Los Angeles Dodgers.

Jay Lucas of the Dodgers, Erica Boeke of the Giants, and private collector Dick Dobbins deserve special mention for assistance in providing photographs. And no baseball book's acknowledgments could ever fail to mention the superb researchers at the Hall of Fame Library. The contributions of Tom Heitz, Bill Deane, Gary Van Allen, and the rest of the Cooperstown team are evident throughout these pages.

Special music legal clearances were made possible by William Stinehart, Jr., legal counsel for Danny Kaye's estate. I am also grateful to Tom Hedden at NFL Films, Warner Fusselle at Phoenix Communications, and James Austin at Rhino Records. Don Tillman, program director at KTTV/Los Angeles and his operations manager, Ray Green, deserve special thanks, as does Mike Scully of the Phoenix Memorial Hospital Foundation. Gary Wright, Jay and Joyce Cooper, Ben Kessler, Gary Reed, Steve Feinstein—and especially Jeffrey Cooper—are good friends who performed valorous tasks during the book's creation.

I want to thank my parents who instilled in me their passion for reading and writing. They were also the ones who mailed me the *1963 Baseball Almanac* while I was away at summer camp, the book which first piqued my interest in the '62 season.

My greatest ally throughout has been my wife, Joan. She shouldered child-rearing responsibilities, skillfully edited the early drafts of the manuscript, and gave me the strength to complete my work. Without her love and support, this book would never have seen the light of day.

David Plaut
Moorestown, New Jersey
October 1993

THE RIVALRY

1

WHERE WERE YOU IN '62?

Nineteen-sixty-two is often considered "the last year of American innocence." It is a label likely attached more for what took place the *following* year: the assassination of a United States president. To many, the shocking death of John F. Kennedy was the cataclysmic event which ended the soothing, if somewhat narcotizing 1950s, and dragged a shaken, stunned nation—and the world—into the uncharted cacaphony of the true 1960s.

Nineteen-sixty-two was also a watershed year within the smaller world of baseball's National League. Two freshly minted expansion teams, an enlarged schedule and the opening of the prototypical modern ballpark signalled the birth of a new era for the game. While these icons of the sport's future were thrusting baseball forward, the season's pennant race was a vivid reminder of one aspect of the game that would eventually be left behind.

In 1958, after more than a half-century in New York City, the Dodgers and Giants had unceremoniously departed Brooklyn and Manhattan for the West Coast. There are those who contend that it was this disruption that brought on baseball's own loss of innocence. But the finality of that loss may have only fully registered after 1962, when the two bitter foes staged, perhaps for the last time, a pennant race that truly equalled the fervor of their New York battles. In a year when so many baseball traditions were challenged, the game's oldest rivals successfully reenacted the drama of a bygone era. There would be other competitive Dodger-Giant races in future seasons, but after 1962, it was never the same.

* * *

The '62 season lasted 191 days, extending over nearly seven full months. Compared against all other major league seasons prior to divisional play, it remains the longest in baseball history.

For a campaign of such uncommon duration, its final result was customarily familiar. For the 20th time in 39 years, the New York Yankees

1

became world champions. That was expected. But much that did occur in '62 could hardly be considered "business as usual."

Unprecedented events commenced in early January, when former Brooklyn star Jackie Robinson became the first black player ever to be voted into the Hall of Fame. More history was made in the summer months, as longstanding big league records were broken with surprising regularity. A *present*-day Dodger infielder, Maury Wills, played in a record number of games and stole more bases in a season than any man before him.

At age 41, Milwaukee's Warren Spahn earned victory number 327, the most ever by a left-handed pitcher. Twenty-seven-year-old Tom Cheney, a journeyman for the Washington Senators, struck out an all-time-high 21 batters in a game, even though it took him 16 innings to do it. Kansas City's Bill Fischer became baseball's ultimate "control freak," pitching a record 841/3 innings without issuing a walk. At age 43, Pirates pitcher Diomedes Olivo debuted as the oldest rookie in major league history. And Bob Buhl of the Cubs established an unenviable mark of slugging futility for a full season by going hitless over 70 at-bats.

No dubious individual deeds could match the pathetic performance of the expansion New York Mets—losers of a record 120 games. And no young team was more inspiring than the Los Angeles Angels, pennant contenders until mid-September and winners of 86 games in only their second season of existence. The Angels' playboy pitcher, flamboyant Bo Belinsky, fired the first of the year's five no-hitters. Another rookie, Cubs infielder Ken Hubbs, set a fielding record for second basemen, handling 418 chances over 78 games without an error.

Hubbs and the Cubs were led by three rotating dugout bosses, the result of a previously untried system known as the "College of Coaches." That was the extent of managerial "movement" throughout the major leagues. For the first time in 20 years, not one manager was fired or replaced during the regular season.

While old records were seemingly shattered almost every week, baseball's off-field business climate was calm by contrast. Ownership continued to rule the game with an iron fist. Free agency, arbitration, and billion-dollar television contracts were still years into the future. The minimum wage was $7,000, the average major league salary $16,000. Spring holdouts were few and player strikes nonexistent—unless you counted the aborted August work stoppage of the Pittsburgh Pirates. The issue—the Bucs' objection to a rainout being rescheduled as a night game prior to a doubleheader the next afternoon. *This* was what passed for heated player-management confrontation in 1962.

* * *

Socially, politically, and culturally, it was also a simpler time. As a people, Americans still basically believed what their leaders told them. They trusted what they read in the newspapers and what they heard on television. And why not? Unless you were poor or black, life was pretty good. No other nation in the world came close to equalling the U.S. gross national product or standard of living. Unemployment was well below six percent. Industrial production totals hit record numbers, as did capital investment for plants and equipment. New automobile orders reached a postwar high, powered by continued economic prosperity—and gasoline prices that were still only about 21 cents a gallon.

Such cheap fuel was also leaded fuel—a deadly energy source that belched out harmful fumes into the atmosphere. The cars' interiors were equally unsafe—seatbelts were not required in domestic vehicles, so nobody wore them.

In fact, much of the behavior America practiced was hazardous to its health. In 1962, the first-ever public service warning about the dangers of cigarettes was aired on television, yet more than half of all Americans continued to smoke. They taxed their hearts further by consuming a diet laden with red meat and dairy products. Illegal narcotics were not the widespread problem they would eventually become, as millions of citizens turned instead to liquor as their drug of choice.

Industrial factories sustained the practice of dumping chemical waste and garbage into rivers and streams, and farmers sprayed a variety of pesticides on their crops with barely a whimper of protest from the government. It wasn't until the November '62 publication of Rachel Carson's seminal book, *Silent Spring,* that the issue of industrial pollution was even addressed in a public forum.

Of greater concern to Americans was the threat of nuclear war. Relations between the United States and the Soviet Union had worsened following 1961's aborted American invasion attempt of communist Cuba at the Bay of Pigs—and an unsuccessful Vienna summit meeting between President Kennedy and Soviet leader Nikita Krushchev. Both superpowers still regularly conducted atmospheric nuclear tests while increasing their weapons stockpile, heightening fears about the future. Such tensions contributed to troubled sleep for children who agonized through nightmares of nuclear holocaust, while also spurring the boom of an American cottage industry—the fallout shelter.

Nineteen-sixty-two proved to be the peak year for these underground havens of "safety." In January, the Department of Civil Defense acknowledged that massive city evacuations simply could not be successful, given the brief warning time citizens would have in the event of enemy attack. The department encouraged instead the amassing of more public and private shelters. For construction firms, lumber and steel companies, and manufacturers of canned foods, cots, and storage units, Civil Defense's official pronouncement guaranteed a healthy fiscal bottom line.

You didn't necessarily have to be in the bomb shelter business to make money in 1962. As Americans gained more leisure time and disposable income, they turned to new products to improve their lives. Pop-top tabs on aluminum cans were invented, the better to open the first low-calorie soda ever marketed, Royal Crown's Diet Rite Cola. Polaroid introduced new color film that developed snapshots in 60 seconds. Improved technology was making color television less expensive and more widely available. These and other modern conveniences could all be purchased at a friendly neighborhood emporium, including a brand new retail center called KMart, which opened its first store in Garden City, Michigan.

Other technological advances contributed to national pride. In February, astronaut John Glenn struck a blow for his country in the space race by becoming the first American to orbit the earth. Further domestic fears about superior Russian satellite technology were soothed in July when AT&T's Telstar beamed the first-ever pictures from space to television screens in the United States, Great Britain, and France. Technology was making the world smaller—even as its boundaries were changing.

Across the globe, colonies and protectorates such as Algeria, Jamaica, Trinidad-Tobago, and Uganda broke from their mother countries to become independent nations. Standing regimes in Syria, Peru, and Yemen were toppled. But these events, while notable, did not directly relate to the sobering cold war conflicts between East and West.

One such flashpoint that did was in Southeast Asia, where the escalation of military action between communist North Vietnam and free-world-backed South Vietnam convinced the U.S. government to increase its number of American "advisers" from 700 to 12,000. An incident of potentially more tragic consequences occurred when Soviet nuclear warheads targeted for U.S. cities were clandestinely installed in Cuba. A tension-filled diplomatic showdown between Russia and the United States lasted for seven nerve-wracking October days before the Soviets finally agreed to dismantle their weapons. The favorable results of the Cuban Missile Crisis proved to be the greatest triumph of John F. Kennedy's presidency, but was only a part of the personal imprint he stamped on his era.

Kennedy was the youngest man ever elected to the White House, and he channeled his appealing youth and energy (or "vigah," as it sounded when spoken by the Boston-born JFK) to launch his "New Frontier." Kennedy beckoned Americans into the service of their country, heightening their enthusiasm with the creation of the Peace Corps and other new programs that were especially appealing to his young followers.

The glamorous aura of the Kennedy family resonated just as deeply among the American people. JFK was handsome, masculine, and witty, yet was also a loving father of two spirited young children. Attractive First Lady Jacqueline Kennedy brought high-brow sophistication back to the nation's capital and set the standard in women's fashion. Her photogenic talents were evident in February of '62 when Jackie guided a nationally televised tour of the White House.

The Kennedys were active patrons of the arts. They frequently hosted operas and classical performances, and held the first jazz concert ever staged at 1600 Pennsylvania Avenue. Educators, philosophers and film stars were included among their closest friends. Blessed with wealth, power, good looks, and incalculable charisma, the Kennedys were the closest approximation to American royalty. Such deification prompted the press to label all things Kennedy as part of the reign of "Camelot."

Even the lampooning of the Kennedy clan was viewed as an expression of affection. A popular 1962 record, *The First Family*, poked good-natured fun at the president, and in so doing became, for many years, the bestselling comedy album of all time. JFK, ever the good sport, admitted he enjoyed the performance but confessed that his alter ego, comedian Vaughn Meader, "sounded more like [brother] Teddy than me."

In other respects, the president was still a man of an earlier time. Kennedy's willingness to wage an aggressive cold war against communism superseded the zeal of some right-wing Republicans. On the issue of civil rights, JFK was more of a Johnny-come-lately. His support proved symbolic and superficial until events such as the '62 Mississippi riots demanded more forceful action. Even so, it was undeniable that his beguiling personality encouraged a national spirit of vitality—a "can-do" confidence that reached its zenith in 1962.

This fresh breeze of enthusiasm inevitably carried over into 1962 mainstream art forms and culture, which had been stifled during the '50s decade of anti-intellectualism. Andy Warhol's startling new "Pop Art" debuted at an exhibit in New York. The Greenwich Village folk-revival movement spawned *The Free-Wheelin' Bob Dylan*, a thought-provoking second (and more widely heard) album from the most politicized voice of '60s music.

On Broadway, the acid-tongued *Who's Afraid of Virginia Wolff?* introduced theatre audiences to language previously unheard on the New York stage. Controversial films *Lolita, Lonely Are the Brave, The Manchurian Candidate,* and *To Kill a Mockingbird* opened, while an increasing number of intellectually stimulating books were also being published. The titles included James Baldwin's *Another Country*, Ken Kesey's *One Flew Over the Cuckoo's Nest*, and Marshall McLuhan's *The Gutenberg Galaxy*. One '62 release that probably had the most lasting influence was *Cosmopolitan* editor Helen Gurley Brown's *Sex and the Single Girl*, her then-shocking polemic on a new code of personal conduct for the modern woman.

Despite these bursts of originality, much of the '62 culture was still grounded in the relative safety of the decade that preceded it. Ranking among the top box-office movie hits were *How the West Was Won*, Walt Disney's *In Search of the Castaways,* and *The Music Man*. *Billboard*'s musical Top 10 included David Rose's orchestral rendition of "The Stripper" and "Johnny Angel" a bathetic teen anthem from Shelley Fabares. Even 1962's number one song was decidedly mainstream. "Stranger on the Shore" a pop-jazz instrumental performed by an English clarinetist named Mr. Acker Bilk, sold more copies than competing singles by Elvis Presley, Ray Charles, Connie Francis, or The Four Seasons.

Another loyal subject of the British Empire rose to the top of his field in '62 when Australia's Rod Laver became the first man to win the Grand Slam of tennis in 24 years. The wait for a champion was considerably shorter in the year's main boxing event. It took barely two minutes of the first round for surly faced challenger Sonny Liston to seize the heavyweight crown from an outgunned Floyd Patterson.

Other sports records were emphatically shattered by Wilt Chamberlain of the Philadelphia Warriors, who became the first player in NBA history to *average* 50 points a game, a figure helped along by Wilt's record-setting, 100-point performance on March 2nd in Hershey, Pennsylvania. Despite Chamberlain's prodigious output, the rival Boston Celtics won their fourth consecutive league title. Other 1962 champions also had the ring of familiarity: Toronto's Maple Leafs earned a 10th Stanley Cup, the Green Bay Packers took their second consecutive NFL football championship, and golfer Arnold Palmer wore his third green jacket at the Masters.

Sports fans also witnessed the first-ever nationally televised fatality—Emile Griffith's lethal knockout of Benny Paret during their welterweight title bout. Paret's stunning death and virtually all live sports of 1962 were broadcast primarily in black and white. Even the increasing number of households with color TVs were limited to monochrome images except in prime time, the only block in the network schedule where color programs could be found.

NBC led the pack, with color available in nearly 70 percent of its evening lineup. It wasn't until 1962 that ABC finally broke through the broadcast color barrier with the cartoon series, *The Jetsons.* Virtually all CBS shows were still living in a black and white world. Despite the color void, CBS was the top-rated network, boasting such hits as *Perry Mason, Red Skelton, Andy Griffith,* and *Candid Camera.*

Westerns still rode tall in the TV saddle in '62. *Wagon Train, Bonanza,* and *Gunsmoke* were among the highest-rated programs, while additional "oaters" *Rawhide, Lawman, Maverick,* and *The Rifleman* also drew sizeable audiences. Domestic sitcoms maintained their popularity: *Danny Thomas, My Three Sons, Dennis the Menace,* and *Dick Van Dyke* were all top 20 programs in the ratings.

The runaway hit of 1962 was the saga of a clan of Ozark hayseeds who accidentally struck oil, got rich, then "loaded up the truck and moved to Beverleee…Hills, that is…swimmin' pools, movie stars…" *The Beverly Hillbillies* debuted in late September, and within six weeks became the number one show on television, the most meteoric rise by any new program since *The $64,000 Question* in 1955. Audiences across America delighted in watching the homespun yokels in the Clampett family trample the ostentatious excesses of Beverly

Hills, outwitting the snooty hoi polloi of the most conspiciously wealthy community in the country.

* * *

Although the basic premise of *The Beverly Hillbillies* was scarcely believable, the Clampetts, in their own way, followed a path that had been well travelled since the end of World War II. The urge to settle the unconquered frontier had always stirred within the souls of restless and ambitious Americans. "Go west, young man," implored Horace Greeley a century before. After 1945, millions followed his advice and headed to California.

Much of the Golden State's attraction emanated from its economic opportunities. Jobs were plentiful, primarily because many California industries contributed goods vital to the cold war: fuels, armaments, aerospace, shipbuilding, atomic research, automobiles. Backed by subsidies from the deep pockets of Uncle Sam, the state economy boomed, allowing workers to plunk down their earnings for a surburban dream home in seemingly no time at all.

Dreams were an essential component of the California migration, particularly in Los Angeles, home to the motion picture and television industry. Moviegoers were initially entranced by the images of "Lotusland" on the big screen in their hometown theatres, then the little screens on their TV sets. The warm climate beckoned to those shivering in the northeast. The mountains and beaches lassoed folks bored with endless prairie flatlands. The glamor of Hollywood hooked just about everyone else.

San Francisco's divergent, yet equally compelling appeal derived from its inherent beauty, international flavor, and high level of sophistication. Most attractive to newcomers may have been the city's "live and let live" morality—an attitude that accepted those with different viewpoints or alternative lifestyles. Some migrants may have been "square pegs" or disenfranchised outcasts in their hometowns, but in San Francisco, they were tolerated, even welcomed.

Appropriately, the state motto is "Eureka!" which, translated from its Greek origins, means "I have found it." For the millions who abandoned a familiar, if stagnating present for California's propitious future, California's official slogan was no empty promise. Whatever "it" was, newcomers by the thousands must have discovered what they were looking for. By 1962, California became, for the first time, the most populous state in the Union.

* * *

The majority of that population lived in the Los Angeles metropolitan area. By strict definition, L.A. was not a city at all, but rather a scattered collection of individual communities linked by ubiquitous miles of serpentine highways. This was exactly the way the pioneer-spirited Angelenos wanted it. As author David Rieff observed, "It was an old Los Angeles conceit, this belief in the automobile as haven in a heartless world, and of the freeways as an untrammeled frontier. Cowboys don't ride buses. The act feels like a demotion from one's Americanness. Traffic jams or no traffic jams, every car trip is a kind of miniature version of the fresh start that moving is felt to represent."

By the early '60s, there were four million cars serving seven million people, and Los Angeles was virtually the only major metro area in the United States that still did not operate a comprehensive rapid transit system.

Many of these motorists drove daily to jobs in shipping, finance, or agriculture, but L.A.'s high-profile industries were tourism and show business. Graying skies filled with thickening automobile smog did not deter the multitudes who visited annually to "catch a wave," tour a movie studio, or stargaze at celebrities.

Nightly network TV programs set in L.A. and Top 40 music extolling southern California beach bunnies were *de facto* free advertising for the Los Angeles Chamber of Commerce, civic boosters who eagerly positioned the city as the mecca of leisure activity. A welcomed ally was the affluent baby boom generation growing up in southern California during the '50s and '60s, teenagers only too happy to perpetuate the casual images marketed by their elders.

By 1962, the surfing craze had grown from a regional California fad to a national obsession, thanks to hit records by L.A.-based acts such as Dick Dale and the Deltones, The Surfaris, Ventures, and of course, The Beach Boys. Pop culture observers Jane and Michael Stern characterized the surfing fad as a "carefree cosmology of twanging guitars, hot-rod cars, the smells of suntan lotion and sizzling cheeseburgers at an oceanside drive-in, and girls in bikinis and guys in tight white Levi's...a fountain of eternal youth, represented by the ocean's waves and a sun that always shone."

Such activity only substantiated the popular notion that southern Californians sought pleasure over other humanly pursuits. It didn't seem to matter. If good times and glamorous looks carried greater cachet than intellectual growth, so be it. Author Aldous Huxley carped disdainfully at Los Angeles when he wrote, "Thought is barred in this city of Dreadful Joy, and conversation is unknown." Most L.A. natives, and nearly every tourist, couldn't have cared less.

Three-hundred-thirty-seven miles to the north lay San Francisco, a city more familiar with fog, rain and brisk winds than L.A.'s perpetual sunshine and gentle breezes. The harsher northern California climate affected its populace sociologically, just as surely as southern California's benign weather sustained the unbridled hedonism of its citizens. Like the weather, the behavior of Bay Area natives could often be construed as cool and blustery.

It wasn't simply the chill in the air that shaped San Francisco attitudes: Here was a city that had once been levelled by earthquake, and its citizens knew another could occur at a moment's notice. This constant fear may have partially contributed to the natives' provincial and protective feelings toward their town. But such nurturing instincts went beyond preservation for survival's sake alone. San Franciscans *knew* they were superior to Los Angeles, and truly believed their city was also the most civilized and sophisticated in the country—perhaps even the world.

Its scenic beauty was unparalleled. San Francisco was built in and around 42 hills overlooking a breathtaking bay, the hub of the shipping industry, core of the city's economy (along with banking and insurance). Unlike the vast sprawl of Los Angeles, the town proper was tightly confined to an area of less than 47 square miles, borders easily travelled by San Francisco's indigenous cable cars or buses. Within these smaller boundaries lived people of varying nationalities, many who had settled permanently upon arriving in the West Coast's busiest port city. Their numbers included the inhabitants of Chinatown, center of the largest Chinese settlement outside of Asia.

At one time Chinatown was bordered on Pacific and Kearny Streets by the "Barbary Coast," a district of opium dens, whorehouses, and saloons that catered to rough-and-tumble seafarers on shore leave during the middle of the 19th century. Although the Barbary Coast's heyday was brief, it set a precedent for the existence of enclaves catering to those with unquenchable prurient interests.

San Francisco's tolerant nature also made it a haven for a variety of Bohemian movements, dating as far back as the 1840s. Writers, poets, and musicians coexisted and even thrived in the community. The San Francisco Renaissance of the 1950s begat the "Beat Generation," disaffected youths who rejected the conventional mores of the Eisenhower era. Influenced by the writings of Jack Kerouac and Allen Ginsberg, the Beats centered in the North Beach area, which, in time, became a magnet for other counterculture interests. Jazz performances became a North Beach staple. Nightclubs such as the *Purple Onion* and *hungry i* featured avant-garde comedians Lenny Bruce and Mort Sahl, and also popularized folk artists such as The Kingston Trio.

In 1962, Students for a Democratic Society (SDS), a group espousing liberal causes, officially formed in Port Huron, Michigan. They were two years behind those San Franciscans who had already made inroads on behalf of social change. As early as 1960, committed activists at the University of California-Berkeley had sown the seeds of Cal's Free Speech Movement by disrupting House of Un-American Activities hearings at San Francisco's City Hall.

Even a perceived moderate such as President Kennedy was not immune to radical Bay Area protests. At least two groups announced plans to picket the president's Berkeley speech in March of '62. They targeted their criticism at JFK's policies on military spending, civil rights, the Bay of Pigs—even America's accelerating commitment to Vietnam. This was happening two years before the war was officially escalated, and five years prior to the national antiwar movement. Clearly, San Francisco could stake its claim as the most liberal of American cities.

Unfortunately, the city also led in areas of a more dubious nature. By 1962, San Francisco topped the nation in suicides, and suffered the country's highest accident rate. San Francisco was also first in mental health patients and alcoholism. More than twice as many San Franciscans died from cirrhosis of the liver than in any other city in the country—including Los Angeles, the despised neighbors to the south.

In 1962 America, it would have been impossible to find two places as geographically close but as profoundly different as San Francisco and Los Angeles. On the map, they were cities in the same state. By all other comparisons, they were worlds apart.

* * *

Los Angeles and San Francisco had long sustained a mutual disregard, hatred blended with a tinge of jealousy for what one town possessed that the other did not. Some, like San Francisco columnist Herb Caen, reveled in the intrastate feud. "The rivalry is a reflex built at birth. It is firmly a part of the mystique of each city—and why not? In this era of blandness verging on torpor, and conformity close to nonthink, it's fun to have an object of automatic disdain so close at hand."

Bay Area native and Baseball Hall-of-Famer Joe Cronin offered a more visceral opinion: "You can talk all you want about Brooklyn and New York, Minneapolis and St. Paul, Dallas and Fort Worth, but there are no two cities in America where the people want to beat each other's brains out more than in San Francisco and Los Angeles." On California's major league baseball diamonds during 1962, Cronin was absolutely correct.

The Dodgers-Giants rivalry was fought on New York turf until 1958, when the two teams moved to California. Since that time, no West Coast version of the rivalry has ever eclipsed the fervor of the '62 hostilities.

The tightly bunched final standings at the conclusion of a feverish pennant race is one measure of verification. Attendance figures provide another: The two teams played head-to-head in 21 games that attracted nearly one million fans. Ratings for Dodger-Giant telecasts in both cities routinely reached 70 percent, and radio broadcasts usually grabbed three quarters of the listening audience. One Bay Area phone service providing inning-by-inning results received in excess of 25,000 calls per day in '62.

Newspapermen in both towns reserved their most acidic barbs for the rival cities. Of the Bay Area's liberal moralities and chilling weather, Jim Murray of the *Los Angeles Times* jeered, "San Francisco isn't a city—it's a no-host cocktail party. It has a nice, even climate: it's always winter." Noting the Giants' past proclivities for failing in clutch situations, *Los Angeles Herald-Examiner* columnist Melvin Durslag issued this sarcastic recommendation: "San Franciscans [who expect a pennant] are advised to stay away from coarse foods... avoid stimulants that irritate the stomach walls...if seized by a choking feeling, lay quietly and well-covered until your physician arrives."

The *San Francisco Chronicle*'s Art Rosenbaum returned the fire by perpetuating the phrase "Smodgers" (in reference to the pervasive smog that hung in the Los Angeles atmosphere), while also penning prose chiding L.A. as "a city whose women would attend the opera in leopard shirts and toreador pants if indeed they attended the opera at all." Colleague Herb Caen tersely added, "Isn't it nice that people who prefer Los Angeles to San Francisco live there?"

The ballplayers on both teams fed on the frenzy—and the lineage of the historic feud itself. Dodgers pitcher Johnny Podres took part in the rivalry on both coasts. "It may not have matched the spirit of the New York days, but it was still a great rivalry. You always got fired up playing the Giants." L.A. shortstop Maury Wills could feel "...definite tension in the air. It reminds me of a homecoming college football game. Each time we face San Francisco, it's different than any other National League series."

Established veterans from Brooklyn taught youngsters such as infielder Ron Fairly to "hate the Giants more than any other team. I'm sure that the Giants weren't too fond of us, either—and that's exactly the way we wanted it." Dodger infielder Jim Gilliam regarded the Giants' Willie Mays as "one of the best friends I ever had in my life, but there was no way we would talk to each other on the field. Not even a hello." Nineteen-year-old L.A. rookie Joe Moeller caught on quickly, too. "Against the Giants, you just tried that much harder. Even if the Giants had been in last place, we would've wanted to beat them worse than the frontrunners."

In San Francisco, the feeling was mutual. Alvin Dark, who played for the Giants in the East and managed them in the West, rejected the view that the California battles weren't as fierce. "I don't care where you play these games—the Dodger-Giant rivalry is always intense." First baseman Orlando Cepeda noticed the difference during pregame batting practice. "Usually, in the batting cage, guys on other teams would come over and exchange ideas, say hi. When we played the Dodgers, we wouldn't talk to them. Every game had a playoff atmosphere."

Outfielder Felipe Alou regarded each series as "a special event that required a much greater level of preparation." Slugger Willie McCovey sensed the difference even before the Giants got to the stadium. "When you stepped off the plane in Los Angeles, you could *hear* the electricity. Even the skycaps at the airports were all wrapped up in the rivalry. It carried over to the hotel and finally the ballpark. The tension was always there."

Since the early 1900s, that tension was sustained over the course of a traditional 154-game schedule, providing the Dodgers and Giants with a minimum of 22 guaranteed meetings every year. But in 1962, that number shrank to 18 while the overall size of the National League enlarged. The American League created two new franchises in 1961; now it was the N.L.'s turn.

This redistribution of talent created a noticeable jump in run production and a shocking regression in overall quality pitching. Seven of 10 clubs finished above .500 by routinely beating up on the three remaining patsies. The on-field performances that resulted demanded sweeping revisions in baseball's record books. Clearly, expansion had permanently reconfigured the competitive—and geographic—landscape of the National League.

After a four-year absence, N.L. baseball returned to New York with the creation of the Mets. Another ballclub, the newborn Houston Colt .45s, was also added. Eight additional games were tacked onto the schedule, a total that, at the time, designated the 1962 season as the lengthiest in National League history.

Even the extra regular-season games were not enough for Los Angeles and San Francisco to conclusively determine which team would win the pennant. A best-of-three playoff series pressed the newly expanded schedule into overtime, adding a significant chapter to the lore of the rivalry. The battle for the 1962 National League championship ranks favorably alongside the storied New York-based feuds that preceded it—and unquestionably remains the most dramatic pennant race ever staged between the Dodgers and Giants within the boundaries of California.

2
WESTWARD HO!
THE RIVALS

By 1962, the West Coast incarnation of baseball's longest, most heated rivalry was clearly established. After four years in the Golden State, the Dodgers and Giants had already battled head-to-head in two turbulent pennant races. In 1959, season-long frontrunner San Francisco collapsed in September, dropping seven of its last eight games. Their egregious slump allowed both Los Angeles and the late-arriving Milwaukee Braves to pass them, en route to a postseason pennant playoff (which L.A. won). The Dodgers and Giants waged another closely contested duel in '61, but neither had enough stamina down the stretch to overtake the surprising Cincinnati Reds.

There would be no legitimate third parties, no other serious intruders to distract the Dodgers-Giants competition in '62. From the first pitch of April until the final out in October, the two California clubs staged a furious pennant fight that was every bit the equal of the fractious feuds waged during the rivalry's New York heyday.

By 1962, the rivalry itself was only a few years shy of its diamond anniversary. The two teams first met as New Yorkers in 1889 during the 19th century version of the World Series. The established New York Giants rallied to defeat the relative newcomers from Brooklyn, who called themselves the Bridegrooms. Subsequent games of that era were notorious for bench-clearing brawls and fistfights between players and fans. Such disorderly behavior became commonplace as the two teams continued to claw and scratch at each other well into the next century.

From the early 1900s through the first decade of postwar America, theirs was the most intense of all rivalries; geography saw to that. The Dodgers and Giants were the only two teams that played in the same town while competing in the same league. But their mutual dislike flourished far beyond the boundaries of the ballpark. In every way, the two neighboring boroughs could not have been more dissimilar, and such differences bred contempt.

Author Eric Walker wrote: "New York and Brooklyn were the aristocratic, cultured gentleman and his scrappy, slum-born cousin who had fought his way up in the world; each openly disdained the other's ways....and the baseball teams they fielded were the chosen armies sent to fight this war, to crush the despised enemy."

Longtime Dodgers broadcaster Red Barber recognized the underpinnings of Brooklyn's second-class-citizen mentality. "Manhattan had the great architecture, all the tall buildings—Brooklyn didn't have any. Manhattan had Broadway and the theatre —Brooklyn didn't have that. Manhattan was the financial center, the cultural center—it was 'The Big Town.' Brooklyn was called the 'Bedroom of New York' and the people resented this. With the Dodgers, the people of Brooklyn had their only instrument to strike back—at New York—and the Giants."

But even on the baseball diamond, the Dodgers usually came out second best. In the first decades of the new century, fans filled the cavernous Polo Grounds to watch manager John McGraw lead his Giants to 10 pennants and a trio of world championships. Playing in considerably smaller Ebbets Field, Brooklyn won only three league flags and no Series titles during the same time. The gap widened in the 1930s, as the Dodgers spent most of their time buried in the standings while the Giants claimed three more league crowns.

Despite such obvious disparity, the rivalry remained a bitter one. In 1934, Giants manager Bill Terry was asked during the winter meetings about the Dodgers' chances. "Brooklyn? Are they still in the league?" he jokingly replied. The woebegone Dodgers viewed Terry's satiric comment as a personal affront—an insult they would not forget. Atop the standings for nearly the entire season, the Giants collapsed when they fell twice to the Dodgers at the end of the year, allowing the St. Louis Cardinals' "Gashouse Gang" to steal the pennant.

And so it went each year, 22 times a year—with most games fought over nothing more than New York City bragging rights. An afternoon with the Dodgers and Giants was two hours of urban combat waged with high spikes, hard slides, and whizzing fastballs under the chin. Salvos of verbal abuse were volleyed from one dugout to the other. Veteran players schooled arriving rookies to despise their foes from the rival borough. Placards hung in clubhouses throughout the respective minor league systems, preaching disdain for the Giants or Dodgers. The rabid fans of both teams needed no signs to tell them who to hate.

The end of World War II begat the golden age of the Dodger-Giant rivalry. Fueled by record crowds eager to forget the war and enjoy baseball, the National League's two New York teams fattened their balance sheets with the financial windfall, providing them with resources to acquire the best players. Much of that talent had been playing in the Negro leagues. Both the Dodgers and Giants expressed a willingness to defy the game's color barrier and sign black stars while the rest of baseball dragged its feet. Such boldness stamped both clubs as instant contenders.

For the first time since the '20s, the Dodgers and Giants were the two strongest teams in the league. Coupled with the existing "hate thy neighbor" sentiments, the rivalry soared to its highest level of intensity during the unforgettable 1951 season.

The Dodgers steamrollered all comers through the first months of the schedule, building a huge lead by midseason. The Giants, meanwhile, struggled just to avoid the second division. But when Brooklyn manager Charley Dressen declared to a group of furiously scribbling sportswriters in July that "The Giants is dead," he did more than evoke the memory of Bill Terry's *faux pas* of '34. Dressen unwittingly set into motion the greatest comeback in baseball history.

New York won 37 of its 44 games to tie the Dodgers for first on the final day of the regular season. A best-of-three playoff series would decide the championship. After splitting the first two games, the Dodgers appeared to have matters well in hand in the deciding game, taking a 4-1 lead into the bottom of the ninth inning. Instead of locking up its second pennant in three years, Brooklyn went down to ignominious defeat as the Giants rallied behind a dramatic three-run home run by Bobby Thomson. It remains the Dodgers' most shattering loss—and the most exalted victory in the history of the Giants.

Brooklyn recovered to win pennants in 1952, '53, '55 and '56, losing out only in '54 to their Polo Grounds rivals. Although the familiar names in the headlines of those years included Mays and Irvin or Snider and Campanella, their on-field accomplishments would eventually be eclipsed by the boardroom maneuverings of powerbrokers Horace Stoneham and Walter O'Malley.

* * *

Since 1919, the Giants had been the property of the Stoneham family, and when patriarch Charles Stoneham died suddenly in January 1936, control of the team was bequeathed to his 32-year-old son, Horace. Horace continued his stewardship of the franchise into the

'50s, just as Walter O'Malley was consolidating his hold on the crosstown Dodgers. Unlike Stoneham, Walter's ownership did not come about through inheritance. During his years of service as team counsel, O'Malley quietly annexed enough stock shares to eventually gain majority control of the ballclub. Once in charge, O'Malley's business acumen transformed the modestly profitable Dodgers into one of baseball's most lucrative teams.

Born into wealth and educated at Fordham Law School, O'Malley was gifted with an inbred understanding of the byzantine world of finance. Complex fiscal problems fascinated him. "I think he'd be very happy if you'd give him a long piece of string, all tangled up in knots, so he could have fun untangling it," noted team broadcaster Vin Scully. Front-office executive Buzzie Bavasi understood O'Malley as well as anyone. "Walter was a businessman—first and only. He was not a baseball man and admitted as much. He left that part to others. Contractual work with television and radio was about all he was interested in. He was not an emotional man and he never got close to any of the players."

Stoneham, on the other hand, lived and died with the Giants' every move, as team vice president Chub Feeney could attest. "He was a real baseball fan as an owner. Winning meant a lot to him and the team meant a lot to him. He was a rooter." Chuck Hiller, who played for the Giants in the '60s, remembered Stoneham as "a loving and caring person. And if people knew all that he did for ballplayers, I think they'd commend him very highly. He did a lot of good things for a lot of guys that nobody ever heard about, and that's how he wanted it."

With slicked-back hair, wire-rim glasses, and a husky build clad in Brooks Brothers suits, O'Malley looked the part of a big city bank president. The chubby Stoneham, with his rosy cheeks, thinning hair, and thick, dark glasses, more resembled a backslapping regional branch manager. While O'Malley affected a patrician, even autocratic air, Stoneham was renowned for his bonhomie. "Horace Stoneham has two occupations in life," quipped Indians owner Bill Veeck. "He owns the Giants and he drinks." Added then-Giants manager Leo Durocher, an occasional imbibing partner of Stoneham's, "To say that Horace can drink is like saying Sinatra can sing."

It would be difficult to find two more contrasting figures than O'Malley and Stoneham, but in the business of baseball they shared a common denominator; the societal and demographic upheaval of postwar New York was slowly but most assuredly affecting the fiscal health of their franchises.

The Polo Grounds (erected in 1891) and Ebbets Field (1913) were parks built for a cloistered populace in tightly defined neighborhoods. Those neighborhoods were changing—and not necessarily for the better. The flight to New York, New Jersey, and Connecticut suburbs had begun, sustained by the advent of single homes, superhighways, and the burgeoning ownership of private automobiles. Space was limited at both stadiums for these newly commuting fans to park those cars.

Crowds for Dodger games were healthy, but Ebbets Field, structured over a full city block, could not realistically be expanded beyond its 32,000-seating capacity. Conversely, attendance was dwindling for the Giants, partially because the Polo Grounds facility was falling apart.

O'Malley commissioned architect Buckminster Fuller, who designed blueprints for a domed stadium to be built at Brooklyn's Atlantic and Flatbush Avenues, above the Long Island Railroad depot. For various reasons—practical, legal, and political—city officials never acted on his proposal.

Although Walter was later vilified by New Yorkers for moving their beloved Dodgers to California, it was apparent that O'Malley, at least in the beginning, made a genuine effort to try to keep the team in Brooklyn. The cash-strapped Stoneham was not so inclined. So bad were the Giants' balance sheets that Horace was even in debt to the Polo Grounds concessionaire. Plummeting attendance turned off to an aging team exacerbated his fiscal woes. For Stoneham, there was only one possible solution: a move to Minneapolis, home of the Giants' successful Triple-A farm club.

For half a century, no major league teams had transferred from one city to another. But the early '50s witnessed a migration of three franchises: the Browns from St. Louis to Baltimore, the Braves from Boston to Milwaukee, and the Athletics from Philadelphia to Kansas City. Each move brought prosperity to the three struggling ballclubs, particularly the Braves. It was a fact that did not go unnoticed by the troubled New York baseball owners.

Modern jet travel made it feasible for big league ball to extend even further—to California. Los Angeles city fathers, aware of the problems in New York and hungry for baseball themselves, invited O'Malley to relocate. "Once Los Angeles showed an interest in the Dodgers, Walter used every means to make it look like he had to leave," said Buzzie Bavasi. "His excuse was that if a new stadium was in Flushing or Jamaica (NY), it wasn't in Brooklyn. Being two miles away was the same as being 3,000 miles away. Walter wanted to own his own stadium, even in New York. And Los Angeles was prepared to help him get it."

O'Malley sold the land under Ebbets Field to a real estate developer, then used the proceeds to swap his Fort Worth, Texas, minor league franchise for Cub owner Phil Wrigley's Los Angeles Angels Triple-A team (at a price tag of $2.5 million). With southern California territorial rights in his hip pocket, O'Malley was packed and ready to leave town. All he needed was a travelling partner.

The Dodger boss was well aware that the National League would not look kindly on a single team relocating to California. But if a pair of teams were to move to, say, Los Angeles and San Francisco, then two stops during western road trips for the remaining teams made more sense. Acutely aware of Stoneham's financial problems, O'Malley convinced the Giants owner to abandon his Minneapolis plans and join him out west. With such a partnership, the longtime rivalry could be preserved, the better to engage fan interest in the rich, untapped markets of northern and southern California.

The city of San Francisco, having already consulted with O'Malley, extended a warm invitation to Stoneham and his Giants. Besides pointing out the countless advantages of the Bay Area, council members painted a dark financial future for Horace if he decided to go it alone without the Dodgers in New York. Stoneham did not much care for that scenario, and agreed to the move.

The Red Sox owned the San Francisco Seals minor league team and territorial rights, but Boston owner Tom Yawkey sold those rights to Stoneham in exchange for the Minneapolis franchise (and some $250,000 in cash). With that transaction, the Bay Area became Horace Stoneham's baseball property.

In May 1957, the National League approved the move of the two teams from New York to California—if both requested "permission" to do so. In August, the Giants announced their departure. The Dodgers bade farewell in October. Fans in both boroughs, hoping for an 11th-hour reprieve, were stunned by the action. New York papers roasted O'Malley and screamed of betrayal. In response, Stoneham regrettably sighed, "I feel sorry for the kids, but I haven't seen much of their fathers recently."

An era of New York National League baseball was over—and the game's two fiercest rivals were heading west.

* * *

On April 15, 1958, California was officially welcomed to the major leagues. An enthusiastic throng of 23,449 fans squeezed into San Francisco's Seals Stadium on opening day as the Giants shut out the Dodgers, 8-0. Crowds would continue to fill the tiny former Pacific Coast League park at 90 percent capacity during both Giants' seasons at Seals, a (then) major league record. For the first time in a long time, Horace Stoneham was smiling.

Three days later, the two transplanted rivals met for the Dodgers' home opener in the Los Angeles Coliseum. The Dodgers won, 6-5, before 78,672, and went on to draw more than 1.8 million fans, despite their seventh-place finish. Walter O'Malley, too, was pleased.

But both team owners knew these existing parks would only be way stations. Seals Stadium was too small, and the property immediately surrounding the park at 16th and Bryant Streets was privately owned and not for sale. Still, Stoneham could wait. As part of its pitch to ensnare the Giants, the city of San Francisco had already passed a $5 million bond issue to build a stadium. The Giants would soon be playing in a new park before substantially larger crowds.

Size was not the L.A. Coliseum's drawback—in fact, the largest crowd ever to see a game (more than 93,000) paid to attend Roy Campanella Night in May of 1959. Built for the 1932 Summer Olympics, the Coliseum adapted adequately for football, but was a disaster for baseball. Its unorthodox structure dictated a right-field corner of 300 feet, straightaway center at 440, and a cozy left field of 250 feet. Within this bizarre configuration, only a few Coliseum seats offered reasonable baseball sightlines.

The Dodgers agreed to pay for brighter lights and other groundskeeping improvements, but even these could not wallpaper over the facility's structural shortcomings. What irked O'Malley most was simply that the Coliseum was not his property. The Dodgers paid rent to the city of Los Angeles while earning none of the revenues generated from parking and concessions.

O'Malley the businessman winced at this bottom line, but could live with these temporary conditions. Attendance figures were astonishing; with hundreds of thousands more than were drawn in New York, his cash register was ringing with gusto. Walter drew even more comfort from the fact that it would be only a matter of time before his very own stadium underwent construction. Before agreeing to move from Brooklyn, O'Malley had swapped the Watts property he had purchased from Phil Wrigley's Triple-A franchise in exchange for a primarily deserted 300-acre landfill. Walter first found his way to the site only after purchasing a road map from a Los Angeles filling station. Its name—Chavez Ravine.

For years, the city of Los Angeles had tried in vain to put the property to use for recreation or development, but nothing of substance was accomplished. Save for a few squatters' shacks and scattered herds of wayward goats, Chavez Ravine remained unsettled territory outside of downtown L.A. in the late '50s.

The Dodgers were eventually granted the property, but not before a number of bitter political skirmishes were played out and several lawsuits were filed. Many voters viewed the land transfer as a "giveaway," and only a closely contested referendum finally decided the issue (the margin of victory was around 25,000 out of nearly 700,000 votes cast).

When groundbreaking ceremonies for Dodger Stadium finally commenced in September of 1959, San Francisco's new ballpark was nearly finished. Candlestick Park was the first stadium ever to be completely constructed from reinforced concrete and would open in 1960—despite its own series of political, contractual, and meteorological problems.

The troubles began with the site selection. Many citizens believed the Giants should stay put in an expanded Seals Stadium, but public sentiment generally favored a new facility. Others pointed to available land near the downtown cable car turntable at Powell and Market Streets. Regrettably, this location which, in hindsight, would have been the best available choice, also had to be ruled out. Local businesses wanted no part of stadium traffic, and thousands of neighborhood residents would have required compensation through the costly legal procedure of eminent domain (estimated by Mayor George Christopher at $33 million).

A search committee finally suggested land off the Bayshore Freeway overlooking Candlestick Cove to the Hunter's Point Navy Yard, a 75-acre plot that was owned by a private citizen named Charles Harney. Harney offered to sell the land to the city for $2.7 million, under the condition that he also be placed in charge of the stadium's construction. In July 1957, Mayor Christopher accepted the deal and an ecstatic Harney pledged that the park would be finished "in eight months."

Stoneham was equally thrilled, primarily because the site boasted abundant parking space. Unfortunately, much of that land was under-water and would have to be filled in by dirt that was removed from sur-rounding hills. Some critics contend that it was those very hills that had acted as a windshield when the site was first surveyed—and no serious weather problems had been noted.

Such problems became more apparent once construction began. One afternoon, when team vice president Chub Feeney came out to check on the progress, he was alarmed to see cardboard boxes and other debris sailing through the air. "Does the wind always blow like this?" a worried Feeney inquired. "Only between the hours of one and five," deadpanned a crew member. According to writer Arnold Hano, such gusts permeated the area with "the smell of clams and pol-luted water…thicker than Los Angeles smog and fouler than Canar-sie garbage."

More ill winds of a political variety began blowing during con-struction. A contest conducted by the City Parks Commission to pick a name for the stadium ended with a panel of sportswriter judges selecting "Candlestick Park" as the winner. The news was not well received by Charles Harney, who had assumed the park would be named in his honor. The work pace began to slacken and Harney backed off from his original—and unrealistic—completion date.

Additional difficulties arose with grand jury probes of payment procedures, both to Harney and the Candlestick parking contract. In September 1959, a Teamsters strike delayed seat installation. Two months later, Harney barred the Giants from the stadium itself because the team found some of his construction to be unacceptable. To cap off the litany of setbacks, the City Fire Prevention Bureau turned thumbs down on the facility, labeling the park "a fire trap."

The problems were barely ironed out in time for opening day, 1960. On April 12th, 42,269 fans witnessed the first game, including Vice President Richard Nixon, California governor Pat Brown, base-ball commissioner Ford Frick, and John McGraw's widow. The Giants beat the Cardinals, 3-1, with outfielder Willie Mays driving in all of San Francisco's runs.

It was only the second time Mays had actually been in Candle-stick. Last-minute delays kept the Giants from taking batting and fielding practice until the cold and windy morning of April 11th, the day before the opener. Mays stepped into the cage, eager to begin taking his practice cuts. Willie swung at the first pitch, then stared down in shock at his bat. The Candlestick wind had sawed the bat in half.

The blustery breezes and chilly weather rapidly became the major topic of Candlestick conversation. Shortstop Eddie Bressoud lamented, "The Candlestick Park weather leaves you depressed." When asked why San Francisco's opponents didn't feel the same way, Bressoud answered, "They know they'll just be there for two or three days, so they give it their best and leave town." Sneered Pirates pitcher Vernon Law, "If they traded me to San Francisco, I wouldn't report." On a frigid April evening, chilled Cardinals broadcaster Joe Garagiola was asked if he wanted some hot coffee. "Never mind the coffee," shivered Garagiola. "Get a priest." Even Giants manager Bill Rigney admitted, "I have to manage two ways this year, for defense in Candlestick and offense on the road."

Pitching coach Larry Jansen attempted to convince his staff of Candlestick's psychological advantage. "No one liked playing there. Every team that came in hated it, but I told the pitchers this was our home and we'd have the edge if we just prepared ourselves mentally and physically. Wear longjohns, wear a choker around your neck and warm up an extra five minutes."

No amount of preventive apparel could avert some of Candlestick's farcical on-field incidents. Outfielder Willie McCovey's pop-up to second base was carried by an eastern jet stream over the wall for a grand slam home run. Pitcher Stu Miller once put his glove against the Candlestick fence and the wind caused it to stick. A foggy night provoked the strangest incident of all. "We were playing Pittsburgh," recalled pitcher Billy O'Dell. "They had a man on second when Don Hoak hit a pop fly into the fog and the ball was completely lost. Nobody could see it. It was ruled a foul. They had to hold the game up fifteen minutes for the fog to lift." The missing baseball was never found.

Candlestick garnered unfavorable publicity on a national scale when it hosted the 1961 All-Star Game. The event was marred by the most bizarre weather in All-Star history. In the early innings, the sunlight was so intense that nearly a hundred fans had to be treated for heat prostration. Suddenly, without warning, swirling winds caused the temperature to drop dramatically. One gust blew National League reliever Stu Miller right off the pitcher's mound, and was also partially responsible for four N.L. errors in the late innings.

First-time visiting American Leaguers, such as the Yankees' Roger Maris, were in shock. "They built this ballpark alongside the bay. They should have built it under the bay." Baltimore's Hoyt Wilhelm quipped, "Chewing tobacco and sand isn't a tasty combination." And *New York Times* columnist Arthur Daley, buffeted by winds in the pressbox, harshly condemned, "Whatever it is, this isn't a major league ball park."

In an effort to neutralize Candlestick's chilling cold, a coiled heating system had been built under the seats, but even when turned on full blast, no hot air made its way to the frozen toes of park patrons. Flamboyant local attorney Melvin Belli sued the Giants the cost of a season ticket for failing to provide functioning heat. At the conclusion of the widely publicized trial, the jury awarded Belli full damages, which he earmarked for a donation to the city to plant trees. "But not at Candlestick," he vowed. "They would freeze out there."

Stoneham paid Belli the money, but held the architects and city accountable for the heating malfunction. Horace then printed a legal waiver in the game program disavowing all future responsibility for the system.

Other structural problems caused more headaches. Women fans complained that the sharp edges of the seats were tearing their nylons. The Giants eventually hired Bay Area college students to sandpaper the rough spots. Even more serious was the alarming frequency of heart attacks that were occurring when fans attempted to walk to the stadium up a steep grade ignominiously nicknamed "Cardiac Hill." Ironically, elevators had initially been planned to help pedestrians scale the slope, but the designated space was reassigned to the hastily constructed heating system—the heating system that didn't work. By the summer of '62, six more fans had been felled by heart attacks, bringing the three-year total to 16 pulmonary victims.

That same year, the city commissioned a Palo Alto firm named Metronics Associates to begin a one-year study of Candlestick wind conditions. For the fee of $55,000, the group was required to determine the park's specific weather patterns, then make architectural recommendations to reduce the wind problems. If nothing else, such measures were a well-conceived public relations gesture. At least the city was attempting to do something about their flawed stadium, a structure that had become a San Francisco laughingstock and major league baseball's biggest boondoggle.

But even with its drawbacks, it should be understood that Candlestick Park was the first ballpark constructed since the '30s, equipped with numerous amenities and architectural wrinkles that had once been unimaginable. Designer John Bolles had no modern precedent as a guiding example, no other facility from which lessons could be learned. The mistakes of Candlestick were not lost on those responsible for building Dodger Stadium. As Bay Area writer Charles Einstein wisecracked, "The architects and engineers for [Dodger Stadium] came to San Francisco to study Candlestick—and decide, rumor had it, what *not* to do."

In June of 1959, bulldozers began moving out the eight-million cubic yards of Chavez Ravine earth that had to be cleared for the construction of Dodger Stadium. The original completion date was targeted for 1961, but continued legal entanglements and occasional mudslides pushed the deadline back. Even so, the Dodgers did not face nearly as much infighting as the Giants endured during Candlestick Park's construction.

The major reason for the relative harmony was that Walter O'Malley was running the operation without outside interference. Once the city of Los Angeles had awarded the land to him, O'Malley took charge of all major decisions. He hired Captain Emil Praeger, a New Yorker, as his chief architect, and the Vanell Construction Company to build the stadium.

An on-site concrete factory was built to create the more than 21,000 precast units (weighing close to 32 tons apiece) necessary to guarantee that every seat would have an unobstructed view. Parking facilities for 16,000 cars were paved surrounding the stadium frame that was actually built right into the land. The once bug-infested underbrush of the gulch was cleared away, and the land was replanted with tropical shrubs and palm trees.

By April of 1962, the first privately funded stadium constructed since Yankee Stadium in 1923 would be ready. Earlier that same spring, Walter O'Malley unveiled another prized possession—his new ultramodern team jet. Never before had anyone built a ballpark quite like Dodger Stadium—and no professional sports franchise had ever flown in a more luxurious aircraft than O'Malley's Dodger Electra II.

THE DODGERS

3
THE ORGANIZATION MAN

While most of the citizens of Vero Beach, Florida, were still rubbing the sleep from their eyes, a group of 50 wide-awake travelers settled in for a champagne breakfast aboard the Dodger Electra II. Walter O'Malley had planned a relaxing day for his guests in San Juan, Puerto Rico: Sightseeing, shopping, dining at the posh Hotel La Concha, gambling. It was March 5, 1962, and this "spring picnic" had become something of an annual rite with the Dodger boss and friends. Yet never had this entourage journeyed in such opulence.

With its own kitchen, sleeping berths, and recreational lounges fore and aft, the Dodger plane was a virtual "Grand Hotel" in the sky. No other baseball franchise could compete with these accomodations, and management hardly kept it secret. In the same year Dodger Stadium was to open, it was a portrait of the Electra II—not the new ballpark—that could be found on the cover of the team press guide.

Apparently, this did not bother Chavez Ravine architect Emil Praeger and his wife, who were among the invited guests. Also aboard were members of the Dodger board of directors, club front-office staffers Fresco Thompson and Red Patterson, Vero Beach mayor Jack Sturgis, and local businessman Bud Holman, the man who first invited the Dodgers to train in Florida back in 1948.

An abandoned, rickety World War II naval air station had become the team's spring workout facility, but by 1962, the old barracks were impressively modernized. The camp's young superintendent, Peter O'Malley, was already planning additional improvements for baseball's only privately owned training facility. Today, however, Peter set aside thoughts of Dodgertown's future to enjoy the ride on his father's jet.

Finishing breakfast down the aisle was an effervescent group of players' wives. Ginger Drysdale, Beverly Snider, Sally Sherry, and Sue Perranoski were happily comparing notes on the day's shopping possibilities.

Noticeably absent from the flight were the wives of any of the black Dodgers, but few had been willing to come to Florida in the first place. When shortstop Maury Wills was asked why he didn't bring his family to spring training he answered, "There's no good accomoda-tions for wives of Negro players down here. I really hope to see the day when the Dodgers train in the west so she has a decent place to stay."

The community of Vero Beach wasn't friendly to blacks, even if they wore Dodger blue. Golf courses were restricted. The few movie houses that allowed black patronage required them to sit in the bal-cony. Designated "white only" drinking fountains were common. Some restaurants flatly refused to serve blacks, others would do so only if they sat in an obstructed area, away from the other players on the team.

White players could hire out local boats for an afternoon of fish-ing, but blacks didn't even bother to try. Once Wills phoned ahead to confirm reservations at an auto rental, but when he arrived at the agency, he was told there were no more cars available. A town barber badly cut catcher John Roseboro while trimming his sideburns, causing an infection that forced the Dodger catcher to see a doctor. After that episode, all the black players cut each other's hair.

Back at camp, the environment was considerably more friendly. By 1962 the Dodgertown complex sported an Olympic-size swim-ming pool and volleyball, shuffleboard, tennis, and badminton courts. There was even a pitch-and-putt golf course and practice greens.

More choices were available after dark. Because Vero Beach's the-atres were hostile towards the black players, team management began the practice of showing their own first-run Hollywood movies nearly every evening. Table tennis, television, and a small library provided additional entertainment.

One of the liveliest social centers in the training complex was the rec hall which housed a billiard table. Inside this cramped room, a few Dodgers amateurishly engaged in friendly games of pool. Oth-ers, such as veteran infielder Jim Gilliam, were so accomplished with the cue stick that no one would even challenge them. Clearly the best pool player in camp was another man not to be trifled with—the quiet but imposing manager of the Los Angeles Dodgers.

* * *

Walter Emmons Alston was beginning his ninth season as the Dodgers' field boss, having recently signed the latest of his perennial one-year contracts. "Anything longer makes me nervous," Alston would respond to reporters who questioned why one of baseball's most successful managers wasn't granted more extended job security. Club policy had long mandated one-year managerial pacts, but in reality, Alston knew he had a guardian angel in the front office.

No one in baseball had higher regard for Alston than general manager Buzzie Bavasi. "Walter knew that he had a job as long as I was there. He was the type of person you liked to have running your business because you knew where he was all the time. If you needed him, you'd call his hotel room and he'd always be there. Walter was a great organization man. He knew talent. He was quiet, didn't say much. If you did your job, that was all he asked. If you couldn't play for Walter, you couldn't play for anybody. But he also wasn't the soft touch everybody thought he was. He was the strongest man I ever saw—physically.

"Every once in a while, he'd challenge a player. The first guy he challenged was Jackie Robinson one time in Louisville. Walt told him, 'Let's go in my office and only one of us is coming out.' Jackie wouldn't go and I didn't blame him."

At 6-2 and 210 pounds, Alston was larger than many of his players. Most managers, then as now, were too old or too fat to fit comfortably in a baseball uniform, but Dodger colors flattered Alston's powerful frame and blacksmith forearms. It was out of uniform where Alston appeared awkward. When forced to wear a coat and tie, he was as ill at ease as a squirming 10-year-old in his Sunday school suit.

Alston's thinning gray hair surrounded the ruddy complexion of a heavyset face. He had a broad, toothy grin, which contrasted starkly with sad, basset hound eyes. Even in happy moments, Walter's expressions made him look as if he were about to cry. But Walter Alston was never one to display his emotions in public.

"Walter was rather aloof—a cool man," observed longtime Dodger broadcaster Vin Scully. "I used to always say that he should have ridden shotgun through Indian country during the days of the covered wagons."

Indeed, Alston was as comfortable loading rifles as he was filling out a lineup card. Hunting, along with woodworking, were lifelong hobbies, two pastimes he had grown to love since early childhood.

Alston was born in 1911 in Venice, Ohio, the son of an automobile worker with his own farm. As a child, Walt gravitated quickly to baseball, earning the nickname "Smokey" as the fastest pitcher on the town team—a team he still played for until he was almost 60. He dropped out of Miami (Ohio) University to get married, then returned when work was scarce during the depression. Alston borrowed money from a local church and took odd jobs to pay his college tuition, while simultaneously captaining the varsity baseball and basketball teams.

The day after he earned his bachelor's degree, Alston signed a minor league contract with the St. Louis Cardinals.

Despite a lifetime .300 batting average, Alston remained trapped in the minors for his entire 13-year career. He made his first and only major league appearance in 1936 (and struck out). Early on, it was apparent that Walter had virtually no chance of advancing through the Cardinals' talent-rich system, an organization that produced future Hall-of-Famers Johnny Mize, Enos Slaughter, and Stan Musial.

In 1940, Alston was offered the position of player-manager with Portsmouth in the Middle Atlantic League and took it, realizing it was likely his only chance of staying in baseball. He supplemented his small baseball earnings by teaching biology and mechanical drawing during the winter, while also coaching the varsities at New Madison and Lewistown High Schools.

Alston the player/manager never finished better than third, and when the Cardinals released him as an active player in 1944, Walter was crushed, fearful he would be relegated to high school biology labs for the rest of his life. Fortunately, Alston got a reprieve when the Brooklyn Dodgers hired him to manage their Nashua, New Hampshire club in 1946. With prospects Roy Campanella and Don Newcombe on the roster, Walter became one of the first two men (along with Clay Hopper in Montreal) to manage black athletes in the professional ranks, and those players helped him win his first league championship. Almost overnight, Alston became a rising star in the system, and Nashua GM Bavasi made certain Smokey accompanied him along every rung up the Dodgers' minor league ladder.

Wherever he managed, Alston got results. None of his teams ever finished lower than third, and all six of his Triple-A entries made the playoffs every season. When the Dodgers decided against retaining two-time pennant-winning skipper Charley Dressen at the end of the '53 season, Alston applied for the job. To the amazement of nearly everyone in Brooklyn, Walt was hired. The front page of one New York paper featured a photo of a sign in a window which queried, "Walter Who?" One sportswriter sniffed, "The Dodgers do not *need* a manager and that is why they got Alston."

The sportswriter was wrong. No Dodger team had ever won the World Series until Alston led the Bums to the 1955 championship over the archrival Yankees. In '56, the Dodgers repeated as National League champs. After their 1958 disaster when the team flopped in its first season on the West Coast, Alston became the first manager ever to take a ballclub from seventh place one season to a pennant and a world championship the next.

Through it all, Walter maintained his quiet, often colorless profile, offering little that could provide hot copy for southern California newspapers. *Sports Illustrated*'s Robert Creamer characterized Alston as "Whistler's Mother with a scorecard in his lap." Another writer remarked, "If you were to meet Walter Alston, you'd come away convinced you hadn't been introduced."

Alston readily admitted to his less-than-scintillating personality, but steadfastly refused to change. He often recited this mantra: "I appreciate a good shotgun. I appreciate a good target rifle. I appreciate a good pool table. The fancy clothes and big dinners don't appeal to me much. Any time a man tries to be something he's not, he's only hurting himself."

Some of his players believed Walter's conservatism adversely affected the way he managed. "He played the game by the book," wrote John Roseboro in his autobiography. "He knew baseball as well as anyone, but he missed some opportunities because he didn't see them soon enough and seize them fast enough. He didn't want to be second-guessed by the press and the public and didn't want to be criticized by the front office."

According to first baseman Ron Fairly, "Alston's greatest ability was to do nothing—having enough confidence with the guys to say, 'Don't let me screw things up because your talent will come out somewhere during the ballgame.' His patience allowed our abilities to eventually surface."

Undoubtedly, there were incidents to substantiate such portrayals, but the facts at least partially belie these views. On the field, Walter often revealed a bold, gambling side. Under Alston, the Dodgers stole more bases than anyone. The hit-and-run was one of his favorite plays. No other manager, not even Philadelphia's superstrategist Gene Mauch bunted as much as Walter. Alston often platooned at two or more positions, and wasn't reluctant to use multiple pinch-hitters in a single game. He loved defensive switches, constantly ordered intentional walks and, if the need arose, would yank even his best starters early and go to the bullpen.

Another Alston paradox was his extremely volatile temper, the flip side of his calm demeanor. When paired with his physical strength (he once beat mammoth outfielder Frank Howard in an arm-wrestling contest), those who faced his wrath tread a cautious path. Pitcher Ron Perranoski remembered such outbursts from the Dodger manager. "He was a man's man and when he talked to you, he looked you straight in the eye. But you just didn't want to fool around with Walter. He could physically break you in two and was capable of doing so till the day he died."

"We didn't let those gray hairs on his head fool us into thinking he couldn't take any of us on," recalled Fairly. "Now and then, maybe once or twice a year, he'd call a meeting, and he'd be so damned mad he'd have a rough time lighting his cigarette. His hands would be shaking, and as soon as we saw that we knew Smokey was angry and we'd better just sit there and shut up. He was not afraid to go around the room and point his finger at different guys and chew them out. He'd lay it on the line and there'd be no mistake as to who was in charge."

Such explosions were rare, however. Walt preferred to confront the guilty party in private, usually the day after the transgression, when tempers had cooled. And Alston was generally tolerant of players who occasionally extended their late-night adventures past the posted curfew. But such restraint vanished in the spring of '61 when Walter caught pitchers Larry Sherry and Sandy Koufax tiptoeing into the Vero Beach barracks well beyond the witching hour. Alston knocked on their locked door, demanding an explanation. When there was no response, the enraged manager punched the door with such fury that his '59 World Series ring shattered in two, jarring the stone from its setting. There were no more curfew violations for the remainder of spring.

* * *

Concerning most team matters, Alston wrote the rules. Alston made out the batting orders. Alston ran the games. But Alston did not pick his coaches. That task was left to the front office. "We don't want bridge partners or cronies for assistants," stated Walter O'Malley. "It is our job to get the most knowledgeable men, and it is the manager's place to solicit their advice and accept it or reject it." Added Buzzie Bavasi, "Walter has the courage to delegate authority. I think he was the first manager to realize managing is not a one-man job."

In the late '50s, the front office populated the coaching staff with former big league field bosses Charley Dressen and Bobby Bragan. Here were two outspoken, opinionated men whose presence might have intimidated some managers, but their appointments didn't appear to rattle Alston. Vin Scully offered this analogy: "Walter was like Perry Como, who could invite another top singer on his show and it wouldn't bother him in the least." Publicly, Alston claimed the last thing he wanted was a dugout full of yes-men. "We've always had a pretty good bunch of agitators as coaches," said Walt. "They get the dry needle out and get back at me from time to time. That's good. But they know when I'm serious and that's what counts."

In 1961, the Dodgers added to Alston's staff perhaps the fiercest "agitator" in the history of baseball. Indeed, the availability of Leo "The Lip" Durocher came about precisely because of his notorious personality.

The Dodgers were looking for a shrewd baseball mind for the coaching staff when Dressen departed in 1960, but assumed Leo wouldn't be available because the expansion Los Angeles Angels were showing strong leanings toward selecting Durocher as their first manager.

From a public relations standpoint, the Angels could not have chosen a better man for the job. There were few figures in baseball with a more colorful background. As a journeyman infielder with the Yankees, Reds, Cardinals, and Dodgers during the 1920s and '30s, Leo was a hitter of little distinction. His low batting averages earned him the unflattering nickname, "The All-American Out." But Durocher played the game with guile and uncommon zeal, and it was readily apparent that greatness would come to him after his playing days were over.

In 1939, Brooklyn hired Durocher to manage the woeful Dodgers, and within two years he brought the first pennant to Flatbush since 1920. On the field, he was a showman who fielded ballclubs that played with unbridled recklessness, yet were also fundamentally sound. He was the game's most savage umpire baiter, but was also one of baseball's premier strategists. At a time when racial tensions were high, no manager communicated with black players as compassionately as Durocher. Off the field, Leo was a godsend to a New York press corps starved for just this kind of wisecracking, Runyonesque figure.

Durocher was compact, wiry, and physically unimpressive. But his charm was so engaging he could dominate even a room full of celebrities. Leo's smile beamed for the cameras, and his back-slapping conviviality made him extremely difficult to dislike.

With movie-star wife Laraine Day at his side, the well-tailored Durocher played the ponies and toured the nightclub circuit, consorting with singers, actors, and members of the underworld. Leo's alleged involvement with gamblers earned him a one-year suspension from baseball in 1947, and in '48 he shocked New Yorkers by switching allegiances to manage the crosstown Giants.

Leo won two more pennants and a World Series in the Polo Grounds, then retired from managing in 1955. For the next five years, Durocher worked for NBC as "liason officer," a troubleshooter who handled any problems between the network and its TV stars. With an $81,000-a-year job, Leo was able to make his permanent residence in Beverly Hills, where he continued his longtime friendships with such celebrities as Frank Sinatra, George Burns, and Danny Kaye. His afternoons were free to play golf at Hillcrest Country Club, his evenings spent at the Friars Club holding court over hands of gin rummy.

Durocher's network job ended in 1959, and suddenly his phone stopped ringing. Only one offer was tendered over the next 15 months, a minor league position in the Giants' organization. In 1960, the Angels' managerial post appeared to be tantalizingly close, but was pulled back at the last minute. Halos GM Fred Haney told team owner Gene Autry, "If we were going to have a winner right away, a really good club, I wouldn't hesitate to hire Leo. But this is going to be the type of team that will test a manager's patience and temper. I'm not sure Leo can handle it."

Durocher was devastated, certain he was being blackballed from the major leagues. "A guy like me makes a lot of enemies. Any opinionated guy does…I'm pretty convinced that my place is in baseball. This is my element, and where I belong."

Apparently, Walter O'Malley agreed. The Dodger owner, respectful of Walter Alston but bored by his tepid personality, was looking for a jolt of excitement the flamboyant Durocher could most certainly provide. The third base coach's job was open, and O'Malley asked Leo if he was interested. A grateful Durocher accepted without even discussing money. Although his new wages were considerably less than the network dollars he once commanded, Leo began the '61 season earning the highest salary ever paid a major league coach.

* * *

Durocher's princely paycheck might have made him feel entitled to royal surroundings in the otherwise spartan accommodations of Vero Beach. When Leo arrived in the spring of '61, he was assigned a room in the single men's barracks, a building creaking with age and plagued by a leaking roof. Durocher hastily applied for quarters off base where he could also house his maid and cook from his Beverly Hills home. Bavasi nixed such a move, citing the team rule that only married personnel could live away from Dodgertown. Within days, Durocher received no less than six marriage proposals from women who found the idea of wintering in Florida appealing.

Leo passed on pen-pal matrimony, forging a different solution to his lodging problems. By 1962, Durocher's suite had been lavishly upgraded with cotton floor mats, a refrigerator, and his own telephone. Not even Walter O'Malley's quarters were so appointed. Leo also got the red-carpet treatment at team meals, having sweet-talked the kitchen staff into preparing him special dinners (chicken cacciatore was a favorite) while the rest of the Dodgers hacked and probed at mystery meat.

Durocher charmed the cafeteria workers as easily as he had enchanted the Los Angeles beat writers. The scribes delighted in quoting The Lip's zesty wisecracks, snappy repartee that sharply contrasted with the droning cliches of the Dodger manager. "We have to face facts," admitted Alston. "Leo is a colorful figure and a bold and amusing talker. I would be a damn fool if I tried to outdo him. We must live our own way and respect each other."

From the outset, the pairing of Alston and Durocher was hardly a match made in heaven. Simply stated, Leo was not Walter Alston's type of guy. Durocher was boastful, blunt, and manipulative—everything Walter was not. When hitting fungoes at Vero Beach, Leo ridiculed the infielders by calling them women's names, a ploy Alston never would have attempted. Once in '62, Leo was standing at the batting cage, watching rookie catcher Doug Camilli take his cuts. Twenty years earlier, Durocher had managed Camilli's father Dolf, a slugging first baseman, back in Brooklyn. "Hey, Doug!" bellowed Leo, "I remember your dad used to hit 'em way up 'there' and you couldn't hit one up 'there' if a hurricane was blowing!" Leo's jabs often drew laughs, but sometimes drew blood. This was not Walter's way.

According to infielder Daryl Spencer, "I really don't think it was Alston's idea to hire Durocher. He might have said he agreed to it, but I'll bet he didn't want him." Pitcher Johnny Podres believed "there was a conflict because Leo wanted Walt's job—he wanted to manage the Dodgers."

Ever the loyal organization man, Walter towed the party line, constantly praising Leo's knowledge, grateful to have his input during games. In reality, Alston had never liked Durocher, dating back to their days as rivals in New York when Leo still piloted the Giants. Their relationship, tenuous at best in '61, would gradually deteriorate throughout the '62 campaign after a series of abrasive incidents.

One event that foreshadowed conflicts to come occurred during the final weeks of spring training. On a humid Florida evening, Durocher was dominating a spirited game of rise and fly pool in the tiny billiard rec room. Under the rules of rise and fly, the loser had to relinquish the stick so a new challenger could face the reigning champion. Opponents came and went, but the gloating Durocher easily dispatched all comers. This surprised none of the 30 spectators crammed around the table. Leo had spent much of his life hanging around pool halls, and that schooling made him a savvy, merciless competitor.

With each victory, the cheering and wisecracks grew louder. Durocher wasn't bothered by the noise; he thrived on it. Suddenly Alston appeared at the door, curious to see the cause of all the commotion. When he spotted Leo chalking his cue tip, Walt began to turn around and leave, but Maury Wills stopped him.

"Hey Skip, come on in and shoot some pool," beseeched the shortstop. Against his better judgment, Walter stayed.

"Leo, we've got a match for you," said Wills. Still busily working the resin, Durocher didn't offer a glance as he boastfully responded. "I'll take anybody. Name him—Willie Mosconi, Minnesota Fats..."

Then Leo looked up. There stood an unsmiling Alston, cradling a stick in his hand. Both men hesitated briefly, but the cacophony of racking billiard balls served as a clarion call to battle. Both understood there was no other choice but to play.

"I remember that night very well. I'm standing there right now," recalled Wills. "It was like a scene from *The Hustler*. There was a burning desire by both men to beat one another—a personal vendetta. Alston had the first shot and he was hot. He couldn't miss."

The Dodger manager ran through two entire racks without difficulty. "Hey Leo, you're losing," chuckled one of the players. For once, The Lip had no retort as he silently stood in his corner, arms folded. Inside, he was seething. Pool was his game and Alston was cleaning his clock.

Finally, Walter missed, but nobody in the crowd dared utter a smart remark. Getting his chance, Durocher rallied, trimming Alston's margin. The spectators roared when Leo briefly took the lead, but Walt responded, sinking two difficult shots to tie the game.

The tension, like the nighttime humidity, pervaded the sweltering hall. Then Alston glanced down at his watch and declared, "Staff meeting at 8:30." He put down his cue and walked out of the room. A moment later, Durocher followed him through the door.

Wills wondered if a meeting was actually scheduled, or whether Alston conveniently created an excuse when the game became dead-locked. No one ever found out; nor would there ever be a rematch—at least at billiards—between the two adversaries.

*   *   *

Leo Durocher wasn't the only issue on Walter Alston's mind dur-ing the spring of '62. After winning the Series in '59, the Dodgers skidded to fourth in 1960, then ran out of gas in '61, finishing second to the less-talented Cincinnati Reds. Beyond the obvious pressure to reclaim the pennant, Alston knew he would have to find a different way to win because now, at least at home, the ground rules had been literally transformed.

After four seasons in the crazy-quilt, slugger-friendly confines of the Coliseum, the Dodgers were ready to move into the spacious new park in Chavez Ravine. The change in address also demanded a change in the way the team did business between the white lines. Longball punch was less critical—pitching and speed were paramount.

Only the lowly Cubs and Phillies posted worse team ERAs than the '61 Dodger staff, but Alston was confident his pitchers would improve dramatically in the bigger ballpark. And in Wills, Gilliam, and Willie and Tommy Davis, the top of the L.A. lineup was the fastest in baseball.

The problem was, where to play all his speed merchants? Wills was set as the opening day shortstop, and Gilliam would man an infield position, but which one? Veteran Daryl Spencer was a proven third base talent. Line-drive-hitting rookie second baseman Larry Burright was tearing up the Grapefruit League and fielding brilliant-ly. One of them would have to be benched in deference to Gilliam.

In the outfield, Alston's dilemma was even greater. Thirty-two-year-old Wally Moon was coming off his best season in the big leagues, with 88 RBI and a .328 batting average. And Duke Snider, even at age 34, was still productive, having hit close to .300 despite injuries.

In '61, Alston took some heat for platooning the Dodgers, but had done so to give younger players, such as the Davises, Frank Howard, and Ron Fairly, an opportunity to find their own comfort level in the big leagues. Now, their seasons of apprenticeship were over. Lefty/righty batting orders would be used as the season began, but Alston secretly knew that a set lineup was inevitably coming, one which placed a premium on speed.

The situation was clear-cut: Dodger Stadium's outfield was simply more spacious than the Coliseum's. Alston knew that younger, faster legs could more easily run down pitchers' mistakes in the power alleys. Moon and Snider weren't slow, but neither came close to equalling the speed of Willie and Tommy Davis.

There were other mitigating factors. Moon's inside-out swing had produced his famous "Moon shots" over the Coliseum's 250-foot left-field wall and off its 46-foot-high screen. Walter feared Wally's pull-hitting punch would be negated in roomier Dodger Stadium. Although he began 1962 as a regular, Moon's playing time was eventually cut in half, and he was never a full-time starter in the big leagues again. It had to be a crushing defeat to one of the brightest, most articulate men in baseball.

The highlight of what had to be Wally's most trying season came on May 7th when the Dodgers travelled to Houston for a series with the Colts. Moon, a Lone Star state native with bachelor's and master's degrees from Texas A&M, was feted at a special luncheon. A&M representatives and Houston's mayor gave him the key to the city while establishing an annual school trophy in his name. The next evening "Wally Moon Night" was held at Colt Stadium.

Snider was also honored in early '62, selected as the first Dodger captain since Pee Wee Reese held the position in 1958. The one-time "Duke of Flatbush" was clearly pleased to be entrusted with his new responsibility. "I don't want to sound immodest, but we have a lot of kids this year that knew about me a long time before they met me personally at Dodgertown. I think they will listen to me when I make suggestions." The choice was a popular one among the players, as well as a clever maneuver by team management to tactfully soften the blow of easing out a franchise legend for younger stars.

* * *

Walter Alston began spring training with one of the shortest pep talks in sports history. Rookie pitcher Joe Moeller recalled, "It was my first meeting as a Dodger. I thought we'd be getting an hour and a half lecture to fire us up, tell us all how we were gonna do it. He walks into the room and says, 'Gentlemen, I'll see you in forty days. Be ready.' That was it!"

Forty days later, Walter Alston ended spring training, having stocked his roster with some of baseball's most youthful players. Beginning with Moeller, the most callow of major leaguers at 19, Alston entered the '62 pennant race with 22-year-olds Willie Davis and (pitcher) Pete Richert, 23-year-olds Tommy Davis and Ron Fairly, and infielders Burright and Tim Harkness, both 24. At 25, Frank Howard was the oldest of the still-ripening farm system prospects. Adding Doug Camilli, the Dodgers opened their season carrying five rookies, an unusually high number of first-year players for a contender.

Yet Smokey would hardly be launching a children's crusade. Both Jim Gilliam and Duke Snider had played for Alston since 1954, his first season as team manager. Don Drysdale, Sandy Koufax, Johnny Podres, and Ed Roebuck were throwing in the majors when the Dodgers still played in Ebbets Field. Stan Williams, Larry Sherry, and Ron Perranoski were established pitching talents. With Norm Sherry or John Roseboro catching, it was like having a coach behind the plate. Lee Walls and Andy Carey gave Alston two more veterans on the bench with versatile skills and exceptional baseball minds. And at 29, the late-blooming Wills had become the best shortstop in the National League.

Rookies and veterans alike rode in style as the ballclub boarded the Electra II for their flight west. After stops in Las Vegas and San Diego to complete the exhibition schedule, the players arrived in Los Angeles in time for the ceremonial christening of Dodger Stadium.

Besides the stadium dedication, there was an additional season-opening ritual to observe. The annual spring Baseball Writers' Banquet on April Fools' Day at the Beverly Hilton was rapidly becoming a tough ticket. TV star Danny Thomas, comedian Bob Newhart, and singer Gogi Grant were on the program, but the unique attraction of the evening would be stage performances by a quartet of musically inclined Dodgers.

After opening "out-of-town" in Vegas during Dinah Shore's show at the Riviera Hotel, banjo-playing Maury Wills and the crooning trio of Sandy Koufax, Don Drysdale, and Willie Davis took their act before the writers' dinner audience. Wills opened the festivities, plucking the strings with his rendition of "Bye Bye Blues." Koufax, Drysdale, and Davis followed, belting out "A Diamond is a Man's Best Friend." The friendly crowd roared its approval.

During the early weeks of April and then throughout the season, sports and show business personalities shared center stage at the new ballpark. In a town where stardom and celebrity meant everything, the marriage between baseball and showbiz seemed perfectly natural. It was a glamorous alliance that had been going strong ever since the Dodgers moved west—and would crest to its high point during the summer of '62.

4
LIGHTS, CAMERA, BASEBALL

Klieg lamps, neon signs, and search beacons have long bathed Hollywood celebrities in a warm glow, but on April 3rd the nighttime skies over Los Angeles lit up for a new leading lady. This was no film premiere, no studio publicity stunt; these beams were for Tinseltown's latest star. With the flip of a switch, eight light towers ("with enough [power] to illuminate the entire city of Seattle," gushed *The Sporting News*) cast their light over Dodger Stadium. Its luster could be seen from miles away.

It made for a pretty picture, but in reality, the switch was thrown because hamstrung building crews were still burning the midnight oil. Dodger Stadium's debutant ball was less than a week away, and unexpected heavy California rains had thrown construction behind schedule. Workers toiled feverishly to complete the final touches, urged on by that one-time engineering school grad, Walter O'Malley. "We saw more of him than our own boss," confessed one crew member.

Construction was completed with virtually no time to spare (the huge twin scoreboards were hoisted by crane for installation only the day before the season opener). On that same afternoon, a lengthy motorcade weaved its way from City Hall, en route to Chavez Ravine for a V.I.P. sneak preview.

The dignitaries included league president Warren Giles and baseball commissioner Ford Frick, whose voice cracked with emotion as he saluted the game's newest park. Comedian Joe E. Brown entertained and Art Baker's orchestra serenaded, as 2,000 invited guests relaxed in the stands, eating box lunches and drinking in the sights.

Perhaps the most interested of O'Malley's guests was Gene Autry, owner of the American League Los Angeles Angels, and new co-tenant of Dodger Stadium. After his first season in bandbox Wrigley Field, Autry knew he would have to move his team to a larger park or risk prohibitive revenue losses. When the Dodgers offered to take them in, the Angels had little choice but to accept. Even though "The Singing Cowboy" was as impressed with the facility as anyone, Autry wasn't completely thrilled to be renting from the Dodgers and O'Malley.

O'Malley's invitation was viewed as a public relations gesture, since he had already extracted $350,000 in territorial rights fees from

41

the Angels when they debuted in L.A. the summer before. O'Malley was also aware of the ill feelings many citizens still harbored over the Chavez Ravine land deal. This was no time to turn his back on a fledgling team in need of a place to play. So Walter welcomed the Angels to his new home—although such a welcome bore a steep price tag.

The Angels would gain no parking revenues and shared in only half the concession profits. They were restricted by the Dodgers in areas of promotion, merchandising, and sponsorship. The Halos had to pay compensatory indemnification to the Dodgers whenever they televised an away game that would conflict with Dodger home dates. Other bills from the Angels' landlords were even more irritating.

The Dodgers charged the Angels for resurfacing the parking area, despite the fact the American Leaguers received no revenue from the lot. The Dodgers solicited the Angels for window-cleaning services, but only the Dodger offices had windows. The Dodgers even wanted to split expenses for toilet paper, although they would draw more than twice as many fans to the park as the second-year Angels.

The unkindest act of all may have been the Dodgers' placement of the Angels' ticket office. Located in the left-field corner near the groundskeepers' storage sheds, Angel patrons had to pass immense piles of manure to get to the ticket windows. On sultry summer days, the stench was overpowering.

Composts notwithstanding, the new park radiated the sweet smell of success, even before the first pitch was thrown. O'Malley sensed The Big Score, certain this was the final piece in the marketing puzzle that would make his team the wealthiest in baseball.

The Dodgers already had a quality product in their contending team. Now this magnificent ballpark would attract more fans entirely by itself. And in convivial broadcaster Vin Scully, O'Malley was blessed with a personality whose silken pronouncements were the siren song that lured thousands of spectators to baseball paradise.

By O'Malley's edict, however, Scully was heard almost exclusively on radio. Back in Brooklyn, fans could pay their way into Ebbets Field or watch the Dodgers on dozens of telecasts. The move west all but banished baseball from the TV airwaves. New Yorkers expected televised games almost as a birthright. West Coast fans had not been so indoctrinated. O'Malley firmly believed the folks in southern California would never "buy the cow" when they could get the "milk" for free. If Angelenos wanted to see the Dodgers, they would have to purchase a stadium ticket.

Excluding the 11 annual road dates with the rival Giants, no other Dodger games were televised on the team flagship station, KTTV. The fans, starved for action, flocked to the flawed Coliseum in record numbers for four years, despite its poor baseball sightlines. In 1962, Walter was confident many more would come to Chavez Ravine, already dubbed "Golden Gulch" and the "Taj O'Malley" by local sportswriters.

So it must have been perceived as a sweeping gesture of charity when the ballclub announced that for the first time since their '58 arrival, the Dodgers were going to televise a home game—the first ever staged in baseball's newest pleasure palace.

"A sellout is assured for the opener, but many thousands more will want to see the game and the new stadium, so we're happy to present this telecast," beamed the magnanimous Dodger owner. It would be many years before another regular-season Dodger home game appeared on a southern California TV set.

What that television audience—and 52,564 paying customers— saw on opening day was a baseball park unlike any other. Among the architectural "firsts" of Dodger Stadium: Dugout boxes, multicolored seats, a message board (Dow Jones stock quotations were posted for business executives during opening day), terraced parking (eliminating steep climbs from car to turnstile), complete unobstructed vision, and 70 percent of the seats located within the infield area.

The price tag for Dodger Stadium was estimated at a hefty $18.5 million—and it showed. A Beverly Hills designer created the ushers' outfits. The ballpark sound system was developed by a West German firm that crafted the acoustics for Italy's La Scala Opera House. The posh Stadium Club restaurant served its members steak, prime rib, or swordfish on custom-crafted china made by the same company that provided glassware at the White House.

"They were even saving a space out in left field where they were going to put waterfalls someday, but they never did," remembered catcher Norm Sherry. "But having been raised in Los Angeles, it meant a lot to be able to play in a baseball park instead of a football stadium where you happened to play baseball. It was gorgeous."

The infield was especially eye-catching. Solidly packed dirt with a crushed-brick base gave off an appealing crimson hue. Publicly, the players had nothing but kind words about the surface. "The infield is perfect," claimed Maury Wills. "It's nice and firm and true." "It's excellent," Andy Carey told the *Los Angeles Times*. Their real sentiments were anything but laudatory.

Daryl Spencer detested it. "The infield was really bad. They had a lot of problems with the clay they brought in that first season. They changed the dirt several times and I'm sure it's a better surface now, but it probably was one of the worst infields in the National League that season."

"That red brick looked pretty against the green grass," Wills later said, "but it would bake hard in the sun and was always cracking. It was hard to run on, hard to slide on and hard to field on."

"It was like running on a sidewalk," said Ron Fairly. "There'd be times you'd run across the infield and your spikes would not go in the ground. It was fast and hard and it took a long time for the dirt to settle in. There were some bad hops out there, and in '62 I was reluctant to get in front of a ground ball. I just didn't know where it was going to go.

"Look, the stadium was just opening and everybody was under the hammer. O'Malley told us, 'Don't criticize the field. We've still got a few bugs to work out.' The boss tells you to shut up, you shut up."

There were also serious problems with the infield grass. Because of the uncharacteristically heavy April rainfall, it had no chance to come in. Thin and colorless, the turf would look pallid for the opening day stadium and TV audience if something wasn't done. Vin Scully recalled how the problem was solved—Hollywood style.

"Walter O'Malley's best friend in the film community was director Mervyn LeRoy. When Mr. O'Malley explained the situation, Mervyn said, 'Why don't you do what we do? Just paint it. Get vegetable dye and cover it.' And so, if you see any color photos of opening day at Dodger Stadium, that infield is not only a verdant green, it is almost *black* green, it is so unusually dark."

* * *

Opening day arrived bright and sunny, a postcard-perfect southern California spring morning. The only issue that concerned otherwise enthusiastic Angelenos was the potential for roadway bottlenecks. Newspaper reports predicting heavy traffic into the stadium so alarmed the fans that many began arriving shortly after breakfast. As it turned out, the only ones who were seriously inconvenienced by the road congestion was the visiting team—defending National League champion Cincinnati.

The Reds had begun the baseball season the day before, losing their traditional home opener at Crosley Field. They hopped a westbound flight immediately after their game with the Phillies and did not land in Los Angeles until 2 A.M. coast time. Eight hours later, the still-drowsy Reds boarded the team bus and headed for Chavez Ravine. Unfortunately, the bus was trapped in the traffic snarl, and when the visitors finally reached the gate, they were unceremoniously charged the standard parking admission fee.

The Reds arrived with little time to spare. Soprano Alma Perdoza sang the national anthem and the owner's wife, Kay O'Malley, threw out the first pitch, concluding the abbreviated pregame ceremonies. Then the batting orders were announced, with the L.A. lineup consisting of Wills, Gilliam, Moon, Snider, Roseboro, Fairly, Spencer, and Willie Davis. Johnny Podres, coming off an 18-5 season in '61, was selected to pitch the first game ever played in Dodger Stadium.

"It was quite an honor for me. To get the call over Koufax and Drysdale was something special. Maybe because the Dodgers knew they already had a sellout, they started me so that those two would draw their usual big crowds the next two games.

"The first pitch I threw was a ball and the next pitch Eddie Kasko hit down the line for a double. Cincinnati later scored the first run. We played 'em pretty good till Wally Post hit a three-run homer off me in the seventh." The Reds spoiled the inaugural party, winning, 6-3.

To everyone's surprise, there were virtually no problems with postgame traffic. "Where's the Jam?" queried *Times* columnist Jim Murray the next morning. Murray's sympathies rested more with the "bugs [in Chavez Ravine] that were wondering where the hell the goats went!"

There were far more problems with the large throng that had queued up at the Stadium Club. More than 5,000 tried pushing their way into a restaurant with a capacity of 750. Hollywood luminaries Jack Warner, Frank Sinatra, and James Stewart were among those turned away. But other than the breakdown of one of the elevators, opening day was a rousing success—save for one glaring omission.

"Where were the drinking fountains?" thundered *Times* sportswriter Sid Ziff. Ziff counted only three, including the one in Walter O'Malley's office.

"We blew it. The architects just forgot to put them in," confessed Buzzie Bavasi. We also forgot to put electrical outlets in the team dressing rooms."

The city Board of Health informed the Dodgers they would be required to install 13 additional fountains as soon as possible. In his column entitled "H 2 O'Malley," Jim Murray speculated the club had held back the fountains on purpose, the better to sell more soda and beer, but Bavasi denied any such scheme. "We simply forgot the fountains. We made a mistake, but it wasn't by design."

There was nearly as much newspaper space devoted to the water fountain fiasco as the opening of the stadium itself. Oddly, however, the front page of the *Times* on opening day did not position the new park as its lead item. "*West Side Story* Sweeps Oscars" read the largest headline above the fold. The Academy Awards, an annual event, was still bigger news in southern California than an historic stadium debut. Whether the Dodgers liked it or not, Los Angeles was first and foremost a movie town.

* * *

The alliance between the entertainment industry and the Dodgers had been struck even before the team left New York for the West Coast. During the feverish debate over the city's sale of Chavez Ravine property to Walter O'Malley, a group of Hollywood celebrities appeared on a local telethon in 1957, expressing their support for the land referendum.

Comedians Jack Benny, Groucho Marx, and George Burns kept their quips to a minimum, going to bat for the Dodgers with partisan monologues that were strictly business. Once and future Screen Actors Guild president Ronald Reagan stared sincerely into the cameras and declared, "For years we have been watching golf courses and other recreation areas destroyed to make room for subdivisions and factories. Where is a baseball stadium to go, in the suburbs, away from the freeways?" The five-hour telethon provided a critical boost for the Dodgers, who eventually gained sale approval from the L.A. electorate.

During the Dodgers' first seasons in the Coliseum, rubbernecking fans could watch the baseball action, or cast a glimpse at such personalities as Gene Autry, Lauren Bacall, Spencer Tracy, and Nat King Cole. Cole was an especially rabid fan, a singer who admitted without embarassment that he'd have gladly traded his recording career for the chance to play ball. He made certain his local concerts were booked to coincide with L.A. homestands, and delighted in catching the Dodgers in opposing parks whenever on tour.

Cole also agreed to coach the very first celebrity all-star softball team, enlisting a lineup that included Phil Silvers, Dinah Shore, Doris Day, and Mickey Rooney. The game became an annual event, with sportswriters and local disc jockeys providing the competition. A memorable highlight occurred in 1960 when the TV series *The*

Untouchables was at the height of its popularity. During a mock dispute with the umpire, a vintage 1930s car drove up on the infield. Out stepped veteran gangster actor Edward G. Robinson, sporting the requisite fedora and toting a violin case. Robinson pulled out a Tommy gun and mowed down the misguided ump to the delight of the Coliseum crowd.

In 1962, the first celebrity game was played in Dodger Stadium, and "Coach" Cole's persuasive arm-twisting produced another star-laden squad: Dean Martin, James Garner, Johnny Mathis, Pat Boone, Bob Newhart, Joe Louis, Soupy Sales, Nipsey Russell, and two ballplayers-turned-actors, John Berardino and Chuck Connors. Connors, a former Dodger, was honored later that summer when he was presented his old Brooklyn uniform during a special "Chuck Connors Night."

Hectic production schedules limited most of the stars to this one annual stadium appearance, but other personalities became Chavez Ravine "regulars," with season tickets or open invitations from Buzzie Bavasi to watch from press level. "Jack Benny used to sit with Walter O'Malley almost every night. I gave Danny Kaye a key to my office and my private box. Rosalind Russell really loved the game. Fred Astaire and Bing Crosby were there a lot, and Randolph Scott, Milton Berle, and Cary Grant were real fans."

"Cary Grant was probably the most glamorous regular—and he was a very good fan," added Vin Scully. "He was not coming to the ballpark because it was *de regeur*, the thing to do. Cary came because he really loved baseball." Joe Moeller witnessed first-hand how much baseball meant to Grant. "Once, when I was going to pitch the second game of a doubleheader, I was sitting next to him and he asked me, 'Is there any chance sometime that I could go in the clubhouse?' So I took him in with me and he was so excited to be there—like a little kid. Believe me, the players were just as much in awe of him."

A 1962 film release with Grant and fellow baseball fanatic Doris Day, *That Touch of Mink*, featured a scene filmed at the stadium, action which had virtually no relation to the plot of the movie. "At that time," said Scully, "a lot of films included shots of the park. It seemed as if the producers, directors, and writers were going out of their way to incorporate Dodger Stadium in their movies."

Creative Hollywood types felt the same way about the Dodger ballplayers, casting many of them in television programs. "Most of the time, we just did cameos, playing ourselves," remembered Stan Williams.

"That way, we didn't have to join the actors' union." Williams appeared in team uniform with Larry Sherry, Sandy Koufax, Ed Roebuck, and Vin Scully on *Michael Shayne*, a detective series—and with Sherry on an episode of *The Tom Ewell Show*, both in 1961.

By 1962, the Dodgers were popping up on network TV almost monthly. Sandy Koufax offered pitching pointers on the kids' comedy *Dennis the Menace*, and the ubiquitous Don Drysdale was featured on no less than four programs in '62. By then, Big D had already logged numerous hours of screen time. In the early '60s, Don played a cowboy on TV westerns *The Rifleman* and *Lawman*, a bit part in *The Millionaire*, and guest shots on variety programs with Red Skelton, Groucho Marx, and Steve Allen. He also had a film cameo with Jack Webb and Robert Mitchum in a service comedy, *The Last Time I Saw Archie*.

In '62, Drysdale appeared twice on *The Donna Reed Show* (and would return in 1964 with Leo Durocher and Willie Mays). Don was also at the opposite end of a hero-worshipping phone call on *Leave It To Beaver*. He capped his busy '62 schedule playing a fictitious ballplayer named "Gomer" in the drama "Flashing Spikes," part of the *Alcoa Premiere* anthology series. The cast included James Stewart, Jack Warden, and Edgar Buchanan and was directed by the legendary filmmaker, John Ford (another big baseball fan).

Drysdale and other Dodgers could also be caught on movie screens during the early months of '62, teaming up with some unlikely partners—their hated rivals from San Francisco.

Experiment in Terror, a thriller starring Glenn Ford, Lee Remick, Ross Martin, and Stefanie Powers, told the tale of a murderous psychopath who kidnaps a young woman for ransom. He is eventually cornered at Candlestick Park during a Dodgers-Giants game—where the explosive climax of the story takes place.

Giants pitcher Mike McCormick was one of the principal players involved. "They told us they were going to film our game that night. We all had to sign releases and were paid $50 apiece for being in it. They just said to go play and not even think about what they were doing.

"I pitched a complete game win that night, so I was on the postgame show in the clubhouse when they brought Lee Remick down and we were introduced. I signed my cap and gave it to her. Then she left because they were setting up to shoot other scenes.

"All the shots with fans in the stands were done after the game. They were there until three or four in the morning. We had no idea what it was all about until we saw the finished film in '62."

Director Blake Edwards (whose credits included *Peter Gunn, The Pink Panther* movies, and *10*) shot additional closeups back in Los Angeles with Drysdale, John Roseboro, and Wally Moon, which were integrated with game footage for the theatrical release. Vin Scully provided incidental play-by-play. With Henry Mancini's taut musical score blending into the action, *Experiment in Terror* did respectable box-office business throughout the summer of '62.

* * *

One player, Andy Carey, spent most of his summer behind—not in front of—a camera. According to broadcaster Jerry Doggett, "Carey was a businessman, a guy who arrived at the ballpark in a three-piece suit. He was also a stockbroker, a shrewd fella." Carey parlayed good commercial instincts with his love of still photography to create a collection of portraits called "Hero of the Day."

"I'd always been an avid photographer and I had my own portrait studio. So one day I brought my Polaroid camera with me to the park and thought if I took some shots it'd loosen the guys up. Well, we won the game and the next night we won again and I took another "Hero of the Day" picture. After a few more wins, it kinda got to be old hat just taking pictures with the guys in their uniform, so I went to John the clubhouse man for help."

John "Senator" Griffin could well have been a character out of a Ring Lardner baseball novel. The impish equipment manager was heavy-set, disheveled, undistinguished. He wouldn't have rated even a second glance except when he wore his "lucky" costumes. A few years before, the Senator began wearing conspicuous apparel of all kinds— grass skirts, flowered hats, loud ties, kimonos—and left the article of clothing on as long as the Dodgers kept winning. As soon as the team lost, Griffin switched to something else. To insure variety, he stashed dozens of props in storage—hats, gag glasses, moustaches—a full range of childish items that could be found in any cheesy novelty store. Griffin's prop collection proved to be the missing ingredient that brought Carey's pictures to life.

"We took his wigs and cigars, plus shaving cream and started having the guys clown around in the picture," said Carey. "By now we'd won eight or nine in a row, so we just kept it going, shooting these pictures after every win the rest of the year. I became the team's official photographer and Daryl Spencer and Lee Walls were my assistants. I took over a hundred shots during the course of the season and *Life* magazine ran five of them that fall."

The '62 Dodgers were also celebrated on record. A beefy male chorus calling itself "The Dodgermen" recorded a 45 featuring "The Dodger Song" and "Dodger Calypso." The record was the standard adoring fanfare, but another ode to "Dem Bums" received considerably more publicity and airplay. The "D-O-D-G-E-R-S Song (Oh Really? No, O'Malley)" sung praises and lobbed some good-natured ribbing at the ballclub. The puckish performer was Danny Kaye.

Kaye fell in love with the Brooklyn team back in the '40s, and remained loyal when they shifted to California. Kaye's wife, Sylvia Fine, collaborated with Herbert Baker to pen a five-minute ditty documenting a "typical" Dodger-Giant game at Chavez Ravine. Familiar names from each team were recited throughout the musical drama, and delighted fans responded by purchasing thousands of copies throughout the state of California.

The ballplayers also approved. "They played it over the P.A. during batting practice or when we were taking infield," recalled Doug Camilli. "We all thought it was pretty amusing."

One person who allegedly was not amused was Walter O'Malley—at least according to *San Francisco Chronicle* columnist Art Rosenbaum. Here is the "offending" verse:

Maury goes, the catcher throws, right from the solar plexus
At the bag he beats the tag, that mighty little waif
And umpire Conlan cries—"Yer out!!" Out? Out?
Down in the dugout Alston glowers
Up in the booth Vin Scully frowns
Out in the stands O'Malley grins—
"Attendance - 50,000."

Rosenbaum claimed that "O'Malley was so burned he ordered all records out of his park, and on the radio which broadcasts Dodger games." Buzzie Bavasi insisted that did not happen. "That's absolutely false. We sold the record at the park all summer. It was a big item at the concession stands. Besides, Danny sat with me almost every night"—even though the entertainer's concluding stanza referred to his favorite ballclub as "a team that's all heart and all thumbs."

Another Hollywood star adored one special Dodger in secret. In 1962, actress Doris Day, 38, began a relationship with 29-year-old shortstop Maury Wills, an affair that lasted well into the next year.

Other Dodgers were known to date actresses and up-and-coming starlets, but this was no ordinary commingling. Wills was married with a family in Spokane, Washington, at the time he began seeing Day. Even more incendiary was the interracial issue—an affair between a black athlete and the screen's simon-pure symbol of perpetual white virginity.

Although none of Maury's teammates ever pried into the matter, rumors still abounded, mostly among show business cognoscenti. Despite constant inquiries from the media, both Wills and Day agreed to deny any allegations. It was only some 30 years later in his autobiography *On the Run* that Wills finally admitted for attribution that the two had been lovers in the early '60s.

"I really cared about her," Wills wrote. "We had a mutual need for one another. We were in love—as I understood it at the time. I only had so much love for another human being because I was so much in love with baseball. As much love as I had, it was extended to her, but it was too much for me. I couldn't handle it. I was a baseball player."

The Dodgers were attracted to Hollywood's glitter, and many took advantage of its opportunities. When it became a distraction— as it did for Wills— he would "pull down the shade and block it all out when I got to the park." His *raison d'être* was the game itself, reduced to its most basic level of competition—and it mattered not one bit that celebrities were there to cheer him on.

Cheer they did, however—as movie stars and ordinary fans alike watched Wills and four other African American teammates burn up the basepaths of the 1962 National League. It was a Promethean brand of baseball whose influence still reverberates in the game today.

5
THE SWIFT SET

In 1962, the country was stricken with a critical case of dance fever. Never before in the nation's history were so many seized by the compulsion to "cut the rug," whether at high school gyms or specialty night clubs. Dancing had become a national obsession.

The "Twist," Chubby Checker's gyrating fad that started it all a few years earlier, was more popular than ever. It spawned a frenzied wave of imitators, including the "Hully-Gully," "Watusi," and "Mashed Potato." Many other dances were immortalized in pop tunes such as Little Eva's "Locomotion", Bobby "Boris" Pickett's "Monster Mash," and the "Peppermint Twist" by Joey Dee and the Starliters. Everywhere you looked, restless Americans with "happy feet" were satisfying their urge to get up and "go-go."

So it must have seemed entirely appropriate when a fleet-footed southern California quintet decided to shake things up by creating some bold new steps of their own. Their performing arena, however, was the baseball diamond, not a sock hop. And while most of the dances of the day eventually receded into pop culture history, the innovations begun by these five athletes would permanently change their game and the way it was played.

Rivals in haberdashery, partners in shower stall three-part harmony, walkie-talkie radio hams, and strummers of eclectic musical instruments, these five friends, (and occasional enemies) kept the Dodgers clubhouse rollicking throughout the 1962 season. They also played fundamentally brilliant baseball and ran wild on major league basepaths. Their names were Wills, Gilliam, Roseboro, and two guys named Davis.

They were "The Swift Set," and they blazed a trail of stolen bases that paved the way for future thieves Lou Brock, Vince Coleman, and Rickey Henderson.

The Swift Set led the '62 Dodgers to the staggering total of 198 stolen bases, the most by any National League team since the end of World War I. "And that doesn't show how many doubles were stretched into triples, how many singles into doubles," observed *Times* columnist Jim Murray. " 'The Los Angeles Larcenists,' they should call them…they should play in masks and blackjacks. You know the Dodgers are in town by the cloud of dust around second base."

The Dodgers led the league in stolen bases a year earlier—with 86—but that was within the cramped confines of the hitter-friendly Coliseum. The '62 move to spacious Dodger Stadium demanded the revival of a baseball strategy built around speed.

·"Dodger Stadium today is still a good-sized park, but the playing field was even bigger back then," recalled Norm Sherry. "Home plate was much closer to the stands in '62, making it at least fifteen feet farther to the fences. And in Dodger Stadium, those coastal breezes made the nighttime air a little heavier, so the ball didn't travel as well."

Among those who noticed the difference were sluggers on visiting ballclubs. Facing the dreaded Dodger mound staff was an imposing task all by itself; the "pitcher-perfect" surroundings of Dodger Stadium made hitting even more problematic. Moaned Cubs skipper Elvin Tappe, "This park separates the men from the boys. There will be very few .300 hitters around here."

Of this Dodger batters were well aware. After clubbing one of his two home runs for the season on April 30th, Andy Carey stated, "I would rather have four singles than one home run in this park. It's a tough place to hit homers, and you have to pull the ball right down the line, or hit one a mile."

At first glance, it was difficult to see how the Dodgers could be affected. Walter Alston's roster was loaded with power hitters: Wally Moon, Frank Howard, Duke Snider, Tommy Davis, and Ron Fairly could boast of at least one or more major league seasons with home run totals in double figures. The future stereotype of Alston ballclubs that scratched and clawed for every score was completely inappropriate for this team. In fact, the 1962 Dodgers plated more runs (842) than the home-run-happy 1961 New York Yankees, still regarded as the most feared hitting ballclub in major league history.

If Los Angeles bats were so robust, why then did Alston transform his games into track meets? First, the Dodger slugging stats were, in some ways, misleading. Besides feasting on watered-down expansion pitching, the Dodger batters did most of their real damage in the cozier parks on the road. Scoring in Chavez Ravine proved to be a considerably harder task.

There was an even more important reason for Alston to unleash his jackrabbits in 1962. Like the climber who, when asked why he'd want to scale Mount Everest, replied, "because it's there," so too did Alston turn loose his mercurial weapons. Veterans Jim Gilliam and John Roseboro, already established as basepath aggressors, were joined by two of the fastest graduates of the L.A. farm system, Tommy and Willie Davis. In '62, both became permanent members of the starting lineup. And at the top of that batting order was the L.A. shortstop, the catalyst of the Dodger running game.

Quite simply, 1962 was The Year of Maury Wills. He shattered Ty Cobb's 1915 record of 96 stolen bases by swiping 104 (and Cobb was thrown out stealing 38 times—Wills only 13). Wills played in all 165 Dodger regular-season games, a major league record that may never be surpassed. He collected more than 200 hits and just missed batting .300. Maury earned a Gold Glove as the league's best-fielding shortstop, and was voted the N.L.'s Most Valuable Player. He even won the prestigious Hickok Belt as 1962's top athlete in any sport.

Just four years earlier, Maury was languishing in the minors. He was merely another light-hitting infielder, seemingly doomed to a marginal career in the bush leagues. Painfully shy and bereft of confidence, Maury Wills was going nowhere.

His insecurities could be traced to a troubled past. Wills was born in Washington, D.C., one of 13 children growing up in a rat-infested government housing project. His father was a minister and naval yard machinist, his mother an elevator operator and domestic. Neither was home much, so Maury looked after himself, learning how to iron his own clothing by age seven. With so many brothers and sisters, the children were forced to sleep in the same beds, but no one wanted to sleep with Maury. He was a chronic bedwetter, and continued to suffer the embarrassment of enuresis as an adult. Even in '62, his greatest baseball season, Wills was still plagued by his bedwetting problem.

Maury was small for his age, but excelled in athletics. By the time he was a high school senior, Wills was all-city in baseball, football, and basketball. Maury also eloped that same year, at the age of 17. His high school bride, Gertrude, was only 16. Soon after, their first child was born.

Nine different colleges (including Syracuse and Ohio State) offered Maury athletic scholarships, but the financial responsibilities of supporting his family forced Wills to sign a professional baseball contract instead. Ironically, the Giants could have nabbed him first, but deemed Maury too small to make it as a big leaguer. The rival Dodgers decided to take a chance, signing Wills for a $500 bonus and a new suit ("it comes with two pairs of pants," noted the

Brooklyn scout). To sweeten the deal, the Dodgers threw in a pair of socks.

Maury's minor league career began in 1951, and there he stayed for the next eight years. It was a difficult period, marked by low salaries, long bus rides, constant separation from his family and racist taunts from fans and players. In 1955, Wills became the first black to break the Texas League color barrier. By 1959, Maury made his permanent residence in Spokane, Washington, home of the Dodgers' Triple-A farm team. And it appeared he'd be staying there until his playing days were over.

That spring, the Detroit Tigers, in dire need of a shortstop, bought Maury's contract from the Dodgers. Wills stuck with the Tigers until the end of the exhibition schedule, when he was unceremoniously returned to his former ballclub. Detroit did not feel Maury was worth the $35,000 they would have had to pay for his rights. A humiliated Wills returned to Spokane, utterly defeated.

At perhaps his lowest ebb, Maury Wills gained critical support from the man who had literally changed his life. In 1958, Spokane manager Bobby Bragan convinced Wills he could be a major leaguer by tutoring him in the art of switch-hitting. Almost overnight, Maury regained his confidence and his batting average improved. In '59, Bragan was there once again to bolster Maury's sagging spirits. Wills responded, blistering Pacific Coast League pitching at a .313 clip. When the Dodgers needed infield help at midseason, Bragan recommended Maury to Buzzie Bavasi. Los Angeles recalled Wills and made him its regular shortstop. The Dodgers went on to win the pennant and the World Series, and Wills deservedly got much of the credit.

The following season, Maury regressed at the plate, hovering perilously close around .200. It was then that a second "guardian angel" appeared in the form of hitting coach Pete Reiser. Reiser began arriving early at the park to work with Wills on a regular basis. "He gave up three hours every day that he could have spent with his family," Maury later remembered. "Pete taught me to believe in myself. He gave me the inner conceit that every athlete needs if he hopes to be great." Within two weeks, Reiser's lessons took hold, and by year's end, Wills had lifted his batting average close to .300. From then on, Maury was a solid big league hitter, finishing his career with a lifetime mark of .281.

Now that Wills was getting on base, he could show off his greatest skill—running. He swiped 50 bases in 1960, and still led the league a year later with 35 steals. The move to Dodger Stadium made him even more dangerous.

"Being a line drive hitter, the larger playing area gave me a better chance to run," said Wills. "The infield was fast so I was now able to hit groundballs through the hole and also beat out a lot of high choppers." Walter Alston was so confident of Maury's ability to take advantage of this new environment that the skipper gave Wills an automatic green light to run whenever he wanted. No other Dodger was afforded that privilege.

"I've never seen a better baserunner," said Alston. "He knows when to take a chance, how to get a good lead, how to get the jump on the pitcher and how to slide." Al Campanis, the team's scouting director at the time, paid Wills the ultimate compliment. "I was always the guy who gave the lectures on baserunning at Vero Beach. But after '62, it was Maury's permanent job. It was the first time we ever had an active ballplayer teach basestealing at spring training."

Wills also knew National League hurlers better than they knew themselves. In *Life* magazine that summer, Maury revealed, "I watch every move the pitcher makes and jot down every item in the book I keep in my head. You always steal on the pitcher, not the catcher.

"Just about every pitcher in the business shows a telltale sign with a man on base—a dip of the head or a turn of the shoulder. These signs tell me that this pitch is heading for the plate and that I'm heading for second."

Wills quickly became the darling of Dodger Stadium. "Go, Maury go!" exhorted the fans whenever Maury reached base. "I called him 'The Roadrunner,' based on the cartoon character," recalled Vin Scully. "And every time he'd steal a base we'd go 'beep-beep!' on the broadcasts, and we'd get the crowd in the stands to go 'beep-beep!,' too."

Crowds on the road were equally captivated by Wills' baserunning. And a national TV audience saw Maury at his best on July 10th at the first of two All-Star Games played in '62.

A capacity crowd packed Washington's brand-new D.C. Stadium, a throng which included President Kennedy and Vice President Lyndon Johnson. Native son Maury Wills made his hometown return a memorable one when he first appeared in the sixth inning. As pinchhitter Stan Musial was taking his practice cuts, Wills told the Cardinal outfielder that if he got on, then Maury would steal a base. "The Man" promptly drilled a single off Minnesota's Camilo Pascual. Maury went in to pinch-run.

Before Pascual had even thrown a pitch to the next hitter, Pirates shortstop Dick Groat, Wills was off. His jump was so big that Twins catcher Earl Battey did not bother attempting a throw. Groat followed with a single and Wills scored easily.

In the eighth, Wills struck again, looping a shallow single. San Francisco's Jim Davenport followed with a hit to left fielder Rocky Colavito, whose throwing arm was among the A.L.'s best. Colavito, as expected, threw to second, but Wills had already taken off for third, sliding in safely just ahead of the relay. The Giants' Felipe Alou then lofted a short pop fly to right. Again, Maury displayed the guts of a cat burglar by tagging up and heading for home. Angels outfielder Leon Wagner gunned his throw to the plate, but Wills slid in safely, beating the tag from Cleveland catcher John Romano. It gave the Nationals the insurance run they needed for a 3-1 victory.

By the end of July, Wills had already equalled his own career high of 50 steals, the goal he initially set for himself during spring training. Realizing that his larceny was winning ballgames (and packing ballparks home and away), Maury began to accelerate his pace—even as the rest of the league was making a concerted effort to stop him.

Giants catcher Tom Haller probably spoke for all opposing teams when he admitted, "The guy that got under our skin the most was Maury Wills. He was so competitive and did so many little things that hurt you. Our perception was that it seemed like everything he was doing was trying to rub it in. Of course, he was just playing hard, but we still didn't like him. We always wanted to beat him—get him, knock him out on the double play, whatever you could do."

A few teams turned to their groundskeepers to do the dirty work, whether it meant watering down infields or letting the grass grow to slow down Maury's high-chop hits. More often, it was the players themselves who went gunning for Wills. "Several pitchers have already aimed for my legs," he admitted. "One catcher deliberately threw at my legs when I was on third base."

Most of Maury's physical damage came from his constant sliding on the basepaths. During the '62 season, Wills endured a bruised right hand, black and blue marks on his left hip, and hamstring spasms. Team trainers Bill Buhler and Wayne Anderson offered relief with vitamins, diathermy treatments, whirlpool baths, and foot massage. To protect his beat-up knees, Maury covered them with inch-thick pads. Wills even enlisted the aid of a local psychologist who applied hypnosis to help the Dodger shortstop overcome his pain. Confiding with

L.A. beat writer Bob Hunter, Wills moaned, "I'm so sore, the very thought of sliding makes me hurt all over."

* * *

Maury sacrificed his health to keep the Dodger running game in motion, but in other ways Jim "Junior" Gilliam may have given up more to help his team. No one in the National League possessed a craftier batting eye, executed the hit-and-run more adroitly, or was better at taking pitches than Gilliam. Batting second behind Wills for virtually the entire season, the 10-year veteran probably forfeited the chance to hit .300 or add to his power totals.

"Sure, I've laid off the ball intentionally," admitted Gilliam. Sometimes the ball will be right down the middle, too. But I'm in no hurry to hit. You only hit but one pitch and I'm in no hurry."

A grateful Wills was more than happy to express his appreciation. "I know Jim sacrificed his own personal gains many times to help me. When he's batting left-handed (Gilliam, like Wills, was a switch-hitter), he obstructs the catcher's view of first base. Jim doesn't pull the ball, so it's impossible for fielders to play him in any specific manner. This gives me a great advantage in keeping the shortstop and second baseman honest. He isn't a first-ball hitter and doesn't jump around going for bad pitches. Before a pitcher finishes with him, usually he has to throw five or six pitches, and that's all I need to pull a steal."

Buzzie Bavasi believed that "without Gilliam, Wills doesn't even steal 50 bases that season. Jim had incredible peripheral vision. He could see out of the corner of his eye if Maury was going or not. If Maury didn't get a particularly good jump, he'd foul the ball off on purpose. He was amazing. There's nobody else I know of who was as good at it—even (Hall-of-Famer) Pee Wee Reese couldn't have done it."

Jim's unselfish attitude was a constant throughout his extensive baseball career. At the age of 16, Junior was already playing in the Negro minor leagues, then signed with Brooklyn six years later. A strong major league debut in 1953 earned him Rookie-of-the-Year honors. For the next 13 years, Gilliam was a vital, if not always heralded part of Dodger success.

No one valued his contributions more than Walter Alston. "He never made the headlines that often, but I would rather see Gilliam up at bat with a man on second base and no one out than anybody I know, because he would do the job for the team." In an interview with Vin Scully, Alston showered more praise on Gilliam. "He was the complete professional. In all the years I managed him, he almost never missed a sign, threw to the wrong base, or made a mistake."

Alston could also have added that Gilliam was never given a regular position. Because of his wide-ranging abilities and the Dodgers' talent surplus, Junior frequently shuttled between second, third, and the outfield. The Dodger manager appreciated Jim's versatility—and durability. "Every year there's been some 'pheenom' who was gonna take his job. None of them has yet. It never shakes him up. Gilliam brings three gloves and waits around and says, 'Well, I'm gonna play someplace.' So you'd play the pheenom all spring and Gilliam would get into 152 games anyway." Because his throwing arm was only average, an endless parade of Dodger "phenoms" were auditioned as potential replacements during Jim's tenure: Charlie Neal, Randy Jackson, Dick Gray, Don Zimmer. The uncomplaining Gilliam replied merely by saying, "A young fellow taking my place can't be good for two days or two weeks. Baseball is an everyday game." Just about the only subject Gilliam ever grumbled about publicly was flying in airplanes, an occupational hazard he feared and despised.

In 1962, the latest "phenom" was second baseman Larry Burright, and Gilliam, ever the team player, went out of his way to assist the rookie. "He told me a lot during spring training," admitted Burright. "He'd move me a step to play the hitters. He's a real great guy."

Baseball fans and the press corps seemed to agree, but teammate John Roseboro occasionally witnessed Gilliam's stormier side. Writing in his autobiography, Roseboro said: "Gilliam was a quiet guy, but he had a mean streak that the players saw, even if others didn't…he was suspicious of people, often curt with them, hard, direct. He said what he thought and he didn't always think things through. He had a chip on his shoulder, waiting for someone to knock it off."

Perhaps these outbursts were a way of venting the frustrations he must have felt over his career-long role of sacrificing himself for others. And Gilliam understandably harbored resentment towards a Dodger management that seemed intent each spring on replacing him with a younger player. It is also possible that Gilliam was basically a bitter man, and compensated for it by creating the persona of someone who would do anything "for the good of the team." Whichever scenario, if any, is accurate, a number of incidents from the '62 season offer indisputable evidence that Jim Gilliam was not completely comfortable or happy with the supportive role he played.

One venue where Junior did not compromise his prowess was anywhere there was a billiard table. He handled a cue stick as deftly as he controlled his bat. One evening during spring training, Jim entered a pool hall in the town of Gifford, Florida, and promptly announced to its patrons, "Rack 'em up. 'The Devil' is here." Gilliam then tossed a $20 bill on the table. "Who wants a piece of 'The Devil?' he challenged. No one did. Gilliam later admitted he was only kidding, but the nickname still stuck, even though it was heard only in the clubhouse, never in public.

*   *   *

John Roseboro was called "Gabby," a nickname that could be traced to ex-L.A. pitcher Roger Craig, who came up with the monicker because of John's noticeably quiet nature. One grimace or grin from Roseboro told a pitcher all he needed to know about his performance. Throughout the Dodger catcher's career, he preferred to express himself with deeds, not words. He spoke only when spoken to, but his replies were thoughtful, intelligent, often witty. Otherwise, Roseboro employed nonverbal methods to convey his thoughts.

"When you have a good catcher like Roseboro, it's probably like the same thing in music," said reliever Ed Roebuck. "You're on the same wavelength. You know what sign the guy's gonna put down before he puts it down." Johnny Podres remembered how Roseboro got a pitcher's attention. "If he thought you were fallin' asleep out there, he'd just fire that ball back and that would wake you right up."

"Gabby could catch," said Don Drysdale, "even if he did have to wear white tape on his fingers during night games so we could see his signs. His hands were that dark." All the Dodgers, including Ron Perranoski, believed they were in good hands with Roseboro. "He knew every pitcher and what they were capable of doing. He never got mad. He was an even-tempered individual, a strong, quiet man. He seldom came out to the mound; I had to call him out if I needed him. And then he'd crack a little joke to take some of the pressure off. Sometimes I'd see him smile at me through his mask."

With Roseboro on the job, Buzzie Bavasi stopped worrying about the catching position. "There was no question that John Roseboro was the boss. I have never heard even one of my pitchers criticize anything that Roseboro ever did behind the plate.. And he had more courage than any catcher I ever saw. On a close play at home, nobody'd ever score because he'd block the plate with his entire body. He was the 'Rock of Gibraltar.'"

John learned much of the catching trade from his mentor, Brooklyn legend Roy Campanella. "I think I was as close to Campy as any man I've known, except my father," Roseboro confessed. But in early 1958, as the Dodgers were finalizing their move from New York to Los Angeles, Campy was seriously injured in a car accident, never to play again. By default, rookie John Roseboro became the Dodgers' starter. "We didn't have anybody else," admitted Bavasi, "but from the moment he put on his L.A. uniform, he became the leader of the club."

Alston also loved Roseboro, and not just simply for his Gold Glove receiving skills. Both were soft-spoken, dependable men from Ohio who lived and breathed baseball. Smokey also didn't mind that Roseboro was the speediest catcher in baseball. During the '62 season, Gabby buzzed the basepaths for an astounding seven triples. He also swiped 12 bases in 15 attempts, the most by any National League catcher since 1928. "He beats out infield hits where old-time catchers had trouble beating out outfield hits," wrote *Times* columnist Jim Murray. "On the fastest team in baseball, he ranks no worse than fourth in a foot race."

* * *

Those who saw him play still contend there was no major leaguer with better speed than Willie Davis. Dodger broadcaster Jerry Doggett: "Going from first to third, there was never anybody who ran as fast as Willie. They'd have races almost every day in Vero Beach and nobody ever came close to beating him, not even Maury Wills." Pitcher Stan Williams: "He wasn't real good at getting out of the batter's box, but once he got it going, he took only about four steps between bases. For a sprinter, he had the longest stride I've ever seen." Buzzie Bavasi: "The best play in baseball was to watch Willie Davis run out a triple."

His God-given quickness was the major reason why Davis was offered the chance to play regularly in '62. Dodger Stadium's outfield was simply too much turf for mere mortals to cover. After one look at the endless outfield acreage in his new park, Alston glanced at the fleet youngster and declared, "He almost has to play center field for us at Chavez."

Willie had been burning up L.A. tracks since childhood. Shortly after his birth in Mineral Springs, Arkansas, Davis, his mother, and brother moved to East Los Angeles. Willie's entrepreneurial spirit prevented him from falling prey to the pitfalls of a tough neighborhood. In grade school, Davis always had cash in his pocket because of a successful newspaper stand. "Gang leaders used to borrow money from me," he recalled.

At Roosevelt High, Davis lettered in basketball and track, but preferred baseball because "that's where the money is." Dodgers scout Kenny Myers signed him for $5,000, but there was still much work to be done.

"Willie Davis was a manufactured ballplayer in the truest sense of the word," said Vin Scully. "The only thing he did naturally was run. Otherwise, everything else was taught to him." Willie was a right-handed-hitting first baseman in high school, but Myers converted him into a lefty who played the outfield. "Kenny Myers made a player out of Willie," recalled Stan Williams. "He took him under his wing, and spent hundreds of hours teaching him to hit and throw." Another scout, Harold "Lefty" Phillips, also tutored the talented but raw youngster.

The hard work paid off. Davis won league batting titles in each of his two minor league seasons, arriving in the majors to stay by 1961. The media was instantly captivated by his talent—and his cockiness. "He looks like a decade of World Series checks," clucked the *Times*. Filmmaker David Wolper selected Willie as the subject of the Mike Wallace-narrated TV documentary, *Biography of a Rookie*. And Davis glowed from the attention. "Confidence? You just cannot take the confidence out of Willie Davis," observed coach Pete Reiser.

Baseball stardom and the bright lights of Hollywood proved to be both a help and a hindrance that Willie could not ignore. "I was a swinging man with the foxes hanging on to me and my money was going fast when Buzzie [Bavasi] called me in. He offered me a piece of cash if I'd get married and buy a house. Man, there was a wedding in nothing flat! And I've been a happier player since."

And a better one, too—although to many it didn't always seem as if Davis was performing at top speed. Few players were blessed with so much talent, yet seemed so reluctant to fully exploit it. Perhaps his baseball skills came too easily. His roguish, devil-may-care demeanor could have also been a factor.

"We had him on the postgame show after his very first game," Vin Scully recalled. "At the end of the night, there was a fly ball to center with the bases loaded and two out. He stood almost at attention and caught the ball with a 'ho-hum' kind of attitude. So I asked him how he could be so relaxed in his first game in the big leagues. Well, Willie has a voice that's as low as the ocean floor. He replies in that rumbling, deep tone of his: 'It's not my life—it's not my wife—so why worry?' "

Nineteen-sixty-two was probably Willie's best overall season in baseball. He scored more than 100 runs, drove in 85, socked a career-high 21 home runs and batted .285. He tied for the National League lead in triples, and his 32 stolen bases were more than anyone else in the majors—except for Wills.

The motivating factor behind this career season? Buzzie Bavasi believed it stemmed from the competition between Willie and his best friend on the team, Tommy Davis. Though the two Davises were unrelated, they were as close as brothers. "Tommy made Willie a good hitter—but not by teaching him. Tommy was doing so well that Willie felt he had to try to keep up with him."

* * *

In the same year Maury Wills won MVP honors, there were those who believed that Tommy Davis was at least as valuable to the Dodgers, if not more so. His collective statistics reveal one of the greatest hitting performances of any single season in baseball history: 27 home runs, 230 hits, 120 runs scored, a .346 batting average, and 153 runs batted in. It marked the first time since 1937 that any National Leaguer had driven in 150 or more runs—and no one in baseball has done it since. In 1962, Tommy Davis was all of 23 years old.

"Tommy was probably the best pure hitter I ever saw," claimed Jerry Doggett. "And he won the batting title that year because he learned how to hit to right field." Buzzie Bavasi applied financial incentives to get what he wanted from Willie Davis; he tried the same approach with Tommy.

"Tommy got off to a slow start in '62, so I called him into the office. In those days, a hundred dollars was a lot of money. I said to him, 'Tommy, you're trying to pull everything. So here's what I'll do: I'm going to give you a hundred dollars for every hit you get to the right of second base.' That cost me $3,500, but it was worth it."

"He was a great clutch hitter," said Ed Roebuck. "It seemed as if he knocked in an awful lot of runs with two outs." Sandy Koufax also appreciated Tommy's timely run-production. "Every time there was a man on base, he'd knock him in. And every time there were two men on base, he'd hit a double and knock them both in."

Beyond his natural ability, Tommy's intelligence enabled him to run clever con games on opposing pitchers. Norm Sherry remembered one Davis deception. "He'd go up there and look bad on some pitches, but he'd do it on purpose. So the pitcher would throw the same thing to him again and he'd knock the cover off the ball."

Davis learned early on in life that he'd have to be street-smart if he was going to survive growing up in Brooklyn's rugged Bedford-Stuyvesant district. Tommy quickly gravitated to sports, advancing from stickball to church league baseball. At Boys High, he starred in baseball and track, but may have loved basketball best. "I couldn't shoot a lick, I was a garbage man. But I made the all-city team with Doug Moe and Satch Sanders, so I was in pretty good company. I was going to go to Providence with my best friend, Lenny Wilkens. But because of my grades, I signed with the Dodgers out of high school."

Tommy dreamed of playing in nearby Ebbets Field before a cheering crowd of family and friends. But a year after Davis signed his contract, the Dodgers left Brooklyn for the West Coast. Disappointed but undeterred, Tommy batted .300 or better at every one of his minor league stops, finishing with a Pacific Coast League batting title in 1959. A year later, he was in the majors.

Throughout the Dodger farm system, Davis was regarded as an immense talent who "needs to be pushed occasionally." So read the year-end report filed by his then-manager at Kokomo, Pete Reiser, who eventually became his hitting coach in Los Angeles. "I'm Tommy's father and his nursemaid," said Reiser. "I figure out what he needs. Sometimes I bawl him out. Other times I treat him nice. I told him he has to be mean and mad at everyone in the world to be a good hitter."

Walter Alston knew Dodger fortunes rested upon the ability to unlock Tommy's potential. "Down in his heart he wants to play, win and bear down as much as anyone. But he likes to relax. It's our job to keep him wound up." One time, after Alston had chewed him out for perceived nonchalance, the normally placid Davis answered back, "This is the only thing I can do well. Don't you think I want to make as good a living out of baseball as I can?"

Tommy performed at his best during pressure situations, due in large part to his own brand of creative visualization. "When I see those ribbies on the bases, it means more money in the bank. When I see men on, I seem 'em as dollar signs." Team vice president Fresco Thompson went a step further. "With no one on, he goes for power and presses. With men on, he concentrates better. He simply is a better hitter with men on base." In '62, the men on base who scored on Tommy's hits were usually the one-two-three hitters in the order: Wills, Gilliam, and

Willie Davis. Every once in a while, Tommy got the chance to knock in number-eight man Roseboro, too. Yet the baseball diamond was not the only place where the Swift Set liked to run together.

* * *

Sitting at his booth in a Milwaukee hotel coffee shop, Tommy Davis strained to hear the garbled voice crackling over his walkie-talkie. Suddenly, the Dodger slugger broke into a wide smile of recognition. "That's Maury! I just got Maury! He's in a store downtown!" He felt better knowing where "Mousey" was, and the portable radios were a terrific way to stay in touch.

The sounds were much more melodious when the Swift Set got together for musical jam sessions. With his silky baritone, Willie Davis was clearly the most talented vocalist, and three others played instruments with some degree of competence. Roseboro confessed that his talent was limited, but still liked "to fool around with a harmonica, bongo drums, and a ukelele."

Wills was a more polished performer. In his second year with the Dodgers, Maury learned to play the banjo, and eventually was good enough to line up professional dates in Las Vegas and New York. But during his banjo apprenticeship, he drove his teammates crazy by repeatedly playing "Bye Bye Blues." Road roommate Roseboro finally had enough and demanded that the Dodgers find him alternate quarters in the hotel. Even the usually placid Sandy Koufax reached the boiling point with Maury's incessant plucking. "You play 'Bye Bye Blues' one more time around here, and I will personally cut the strings off your banjo," he threatened.

Occasionally, Tommy Davis joined Roseboro and Wills for a musical trio, with Maury playing banjo to their accompanying claviettas—an instrument described by Wills as "a wind instrument that's a combination harmonica and accordion." In 1963, the threesome would cut a single on Lionel Hampton's personal record label. "We like standards," admitted Tommy D. " 'My Funny Valentine.' 'Stella by Starlight.' You can get a bad clavietta for $12 or $14. I had one of those but now I got a $40 clavietta. 'Moon River' is nice on the clavietta."

More often, Tommy simply enjoyed listening to jazz on the portable phonograph that seemingly never left his side. Many of his albums were from the Capitol label, the record company that employed Davis in its promotions department during the off-season. Roseboro also carried his records and phono from one league city to another. Among his favorite artists was Ray Charles, who also happened to be the Dodger catcher's business partner in a local travel agency called Gulliver's.

Whenever possible, the Davises liked to sneak in a round of golf. Willie in particular became a fanatic, studiously digesting every golf book he could find. Eventually, he lowered his score into the 70s. Roseboro played with Tommy and Willie for a while, then began devoting more of his time to chess and reading.

Gabby also took special pride in his appearance. So fastidious was the catcher that Vin Scully referred to him as "the 'Iviest' guy in the league." *Times* writer Jim Murray claimed that "on road trips, if John Roseboro isn't at a movie, he's at a laundry. He has more wardrobe changes than Loretta Young."

Indeed, what most distinguished The Swift Set was its impeccable taste in clothing. *Sports Illustrated* noted that, "When The Swift Set sits in a hotel lobby, everyone marvels at its splendid sweaters."

"Look, I spent eight and a half years in the minors, came from a family of 13 kids and had six of my own," said Maury Wills. "I never had much to spend on clothes until I got to the big leagues. So it was important for me to look nice.

"Other players drove flashy cars. I was happy with my Ford station wagon. But I wanted to look sharp. We did a lot of our shopping at Cy Devore's in Hollywood. That was the ultimate, because that's where the movie stars went."

The Swift Set enjoyed squaring off in card games or golf, but the competition was fiercest when it came to who was the best-dressed Dodger. Wills remembered that occasionally the feuding got ugly. "Tommy Davis lived four houses away from me. He came over for coffee. Our kids played together. But when we'd get to the ballpark, we fought like cats and dogs.

"One time on the team bus in Milwaukee, he started riding me unmercifully about a new sweater I just bought. I had really picked it out with care, but he says, 'Where'd you get it—at a fire sale?' Soon everybody on the bus was laughing at me. Jim Gilliam, who was an excellent dresser, too, also used to criticize my wardrobe, but not in front of everybody like Davis was doing. At the park I challenged Tommy to step outside the clubhouse. When he got there, I was already in tears.

" 'C'mon, let's fight,' I said. 'I'm tired of this crap.' Tommy just laughed. 'I'm not gonna fight you. You're too little.' But I kept shoving him in the chest. My pride and ego were hurt, but he refused to fight me and he wouldn't apologize."

During another game, the two almost came to blows when Wills got a signal from the bench to reposition Tommy in the outfield. Davis ignored Maury's signals, then finally gave him the finger. At the end of the inning, Wills approached Tommy to ask him why he kept ignoring him. Before Maury could finish his question, the 200-pound Davis began punching the 160-pound Wills. Frank Howard, the biggest player on the team, moved in to break it up.

Perhaps the year's most disturbing internal squabble occurred between Wills and Gilliam—a clear indication that all was not well between the Dodgers' number one and two hitters. During a game in Los Angeles, Maury was drawing close to a dozen throws at first while an angry Gilliam impatiently waited in the batter's box. With two strikes on Junior, the Dodger shortstop took off. Gilliam took a called third strike, slammed his bat down in disgust, then shot a menacing look at Wills who was sure "it was his way of saying that I had shown him up."

In the dugout, a now-equally angry Wills screamed, "You do that again and I'll stomp you right through the ground!" "Up yours!" Gilliam retorted. Johnny Podres was in the dugout when the confrontation occurred and overheard Gilliam scream, "I've been taking enough pitches all year long to let you steal bases!" The two headed toward the runway and began exchanging blows when, once again, Frank Howard played the role of peacemaker.

"What are you guys doing?" Howard asked incredulously. "You guys can't fight. We're all on the same team." Howard held both players in midair until tempers cooled, then finally dropped them. Without the intervention of the Dodgers' Gentle Giant, several members of The Swift Set might not have survived the season.

* * *

The pressure of a pennant race can by debilitating for a baseball team with no sense of humor. Fortunately for the Dodgers, there were a number of comedic (if not sophomoric) episodes that managed to defuse clubhouse tension during the pressure-cooker '62 season. One ongoing ritual was Andy Carey's zany "Hero of the Day" photo sessions. Another was the recurring "Dr. Frankenstein" routine staged by the diminutive Maury Wills and the Brobdingnagian Frank Howard.

The bit went something like this: Wills takes an imaginary phone call from an irritated Walter O'Malley, who demands more punch in the lineup. Maury assures the boss he'll build him his "monster." The shortstop summons Howard, barking out various verbal hitting commands to his "creation." Frank follows every order with stiff, robotic motions, gripping the bat and swinging lustily. Suddenly, without warning, Howard mysteriously goes berserk until "Master" Wills orders him to desist. Maury then picks up the "phone" and informs O'Malley, "Your monster is ready. He will be in right field today wearing number 25."

At 6-7, 250 pounds, Frank Howard truly was a monster—the biggest man in the big leagues. "He wasn't born—he was founded," chuckled the *Times'* Jim Murray. "He answers to the nickname 'Hondo' because he's the only guy in the world outside of organized basketball who could call John Wayne 'Shorty.' " Only Howard's majestic home run blasts seemed more towering than the man himself.

The former Ohio State basketball and baseball All-American signed a then-staggering $108,000 bonus with the Dodgers in 1958. In 1959, he was voted *The Sporting News* Minor League Player of the Year, and National League Rookie of the Year in '60. During that first season in Los Angeles, Howard's offensive feats were near-mythical—and his squeaky-clean personality also seemed too good to be true.

Of the young Howard, Al Campanis said, "He would 'yessir' you to death." Stan Williams agreed. "He was such a courteous young man that you'd feel kind of silly. It was like meeting a 12-year-old boy who was nine feet tall. He'd call everybody 'Mister,' then shake your hand and almost tear your arm off."

Vin Scully viewed the young Howard as the living embodiment of the world's largest eagle scout. "Because he was so polite, other players teased him, and he was often the butt of jokes. But he was very good-natured, thank goodness, or he would have dismantled the clubhouse."

One thing Howard routinely demolished was the menu of any restaurant he patronized. "You never wanted to go out to dinner with Frank," shuddered Johnny Podres. "By the time you'd eaten one steak, he'd already have polished off three. He was the biggest eater on the team—by far." Legend has it that during one team flight Howard inhaled six airline dinners in one sitting. "Absolutely not," Hondo insisted. "Only four."

The free-swinging Frank was plagued by strikeouts and was not a fundamentally sound baserunner. His throwing arm was a cannon, but wasn't always accurate. And after tailing off in his sophomore season, Howard began the '62 campaign on the bench behind Wally Moon. Slowly, Howard began to work his way into the batting order, and by the middle of June he became a starter. Everyday duty did wonders for his confidence, and Hondo went on an offensive tear that sent chills down the collective spines of opposing teams. Over the next 26 games, Howard drove in 41 runs, hit 12 homers, and batted .381. He finished the year at .296, with 31 home runs and 119 RBI, his best season ever with the Dodgers.

Nearly as entertaining as his tape-measure blasts were his relay pegs from right field. He threw out 19 baserunners, tying him for second in the league with Pittsburgh's Roberto Clemente. His arm elicited perhaps the most audible response from the Chavez Ravine grandstands, but it was not the most valuable appendage on the Dodgers.

That arm could be found somewhere among the men who comprised the Los Angeles pitching staff, the most dominant in the major leagues.

6
THE ARMS OF LOS ANGELES

The Milwaukee bartender had long since finished washing the last glass. Now he was stacking chairs on the tables, but they still wouldn't leave. The mop and bucket were next, and if that didn't work, he'd have to turn out the lights and lock up the joint. Nearly a half hour had passed since "last call," but the Dodger pitchers paid no attention. Instead, their debate raged on over how to get the heater past Henry Aaron, the only guy on the Braves who'd been hitting the L.A. staff all year.

When the barkeep had just about given up hope, the five Dodgers stood up at once and dug into their wallets, tossing wads of bills on the table. These guys could drink, but they were also generous tippers. "Thanks, buddy," smiled Stan Williams. "We'll see ya tomorrow night." With that, the ballplayers exited, still arguing contentiously about Hammerin' Hank.

For years the Dodger pitchers had capped off their summer evenings in Wisconsin by heading for The New Yorker, a saloon whose regal name belied its otherwise seedy trappings. But it was just what the players wanted—cheap beer in an atmosphere ideal for unwinding after a game. "When we first started going there, the place was a real dive," recalled Williams. "But we spent so much dough there that they started fixing it up. They cleared the peanut shells off the floor and put down red carpet. It got too nice, so we had to go someplace else."

Wherever they went, it was as a group—according to Ron Perranoski. "We'd go to dinner together, have drinks together, and talk baseball together. We were a very close-knit pitching staff." Tenth-inning bull sessions were one of Johnny Podres' fondest memories. "Playing at home in L.A., we used to sit around in the clubhouse an hour or an hour and a half after the game, have a couple of beers and talk about baseball. When we went out, it was pretty much just us. We generally didn't let too many of the other guys come along. It was a pitchers' fraternity."

Theirs was a comraderie founded on friendship and forged by success. Indeed, it is difficult to name a better overall pitching corps of that era than the Dodger staff of the early 1960s. It included two future Hall-of-Famers (Sandy Koufax and Don Drysdale), two previous winners of World Series MVP trophies (Podres and Larry Sherry), and one of the game's most dominant relief pitchers (Perranoski).

"I loved to catch these guys because they could all throw to spots," remarked John Roseboro. "They could pitch away from the hitter's power. It became a chess match between the pitcher and catcher and hitter, and the odds were in our favor because they could throw the ball over the outside of the plate all day long."

And "pound the Budweiser" all night long. The Dodger pitchers liked their beer cold, the women adventurous, and the opposing hitters nervous. National League batters seldom dug in against the Arms of Los Angeles. "Those guys were a lot alike," observed catcher Norm Sherry. "If they didn't like the way that batter was standing in the batter's box, they'd do something about it." It was a lesson absorbed by nearly every pitcher who was brought up through the L.A. organization.

* * *

Ron Perranoski was the only member of the '62 staff who was not originally signed and developed in the Dodger farm system. The native of Paterson, New Jersey, passed on a contract from the White Sox to attend Michigan State University, but the Cubs reeled Ron in with a hefty $30,000 bonus after his senior year in 1958. He marked time in the minors for two seasons, then was swapped to the coast with two other players for infielder Don Zimmer. In 1961, Ron started the first and only game in his 13 major league seasons. After that, the bullpen became his permanent residence. Even as a rookie, it was clear Perranoski possessed the talent and temperament of a born relief pitcher. "I don't care if I never start another game as long as I live," he declared. "I can't wait to throw the ball when I get in there."

For Norm Sherry, catching Perranoski was pure pleasure. "He had that good, hard sinker and a real slow curveball that threw hitters off. He had great control, kept the ball down and away from righthanders and would get a lot of groundballs for you."

Perhaps Ron's greatest asset was his stamina. In '62, he appeared in 70 games, a record at the time for a lefthander. His 20 saves led the team and ranked him second in the National League. Perranoski relished the extra duty. "I loved it. The more work I got, the better I felt. I had the type of arm where it never bothered me to throw every day, and if I threw four out of five days, I would have better stuff and better control on the fourth day than I would on the first."

In 1961, Ron was used primarily against left-handed hitters, but his role expanded in '62. Although the term "closer" was not yet in vogue, Perranoski became the ace of the Dodger relief corps, supplanting Larry Sherry. After three seasons as L.A.'s bullpen mainstay, Alston looked to Sherry primarily for long relief, a role that gave Larry, a frustrated "starter-in-waiting," the chance to prove he could pitch over protracted stretches. His best performance of the season was seven innings of shutout ball in an extra-inning victory over the Cubs. Still, he never was able to crack the rotation.

It was a medical marvel that Sherry made it to the major leagues at all. The Hollywood native was born with two clubbed feet, but corrective surgery at age six—and persistent exercise—enabled Larry to overcome his defect. The difficult episode imbued him with a competitive, even irascible attitude. Older brother Norm remembered that back in the neighborhood, "He was a little troublemaker, always fighting. If he didn't like the way a game was going, he'd break the bat."

At 6-2 and 205 pounds, Sherry's physical presence complemented his combative nature. Larry's piercing eyes and dark, arching brows cowed plenty of hitters, including those on his own team—even his own family. During an intrasquad game at spring training in 1959, Norm ripped two solid hits off Larry, then got dusted during his third at-bat. "Nobody's digging in against me," Larry vowed. "Even if it's my brother, I'm going to brush him back."

Word of Sherry's proclivities spread quickly. To bullpen mate Ed Roebuck, "Larry was a guy who would enter a ballgame and take over. He would knock you down if you didn't play his way." So notorious was Sherry's reputation that Roebuck annointed him, if only partly in jest, "The Rude Jew."

That same autumn, Sherry became an overnight national hero. The rookie righthander was the winning pitcher in the opening playoff game against Milwaukee, then won two and saved two others versus the White Sox in the World Series, a performance that earned him the Series Most Valuable Player award. Three days later, he appeared on *The Ed Sullivan Show*. "I had to go out and buy a suit for that," Sherry confessed. "I didn't own one. I didn't even make the minimum salary that year."

The following season, Larry led the league with 13 relief victories, but a sore arm limited his effectiveness in 1961. Sherry rebounded strongly in '62, with seven wins and 11 saves in 58 appearances, despite continuing shoulder problems. But compared to Ed Roebuck, Larry was the picture of health.

Roebuck, who began his Dodger career in 1955, was the oldest pitcher on the staff at 30. Nineteen-sixty-one was Ed's lost season when he was sidelined by what would today be diagnosed as a torn rotator cuff. Team doctor Robert Kerlan told him he'd probably never pitch again. Scout Kenny Myers thought otherwise. "What do doctors know about baseball?" he asked Ed. "You come with me and we'll try a program and see what happens."

The man who had made a ballplayer out of Willie Davis was also responsible for reviving Roebuck's flagging career. Under Myers' supervision, Ed began simply by throwing hundreds of baseballs against a fence. The process continued for months. The repetitive motion tore the adhesions in Roebuck's arm, so much so that his muscles bled. "It was a very painful, but positive process. By just throwing every day, my arm got better, not worse," he recalled. "Myers had some background as a trainer. He understood muscles and nerves. He'd stretch, rotate, and manipulate my arm.

"Near the end of '61, I was back with the Dodgers. It was almost miraculous. Dr. Kerlan said to me, 'You must really be crazy about baseball to have put yourself through this.' Two other players, [Braves catcher] Del Crandall and [Pirates pitcher] Vern Law heard about what I did and went through the same program to fix their arms, too.

"One of the reasons I was able to come back was that as a sinker-ball pitcher, I didn't have to throw hard. And I could pitch quite often. Really, I just had the one pitch and I'd throw it low and away to everybody."

Getting back into the big leagues was only one obstacle Ed faced. Both his father and brother had died within the year, and their deaths, along with the physical strain of rehabilitation, took its toll. "For the first time in my life, I had insomnia. I was always tired. The whole year of 1962 was unreal to me. Losing two people who were close, being back with the Dodgers—I thought I was in a dream. I couldn't separate the reality from the unreality."

Roebuck's 1962 performance also bordered on the unreal. Pitching in both short and long relief over nearly 60 appearances, Ed breezed through several stretches without allowing so much as an earned run. He won 10 straight games, and wasn't even tagged with his first loss until the final week of the season. "It was almost as if I were in a trance. I was making great pitches, I felt I couldn't lose—I didn't even care how or when they used me; short or long relief, starting—it just didn't matter."

* * *

The starters in the rotation revered Roebuck because he seldom blew leads and almost never lost. Stan Williams, who only completed four games that season, was especially appreciative. Stan had also once been Roebuck's next-door neighbor. A few years earlier, Williams, Roebuck, pitcher Roger Craig, and first baseman Norm Larker all decided to build homes on the same street in the suburb of Lakewood. But Craig and Larker were taken in the expansion draft at the end of '61, and a growing family convinced "Big Daddy" to move to Long Beach.

"I got *that* nickname because my son was the first Dodger baby born on the West Coast," said Williams. "They later changed it to 'Big Hurt,' because everytime I pitched, it seemed like someone got hurt. That was also the same time that the song 'The Big Hurt' came out."

Maury Wills remembered another reason why Williams may have earned that sobriquet. "He was big and powerful, and he'd come up to a teammate from behind, the way kids do, and put a half nelson on him until he screamed for help." "You never turned your back on Stan," advised Joe Moeller. "I guess I was kind of a playful giant with a lot of extra energy," the 6-4, 225-pound Williams acknowledged.

He may also have been the hardest thrower on the Dodger staff. "My hand was much sorer catching Williams than Koufax," revealed Norm Sherry. The ball may have arrived quickly, but Stan took his time before he threw it; he was one of the most deliberate workers in the league. "What's the rush?" he teased. "I give the fans more baseball for their money—four hours instead of three."

Stan's career debut in the minors didn't even last three minutes. He may be the only person in the history of the sport to have been ejected even before playing in his first game. At Shawnee in 1954, Williams arrived late, quickly put on his uniform, and ran to the dugout. As soon as he arrived the umpire threw him out of the game. The ump had overheard a caustic remark from the bench and wrongly believed Stan to be the guilty party. Williams spent the rest of the afternoon sitting by his locker—the victim of baseball's fastest-ever ejection.

Afterwards, Stan's fortunes improved dramatically. He posted 18- and 19-game winning seasons in the minors, finally making the Dodgers' roster during the '58 season. By 1960, he was an established member of the rotation, and was named to the National League All-Star squad. In '61, he finished second in the N.L. with 205 strikeouts, trailing only Sandy Koufax.

Stan relied on his massive size and blazing fastball to intimidate hitters, wielding that power and heat to move batters away from the plate. Those opponents who did solve Williams knew they'd eventually pay for it. "Stan would make notes, keep a little book of guys he had to hit," admitted fellow chin-music afficianado Larry Sherry.

Williams' occasional wild streaks also scared batters. During his best year, 1960, Stan's walks-to-strikeouts ratio was a career best, but an arm injury that same season affected his control. By 1962, Williams was fanning nearly as many as he walked. He ran deeper counts, worked longer, and ultimately wasn't able to finish most of the games he started.

Because of such problems—and his gregarious, playful nature—Stan found himself in Walter Alston's doghouse. "We were never very close. I always had the impression he thought I was a big dummy, and even when I pitched well I didn't feel a lot of respect coming from him. I never cared a lot for Walter and I think he felt the same way."

Williams did win 14 games for the '62 Dodgers, but it clearly was his most discouraging season in Los Angeles. During a month-long stretch that summer, he failed to either win or complete a game. In one particularly ugly relief appearance against the Mets, Stan walked eight batters in five innings. But a week later in the nightcap of a doubleheader against Philadelphia, Williams pitched a shutout and, for the first time in two years, did not issue a single base on balls.

It was a brilliant performance, but it couldn't surpass the gem crafted by Johnny Podres earlier that same evening. Podres' win may have been even more crucial; he had been battling through a worse season than Williams. The man who'd been chosen to start the first game in Dodger Stadium history still hadn't won a game in Chavez Ravine until he finally beat the Phillies, 5-1. In fact, Podres hadn't won anywhere in more than six weeks. On the night of July 2nd, he pitched the game of his life.

Podres retired the first 20 batters he faced before yielding a single to outfielder Ted Savage with two out in the seventh. More impressively, he tied a major league record by striking out eight straight Phillies hitters. It turned Johnny's season around, and he finished the year with 15 victories.

John never pitched better, but no Podres performance carried greater impact than his legendary shutout in game seven of the 1955 World Series. His 2-0 win over the Yankees gave the Dodgers their only Brooklyn world championship, and would forever remain the defining moment of Johnny Podres' career.

Podres was born inside an unheated 8 x 10 room in Witherbee, New York, on September 30, 1932. At the time of his birth, John's mother was stricken with double pneumonia. His father worked in a mine across the street for $18 a week. It was a hardscrabble existence, but Podres felt a sense of belonging in the community, and made it his permanent residence even after arriving in the big leagues. "A small town is the only place to live. I know everyone and everyone knows me, but nobody bothers me. I can find more friends there in one day than in the rest of the world over."

Ice fishing and baseball were two of his passions, and by the end of high school, he was good enough to get a $6,000 signing bonus from the Dodgers. John's father was his guiding force, coaching him, taking him to tryouts, offering support when Johnny's confidence waned in the low minors. A serious back injury later slowed, but did not stop Podres from permanently making the Dodgers in 1953.

At the age of 23, his two World Series wins made him the toast of Brooklyn, but this was a rare moment in the spotlight. Podres spent most of his career standing in the shadows of more prominent Dodger stars—Carl Erskine, Don Newcombe, Don Drysdale, and Sandy Koufax. Yet each year, John could be counted on for at least a dozen or more victories, and no pitcher was better in the clutch.

Podres was aware of his reputation. "When something was on the line, I guess I rose to the occasion more than I did during other times over the course of the year." Ron Perranoski agreed, calling him the Dodgers' "money pitcher, who also threw one of the best changeups in the history of baseball." Added Norm Sherry, "John had what we called the 'pull-down-the-window-shade' change. It's the kind of pitch that's very difficult to learn, but he mastered it as well as anybody."

Buzzie Bavasi unabashedly stated, "Johnny was my favorite. This is a tough thing for me to say because I've had some great ones, but if I had to win one game today, Johnny Podres would be the man I would pick and the man Walter Alston would pick. He was a great pitcher and he had the great desire to succeed."

John pursued *la dolce vita*—the sweet life—with just as much enthusiasm. Still a bachelor at 29, Podres was renowned for his amorous escapades. Women seemed dazzled by his distinctive good looks. Johnny's round face was highlighted by fiery, narrow eyes and a dimpled chin. Teammates called him "The Point" because the top of his head resembled the end of a spike. This did not seem to discourage the ladies, many of whom pursued him—and not the other way around.

Podres also enjoyed following the horses at Hollywood Park, although he was seldom more than a two-dollar bettor. And he liked to bend the elbow as much as any Dodger. This behavior was an occasional annoyance to Alston, but it bothered team GM Bavasi not one bit.

"I never thought malted milk drinkers were good ballplayers, and that's why I've always had a soft spot for guys like John. And he never changed. Throughout his whole career, he never got drunk or made love to a girl the night before he pitched. The other three nights he figured it didn't make any difference. In all the years he played for us, I never saw Johnny with any woman except the one he finally married."

Johnny posted his best record in 1961, leading the league in winning percentage with a career-high 18 victories against only five defeats. Late in the year, he had his first realistic chance to win 20. Unfortunately, Podres missed several turns in September because his dad was dying from lung cancer. Johnny hopped an emergency flight home, but arrived too late. It took a long time to recover from the loss of his father, and may at least partially explain why Podres pitched ineffectively during the opening months of the '62 season.

* * *

By contrast, the month of April represented a new beginning for Don Drysdale. No man was more pleased to bid farewell to the Coliseum and say hello to Dodger Stadium than L.A.'s fireballing right-hander. Steve Gelman in *Sport* put it best when he wrote, "[For Drysdale] the shadow of the Coliseum's short left-field fence is gone. At the Coliseum his best pitch, a fastball on the fists, became a fastball into the seats."

No L.A. starter won more games during their four years in the converted Olympic stadium, but no one complained louder—or more publicly—about its shortcomings than Drysdale. One time, after yet another cheap hit off the outfield screen sent him to an early shower, Drysdale exploded. "I'll never win in this place as long as I live. They should trade me and put me out of my misery. I'll go anywhere." "Even to Philadelphia?" inquired a reporter. "Even to Cuca-monga," snapped Don.

Angelenos were noticeably upset, as they had been over previous Drysdale remarks. As usual, he eventually apologized. Still, Don remained the primary target of local boobirds who felt he complained too much and won too little. The verbal tirades must have been par-ticularly hurtful to the southern California native son, who would otherwise have been the toast of the coast.

Drysdale was born and raised in Van Nuys, a suburb in L.A.'s San Fernando Valley. His father, a one-time semipro pitcher, began teaching his son baseball fundamentals at an early age. He also encouraged his three-quarter throwing motion, one that seemed to come naturally to the younger Drysdale. After spending his forma-tive years as an infielder, Don's father made him a pitcher at the Amer-ican Legion level. During the winter of 1954, his senior year in high school, Drysdale pitched in an amateur rookie league sponsored by the Brooklyn Dodgers. Upon graduation, the Dodgers came calling again, this time with a contract.

They were only one in a long line of suitors. Both the University of Southern California and Stanford offered athletic scholarships. The Giants, White Sox, Yankees, and Cardinals were also interested. It was the Dodgers who finally won the Drysdale Sweepstakes. "I had played in their rookie league and I felt some loyalty. Also, they were a first-place club and you can just bet that's where I wanted to be."

Within two years, the 19-year-old got his wish, earning a spot on the '56 Dodger roster. In his first big league start, Drysdale won, 6-1, striking out nine Philadelphia hitters. Brooklyn went on to win the National League pennant, but the rookie picked up far more that sea-son than simply a World Series check.

Drysdale was the beneficiary of a graduate course in the school of hard knockdowns, studying alongside the master of intimidation—teammate Sal Maglie. No pitcher in baseball better understood the art of moving hitters off the plate than the man nicknamed "The Barber," and Drysdale became his most devoted disciple. "Just remember," taught Maglie, "every time a batter gets a hit off you, it's like he picked your pocket for a dollar."

The following year a new, improved, and meaner Drysdale won 17 games. Throwing with his camouflaging three-quarter sidearm motion, the 6-6 righthander blazed pitches that were always difficult to pick up, and often impossible to escape. His five seasons leading the

N.L. in hit batsmen is still a league record, and he also holds the modern baseball mark for most batters hit in a career. It made Don Drysdale the most feared pitcher in the game.

"Everybody knew about it and they were scared to death of him," said John Roseboro. "Hitters came to the plate talking nice to me in hopes I wouldn't call for the close pitch....if you've ever had a ball come about ninety miles an hour at your head, it screws up your thinking patterns. You've gotta think about safety before you think about hitting that ball hard—and Drysdale lived on that."

Don did his best to look the part of the villain. "On the days he would pitch he did not shave," recalled Ron Perranoski. "He had a mean streak and he wasn't going to give in to you. If he had to knock you down or brush you back, he'd do it. He was a tough pitcher to hit against."

"Batting against Drysdale is the same as making a date with the dentist," groaned Pirates shortstop Dick Groat. Quipped Reds reliever Jim Brosnan: "Drysdale's idea of a waste pitch is a strike." Added San Francisco's Orlando Cepeda: "You just try to hit him before he hits you." But throughout his career, Drysdale insisted he had malice towards none.

"I never deliberately hit a batter in my life," Don claimed. "I pitch 'em tight and I don't intend to alter my style. It's my bread and butter. What do you want me to do, throw it down the pipe? Sometimes a pitch is a little too close, but I can't worry about that. My success as a pitcher determines the size of my salary. My salary buys the food for my wife and daughter."

To Drysdale, the brushback was also a protective weapon. "If one of our hitters goes down, then it's two of yours. And if two of our hitters go down, that makes four. Just add it up. You don't have to go to Yale or Harvard to figure it out."

Don brought his reputation with him when the Dodgers moved west, but the long-anticipated L.A. homecoming was not a happy one. Drysdale took one look at the Coliseum's cozy left field and it was hate at first sight. "My knuckles are scraping that wall every time I throw a pitch," he muttered. His ERA soared, his win total plummeted and the Dodgers sank to seventh place.

A year later, Don bounced back with 17 victories as L.A. made it to the World Series, but along the way Big D got himself into more trouble. When several umpires publicly stated that Drysdale threw beanballs, he threatened to sue the league for what his attorney called "character assassination." In another incident where the newspapers reported that Don had criticized the Dodger coaching staff, Buzzie Bavasi had an engraved plaque sent to the fiery pitcher. The inscription: "To be seen, stand up. To be heard, speak up. To be appreciated, shut up."

It was difficult advice for Drysdale to take. "I don't believe in keeping my anger inside," he confessed. "I don't want to get ulcers." On this Walter Alston agreed. "Don shows lots of emotion. I wouldn't want a guy who didn't give a damn. I like a player who gets a red neck once in a while." Or a pitcher like Drysdale, who was never injured. "Don was paid not for winning games but because Alston knew he was ready and available every fourth day," said Bavasi.

Drysdale finished his reluctant Coliseum tour of duty with 15 and 13 wins in the Dodgers' final two seasons. He may have vented his frustrations in the '61 curtain call by plunking 20 batters, the most by a National Leaguer in more than a half century. In a final cathartic act, Don and some of the other pitchers gathered at the Coliseum that winter. With press photographers in tow, recording the act for posterity, the Dodger hurlers proceeded to tear down the despised left-field fence for good.

To Drysdale, the new Chavez Ravine address must have seemed like heaven. A pitching style turned inside-out in the Coliseum could finally be restored to its more familiar patterns. Dodger Stadium enabled him to throw more smoothly, which, in turn moderated his occasionally volatile temper. He dropped excess pounds while the L.A. lineup supported him with more runs. It added up to the best season in Don Drysdale's career.

He led the majors in starts, innings pitched, strikeouts, and victories, including one stretch of 11 in a row. By August 3rd, he'd already won 20 for the first time in his life—and eventually reached 25, good enough for the Cy Young award as the top pitcher in either league.

Such prosperity brought with it an abundance of off-field opportunities. The Hollywood-handsome Drysdale made a half dozen network television and film appearances throughout the season, opened a cocktail lounge in Van Nuys, and drew a healthy side salary working in public relations for a southern California dairy. "The Meanest Man in Baseball" also donated numerous hours to charity work, which including dressing up as Santa Claus for a Christmas party at a local orphanage.

His tough-guy image took another hit when wife Ginger, a former

Tourament of Roses princess, informed the press: "Don helps me around the house, waxes the floor, does the dishes, and I never have to ask him to do a thing." And at the ballpark between starts, Drysdale played the gracious host to visiting ballplayers—swapping lies, cracking jokes, or doling out bear hugs—occasionally to those he'd knocked down the night before.

Don's dominant pitching accomplishments, coupled with his ubiquitous appearances on television, made him the most visible of the '62 Dodgers. Two other pitchers on the roster were as reclusive as Drysdale was conspicuous—one by choice, the other by circumstance.

* * *

At 19, Joe Moeller, barely a year out of high school, was the youngest player in the major leagues. It was only his second year in organized baseball. During his first, at three different minor league levels, Moeller amassed 20 wins and nearly 300 strikeouts. The following spring at Vero Beach, Joe had been so impressive that Walter Alston was forced to find a place for him on the roster. "Everything he throws jumps and moves," noted *Sports Illustrated.*

Moeller finished the year at 6-5 with a swollen 5.23 ERA, and was even farmed out to the minors for a month. None of this seemed to faze him. "Everything I had ever wished for from baseball came true for me in 1962. I grew up in Manhattan Beach and was a big Dodger fan as a kid. Two years before I signed, I was still getting players' autographs. I collected every article about the Dodgers, going back to when they were in Brooklyn. I got higher offers from other ballclubs, but I really wanted to play with the Dodgers."

Moeller's large bonus, coupled with the fact that he had risen to the majors so rapidly, probably rubbed veteran Dodger ballplayers the wrong way. Many of them earned less money, and were undoubtedly resentful of a kid who hadn't really "paid his dues" with a lengthy minor league apprenticeship. "I wasn't even old enough to go out drinking with them, and they thought they'd have to babysit me.

"I was probably one of the first players to have his own room, because nobody wanted to room with me. It was a pretty lonely existence. I was an outsider—and it was obvious a lot of guys didn't like the idea that I was there. I wasn't treated badly—they just ignored me."

* * *

It is entirely possible that Sandy Koufax may have looked wistfully upon Moeller's enforced seclusion. Like everyone else connected with the Dodgers, Vin Scully admired, respected, but never fully understood the reclusive lefthander. "There probably wasn't a nicer man on the ballclub—charming, always cooperative. A lovely guy. But Sandy was usually off by himself. His close friends on the team would always be those who were not in the limelight—backup catchers or utility infielders. He was distant, but in a friendly way."

During his two years with the Dodgers, Daryl Spencer occcasionally roomed with Koufax. "He didn't go out too often, ordered a lot of room service. It seemed like we spent a lot of our time in the hotel. I don't even remember him going to movies much."

Koufax may have been reclusive, but he was no snob. Johnny Podres recalled that "once in a while, Sandy would go with the other pitchers after a game. He'd have one drink with us, put fifty bucks down on the bar and say, 'okay, boys, have a good time.' Then he'd finish his drink and go home."

Sandy's North Hollywood rancher offered the seclusion he so obviously craved. When Koufax biographer Ed Linn initially trudged out to visit his subject, he encountered "a home on a sharply ascending curve of a narrow street…set back behind a high retaining wall with a heavy growth of landscaping. If you didn't know what you were looking for, you could not possibly have found it."

The Studio City residence was a polyglot of decorating styles: contemporary living room, early-American kitchen, a den in Oriental. Stacked high along the shelves were dozens of books and more than 300 record albums.

"He enjoyed music, and the one thing he really loved to talk about was hi-fi components—woofers and tweeters," recalled Scully. To ensure enjoyment of his favorite selections on road trips, Koufax even built a do-it-yourself "boombox" before such a thing existed. He purchased a large attache case, equipped it with a radio and tape recorder, then wired a speaker into the lid. No matter where he went, Sandy could hear his favorite Broadway show albums and classical selections. According to Doug Camilli, another Koufax roomie, "He seemed to like all kinds of music, except jazz."

Koufax could also hear such music on the FM radio station he co-owned in nearby Thousand Oaks. Sandy's other interests included fine dining, the theatre, gardening, golf, and the company of attractive women—although on the latter he was the most secretive of all. L.A.'s most eligible bachelor athlete never discussed affairs of the heart, and likely preferred as little dialogue as possible on any subject that pertained to himself.

The man Ed Linn described as "a wall of amiability" so effectively guarded his personal existence that no one was ever afforded the opportunity to learn the reasons behind Koufax' craving for privacy. "Whatever I do off the field, after baseball, is my own business, so long as I don't cause any trouble," he told *Sport* magazine. "If I live alone, so what? If I like to do something, who has to know? Who cares? I figure my life is my own to live as I want. Is that asking too much?"

He began his life as Sanford Braun, born in Brooklyn in 1935. At the age of three his mother divorced, then married Irving Koufax when Sandy was nine. The boy quickly adopted his stepdad's surname as his own, then made it a household name as one of the neighborhood's most talented athletes.

Sandy loved to play all sports, but did not really follow baseball as a fan—an odd circumstance in Dodger-mad Brooklyn. Clearly, basketball was his favorite game. He was captain of the local Jewish Community House team that took the 1952 National Jewish Welfare Board title, and later starred at Bensonhurst's Lafayette High School.

During Sandy's senior year, the NBA's New York Knickerbockers played the Lafayette varsity in a charity game, and Koufax more than held his own against their best player, Harry Gallatin. After the final buzzer, an impressed Gallatin came up to the youngster, took down his name and declared, "I'm going to be looking for you in future years." That spring, for the first time, Sandy finally went out for the school baseball team and made it as a first baseman, viewing the sport merely as a way to pass the time until graduation.

That fall, Koufax entered the University of Cincinnati on a basketball scholarship, then averaged nearly 10 points a game for the freshman squad. At season's end, Sandy planned to devote more time to his studies, but when he heard that the Bearcats baseball team had included a trip to New Orleans on its schedule, it gave him the impetus to try out for the varsity.

His blazing fastball eventually earned him a contract with the hometown Dodgers. A $14,000 bonus guaranteed that the 19-year-old could return to college if his baseball career didn't work out, but it also sentenced him to years of virtual inaction on the Brooklyn bench. Existing rules required all clubs to keep bonus babies on the major league roster for their first two seasons, a measure which prevented wealthier franchises from stockpiling talent. Instead of getting much-needed work and instruction in the minors, the seldom-used Koufax sat and watched Erskine, Newcombe, Podres, and Company dominate the rotation.

Like most hard throwers, Sandy was beset by control problems. He walked too many batters and even led the league in wild pitches one season. "Facing him in batting practice was like playing Russian roulette," cracked Duke Snider. At spring training, an embarrassed Koufax often practiced behind the Vero Beach barracks, out of sight from the rest of the team.

When the club moved west, Koufax was given more opportunities to pitch, but was still inconsistent. In one 1959 start, he tied Bob Feller's big league record by striking out 18 batters in a game. On other occasions, Alston had to send Sandy to the showers by the third inning. Because Koufax ranked among the hardest throwers in baseball, the Dodgers ignored all trade offers, hoping he would eventually mature.

The turning point of Koufax' baseball life occurred in the most innocuous of settings—a plane ride to a spring 'B' game against the Minnesota Twins in 1961. Roommate Norm Sherry offered Sandy some simple, but sage advice. "This is just a B game today," said Norm. "If you get behind the hitters, don't try to throw hard, because when you do, your fastball comes in high. If you get in trouble, let up and throw the curveball to spots instead of trying to fire the ball past the hitter."

Sandy had heard it all before, but this time, it finally registered. "For once, I was rather convinced that I didn't have anything to lose. There comes a time and place where you are ready to listen." Throwing easily and without pressure, Koufax fired a seven-inning no-hitter. That afternoon, Sandy Koufax became a great pitcher.

Koufax went on to win 18 and struck out a National League record 269 batters. Stan Williams, the Dodgers' other strikeout king in '61, appreciated Sandy's pitching artistry as well as anyone. "He'd throw his fastball that started at the letters, but by the time batters would swing, the pitch was already out of the strike zone. His curveball started so high that hitters gave up on it and it ended up at the knees. He never threw anything that looked like it was going to be a strike, but it always was. Plus he was able to throw everything in a good location while changing speeds. He was the finest pitcher I've ever seen."

In 1962, Koufax was determined to prove the previous season was not an aberration. His first start came in the second game of the season, designated by the team promotions department as "Chinatown Night." Koufax was wheeled in on a rickshaw, then took the Reds for a ride with a 6-2 win. It was the Dodgers' first victory in their new stadium. Two weeks later, Koufax collected his third win by striking out 18

Cubs, becoming the only pitcher in baseball history to twice fan that many hitters in a ballgame.

By the beginning of summer, Koufax had already won 10 games, and was the league leader in both strikeouts and earned-run average. Those numbers improved dramatically on the night of June 30th, when Sandy faced the New York Mets at Dodger Stadium.

A crowd of more than 32,000 watched Koufax strike out the first three Met hitters on nine pitches. From the bullpen Ron Perranoski cannily observed, "This team is in a lot of trouble today." L.A. then put up four quick runs in the bottom of the first, all but deciding the game's outcome. The only issue still to be settled was whether the Mets would get any hits against the Dodger lefthander.

In the second, Frank Thomas ripped a grounder towards the hole at shortstop, but a backhanded stab and throw by Maury Wills nailed New York's cleanup hitter at first. Sandy later walked four batters, but was rescued by a pair of double plays. In the last of the seventh, Frank Howard belted a solo home run to pad the lead to 5-0. By the eighth, Koufax had racked up 13 strikeouts. "Either he throws the fastest ball I've ever seen, or I'm going blind," lamented the Mets' Richie Ashburn. Entering the ninth, the Mets were still looking for their first base hit.

Pinch-hitter Gene Woodling led off and coaxed the fifth walk from Koufax. Next was the two-time batting champion Ashburn, still dangerous even in his final major league season. After slamming a pitch down the left-field line that curved just foul, Richie grounded into a force at second. Rod Kanehl followed with another forceout. Now only second baseman Felix Mantilla stood in Sandy's way.

In a spring training game four months earlier, Mantilla had beaten Koufax with a ninth-inning single. Better then than now, thought Sandy. Mantilla bounced a 2-1 pitch to Wills who flipped to second baseman Larry Burright for the final out. At the age of 26, Sandy Koufax had authored a no-hitter, the first of four he would eventually throw during his illustrious career.

What made the performance even more remarkable was that Koufax had been pitching with a numb index finger on his throwing hand since mid-May. The cause of the injury was never conclusively determined. "It had a white, dead look about it," Koufax wrote in his autobiography. "I could press the fingernail of my thumb into it, and instead of having the flesh spring back out, the impression would remain there, almost as if it had been made in wax. [But] I had spent too much of my life not pitching to think about missing any turns."

Through six weeks there was no improvement, but it obviously wasn't affecting Sandy's abilities. Besides the no-hitter, Koufax even clubbed the first home run of his major league career off Milwaukee's Warren Spahn. His next start after the Mets yielded another excellent outing, a win against Philadelphia on Independence Day. With the All-Star break approaching, Koufax was scheduled to pitch one more time, facing the Giants on July 8th.

During his warmups, Sandy realized something was terribly wrong. "The finger had turned reddish…and when I pressed my finger against the ball in throwing the curve, it was as if a knife were cutting into it." Koufax would have to rely solely on his fastball, and it didn't take long for the Giants to figure out that was all he could throw. Even so, San Francisco did not get its first hit until the seventh inning. Entering the ninth, Sandy was still clinging to a 2-0 lead.

By then, his hand was numb on the webbing between the thumb and finger. With a two-ball count on Willie Mays, Koufax could no longer continue. Don Drysdale relieved and retired the final two batters to preserve the win.

Koufax flew to Washington for the All-Star Game but did not see action. Meanwhile, the condition of the finger only grew worse. Its color turned blue, and a blister began to form at the tip. Nevertheless, Alston decided to start Sandy in the first game after the break. Still unable to throw a curve, Koufax shut out the Mets for seven innings, then lost all feeling of the ball in his hand and was lifted. The Dodgers still prevailed, 3-0, for Sandy's 14th—and final victory of the 1962 season.

His next turn was in Cincinnati, but after just one inning, Koufax was finished. "The damn thing split open. There was no blood to come spurting out; it was just a raw, open wound." Sandy was ordered to fly at once to Los Angeles for an examination by team physician Robert Woods.

Woods took Koufax to a cardiovascular specialist, Dr. Travis Winsor. Winsor's tests concluded that a blood clot had reduced circulation in the finger to only 15 percent. Drugs, shots, and ointments were immediately prescribed. Had Koufax delayed the exam just a few more days, he might have lost his finger, and his career would have probably ended.

The symptoms were the same as a circulatory ailment known as "Reynaud's Phenomenon," a term that quickly found its way into sports pages across the country. Once the clot was dissolved, the natural blood flow and medical treatment could heal the finger. But Koufax would not pitch again until late September.

To the Dodgers' credit, the team did not use the injury as an excuse. Instead, they reeled off 17 wins in their next 21 games, while opening a five-and-a-half game lead on August 8th, the largest of the season. But the loss of a player as important as Sandy Koufax was bound to take its toll sooner or later.

"If we'd had Koufax the whole season we would have waltzed to the pennant," insisted Norm Sherry. Another interested party emphatically agreed. "His injury was the opportunity that gave us a chance to get back in the race." Those candid words emanated from Alvin Dark, manager of the San Francisco Giants.

THE GIANTS

7
ALVIN'S BASEBALL BIBLE

At his home in Atherton, California, it was likely Alvin Dark was not pleased as he absorbed the news in the headlines. Not since the 1954 landmark ruling on *Brown v. Board of Education* had a legal decree provoked as incendiary a response from the public. The date was June 25, 1962, and the United States Supreme Court had handed down its long-awaited decision on the case of *Engel v. Vitale*: Prayer in American public schools was declared unconstitutional and would no longer be permitted. This could not have been well received by the Giants manager, a devout Southern Baptist. The nationwide outcry of dissent was even more volatile. Clerics from coast to coast were furious. In California, Bishop James Pike accused the Supreme Court of "deconsecrating the nation." Dozens of politicians expressed similar sentiments, including former President Eisenhower. Another ex-chief executive, Herbert Hoover, labelled the decision "a disintegration of one of the most sacred of American heritages." Before the day was over, bills were introduced in both the House and Senate to override the ruling by Constitutional amendment.

Of all the men who managed in the major leagues, none was more deeply committed to the worship of divinity than Alvin Dark. He was an avid churchgoer who tithed generously. If time permitted, Dark appeared as a featured speaker at religious functions. When packing for road trips, Alvin's suitcase always contained his toothbrush—and a Bible.

And yet, by his own decree, Alvin Dark had insisted upon his own version of *Engel v. Vitale* from the moment he became San Francisco's manager. Among the first to learn of Alvin's policy was outfielder Felipe Alou, the most religious player on the Giants. "He had a rule against presenting his Christian testimony or preaching to any of the players while in uniform, a rule I was also to abide by. He told me that he felt there was ample time to talk about my beliefs, but that while I was in the clubhouse and on the field I was to be dedicated to winning baseball games."

The press was also aware of Dark's pietistic leanings, but Dark was leery of engaging them in religious discussion. Only occasional parables were drawn, and even then they were more amusing than ecumenical. During a '62 spring training drill, Alvin preached this liturgy of baseball fundamentalism: "The cutoff play is just like the Bible. You don't question it, you just accept it."

Consistent with his Christian views, Dark neither smoked nor drank. Yet in other ways his personality was full of intriguing contradictions. His off-field life, so clearly governed by caution and moderation, contrasted sharply with a gambling, against-the-grain managerial style. Dark's devotion to the Scriptures did not guarantee a passive nature. Quite the contrary. Few players or managers came close to matching Alvin's competitive fire. "He instilled an aggressiveness in that ballclub," recalled catcher Tom Haller. "He wanted us to play hard. Alvin loved to win, but hated to lose. And he did curse. He'd get hot under the collar and could get quite angry at times."

On one occasion, Dark spewed forth a tirade of profanity while arguing with umpire Shag Crawford, then later apologized for using such language. "It wasn't a Christian thing to do. The devil was in me," Dark confessed to the *San Francisco Examiner*. "Never before have I so addressed any man—and with the Lord's help, I hope to have the strength never to do so again."

Perhaps the most striking contrast within Alvin's personality was his capacity for deeds of both kindness and callousness, sentiments that could, on occasion, manifest themselves simultaneously. In striving to be fair with the team collectively, Alvin could hurt, even embitter some of his players individually, often without his even realizing it.

Years after leaving the managerial profession, Dark acknowledged his mistakes, many which had initially been paved with good intentions. "I would certainly do a lot of things differently today. I tried to treat all the players the same then. I would treat them all differently now."

* * *

Alvin Ralph Dark was born on January 7, 1922, in Commanche, Oklahoma, the son of an oil well engineer. Soon after, the family of five moved to Lake Charles, Louisiana, where Alvin spent his formative years. Dark's parents, particularly his mother, provided him and his three siblings with a staunch religious upbringing. The state of Louisiana, like much of the Deep South, was heavily Baptist, and the Dark family was a paragon of pious devotion.

The South of his youth was also structurally divided by the laws of segregation, and Alvin grew up unavoidably inundated by the region's preconceived notions regarding blacks.   Many of these statutes and pervasive beliefs had been on the books or considered socially acceptable since before the Civil War.

Even by 1956, many years after Dark left Lake Charles for the big leagues, the racist attitudes of his adopted hometown impacted directly on one of his future players. After signing with the Giants organization, Dominican-born Felipe Alou and another minority teammate were assigned to the Class C Lake Charles farm team in the Evangeline League, only to be permanently banished from action after only a few games. Their crime: violation of a Louisiana statute which prohibited whites and blacks from playing with or against each other in athletic competition.

It is a virtual certainty that Alvin would have objected to such action, seeing as he played harmoniously with black and Latin teammates right from the start of his major league career. Other events in Dark's life offer additional evidence of his absence of hatred for minorities, but Dark's upbringing, perhaps unconsciously, still held him captive to some of the South's stereotypical beliefs towards blacks.

Exacerbating the problem was an inability to always communicate his feelings accurately or appropriately. Accepted Lake Charles idiom was often considered insulting or ignorant to those outside of Louisiana. "Since I had been a kid," he later admitted, "the ways I have used to express myself have been mostly physical...I was not good at expressing my thoughts verbally or on paper."

In Jackie Robinson's 1964 autobiography, *Baseball Has Done It*, Alvin offered a quote that he most assuredly believed was an illustration of his racial tolerance: "I felt that because I was from the South—and we from the South actually take care of the colored people, I think, better than they're taken care of in the North—I felt when I was playing with them it was a responsibility for me. I liked the idea that I was pushed to take care of them and make them feel at home and to help them out any way possible that I could in playing baseball the way that you can win pennants." It was a well meaning, but utterly patronizing statement whose antecedents were perhaps more a product of the region than of the man himself.

For Alvin and much of the Deep South of his youth, the three pillars of community were God, family— and sports. From an early age, the youngster displayed exceptional athletic talent. "The choice was made when I was six years old...I enjoyed football, but when football was over, my thoughts were entirely on baseball. I played basketball too, but baseball was my life."

By the time he was 10, Alvin was already competing in leagues with players as old as 19. In high school, Dark earned all-state football honors and captained the basketball team. His play at point guard earned him a scholarship to Texas A&M, but when Louisiana State offered Alvin the opportunity to play baseball as well as football and basketball, he elected to remain in Bayou country for his college education.

During his sophomore year in 1942, Alvin was the featured star in LSU's backfield, running behind the crunching blocks of a fullback by the name of Steve Van Buren. Van Buren went on to become an NFL legend with the Philadelphia Eagles, and an eventual enshrinee in the Pro Football Hall of Fame.

With the outbreak of World War II, Alvin enlisted in a Marine Corps program that assigned its officer candidates to college units. While billeted at Southwestern Louisiana State during his junior season, Dark earned All-America football honors. He played halfback on overseas service teams in 1945, then completed his tour of duty in China. After receiving his discharge, he was drafted again—this time by two different professional football franchises. Neither had a chance of signing the ex-Marine. Alvin Dark was intent on fulfilling the baseball pledge he had made to himself back in the first grade.

Dark signed a contract with the Boston Braves, appeared with them briefly at the end of the '46 season, then played all of 1947 with their Triple-A Milwaukee farm team. Installed at shortstop, Dark led Milwaukee to the Little World Series championship, then made it to the major leagues to stay in 1948. He was 26 years old.

Alvin's first full season was almost too good to be true. Veteran second baseman Eddie Stanky took to his new shortstop immediately, and the two became inseparable pals, sharing a passion for the intricacies of baseball strategy. With Dark and Stanky strengthening the middle of the infield, the Braves won their first National League pennant since 1914, and Alvin's .322 batting average enabled him to nose out Philadelphia's Richie Ashburn for Rookie-of-the-Year honors.

A year later, Alvin's batting average dipped nearly 50 points and the Braves slumped to fourth place. Boston's drop-off may have been caused in part by the *laissez-faire* nature of manager Billy Southworth, who was distracted by personal problems. Still mourning the untimely death of his son, Southworth drank heavily, which must have disturbed the teetotaling Dark. And neither Dark nor Stanky respected Southworth for failing to challenge the front office on behalf of those players who deserved raises. That was a transgression Alvin vowed he would never commit if he ever got the chance to become a major league manager.

Boston ownership seemed eager to rid themselves of their hot-tempered, opinionated infielders and acquire some longball punch at the same time. They achieved that goal in a stunning winter trade with the New York Giants, sending Stanky and Dark to the Polo Grounds for sluggers Sid Gordon, Willard Marshall, and two other players. The transaction may have been the most influential event in the baseball career of Alvin Dark.

Alvin's keen interest in the game's nuances was evident to his new skipper Leo Durocher, a man with Dark's same fiery competitiveness and will to win. When the nonsmoking Alvin lost the chance to make $500 by turning down a cigarette advertising endorsement, Durocher named Alvin captain of the Giants, a job that paid the same amount. Leo's largesse went beyond simply trying to get one of his athletes more money; Durocher regarded his shortstop as a player-coach, and entrusted him with a captaincy that would allow Dark to freely command on the field. "You're involved with cutoffs, with relays," Dark noted. "You watch the catcher give signs. You pass the signs on to other people on your ballclub. You're running everything a manager does on the bench."

Dark's leadership qualities were obvious, as was his innate intelligence for baseball. Alvin was saddled with limited fielding range and only average bat speed. He compensated for both shortcomings by learning the strengths and weaknesses of league opponents—as well as the virtues and limitations of his teammates. Alvin's technique wasn't pretty (Leo called him "my upside-down shortstop"), but his natural grasp of baseball strategy always kept him thinking a step ahead of the action, an essential quality for anyone with coaching aspirations.

"My eventual managing style was incorporated from people like Billy Southworth, Durocher, Gene Mauch, Charley Dressen, Fred Hutchinson—all the guys I played for. As a shortstop, I would be out there in the middle of the diamond thinking along with the manager, and thinking along with what he would do defensively. It gave me an awareness of how each of them thought. You get the chance to learn managing from a Durocher or a Mauch—that's a pretty good education."

Dark and Durocher were together for six New York seasons, winning two pennants and a World Series during that time. Leo left the

Giants at the end of 1955 and Dark departed the year after, the key figure in a trade to St. Louis. Alvin later toiled for the Cubs, Phillies, and Braves, teams that appreciated his teaching abilities and steadying influence as much as his infield skills. Lee Walls, Dark's roommate in Chicago, never forgot one of Alvin's regular rituals. "Dark did something as a player that only one other man in baseball did to my knowledge. When a new man joined the club, Alvin would take him out to dinner. He wanted to know all about this man as a person and as a player."

At the end of his 14th and final season, Dark had compiled more than 2,000 hits and a lifetime .289 batting average. In late 1960, Milwaukee traded him to San Francisco for shortstop Andre Rodgers. After a five-year hiatus, Dark once again donned a Giants uniform, this time as their field manager.

Willie Mays, San Francisco's star player and former teammate of Dark, was delighted to hear the news. "I never thought I'd say this about anybody," Willie told sportswriter Charles Einstein, "but I actually think more of 'Cap' [Dark] than I did of Leo. You know what he did when they made him manager? He sent me a letter, telling me how glad he was we were going to be back together. How can you not want to play for a guy like that?"

* * *

Horace Stoneham's decision to select Dark was entirely consistent with his previous record of hiring established former Giants players to manage, a group which included Bill Terry, Mel Ott, and Bill Rigney. To Stoneham, loyalty was a virtue to be cherished.

But so was comraderie, and Horace delighted in cementing such friendships over a late-night cocktail or two. As Bill Veeck observed, "Normally, Horace insists that his managers drink with him. It goes with the job. When he drinks, everybody drinks. Especially if he is paying their salaries."

Dark's immediate predecessors, Rigney and midseason replacement Tom Sheehan, accepted these conditions happily, but Alvin's ethical code prohibited any imbibing. Stoneham was obviously disappointed, but Dark's years of devotion to the Giants carried significantly more weight. Horace remembered Alvin's bone-jarring takeout slides, the clutch hits, the rallying clubhouse speeches. Alvin Dark *deserved* the job because he had been a staunch, unwavering soldier in the service of Stoneham.

Dark picked his coaching staff with the same principle in mind, selecting three former Giants teammates he knew and trusted: Larry Jansen, Whitey Lockman, and Wes Westrum. "He had a lot of faith in our judgment when we were players," said Jansen. "Wes was a solid defensive catcher and a great guy. Lockman really knew how to deal with people, and I guess Alvin thought I knew enough about pitching to help him."

"I know what each of us can do," Dark told the beat writers. "When I assign them their work at spring training, I can relax. I know the job is getting done because they know what I want done. And they do it." Each displayed a capacity for boundless enthusiasm, primarily because they were also one of the youngest coaching staffs in major league history. Westrum was only 38, and both Jansen, 40, and Lockman, 34, had been active players the previous year—as had the 39-year-old Dark.

But Alvin's energetic zeal could be a double-edged sword. Even as a manager, the wrathful temper made famous during his playing days could explode without warning. "We were playing the Phillies and lost three straight games by one run," Dark recalled. "We had our opportunities, but couldn't score. After one of those ballgames I heard some guys at the other end of the clubhouse laughing. What they were laughing about, I don't know. It was probably something I should have found out before I got so mad. But it hit me all at once. How could anybody laugh in a situation like this?" An enraged Dark picked up a stool and angrily threw it against the door. Unfortunately, part of Alvin's right hand was caught in the chair as he let fly, costing him the tip of his little finger.

Mike McCormick remembered Alvin "turning over a food table at least once in Houston. The food went flying all over the place and it ruined one of Willie McCovey's suits. The next day, Alvin apologized and gave Willie a check for two or three hundred dollars and told him to go out and buy a new outfit."

"He still had the mentality of a baseball player," observed Felipe Alou. "He made the jump right to managing and they're aren't many people who've done that. He was still learning." Wrote *Chronicle* columnist Charles McCabe: "[Dark] still hasn't gotten the playing out of his blood. He is always the tenth man on the field. This can be a very dangerous thing. Like, he has to win every game himself."

During 1960 Giants ballgames, both Rigney and Sheehan preferred a comfortable spot on the bench, but Alvin always stood erect in the dugout, one foot on the steps, arms folded, surveying the action with steely eyed focus. Local writers quipped that "he looked like Washington crossing the Delaware." Dark disregarded the wisecrack. "I had experienced too many managers who sat there and watched the game go by, leaving nothing more to mark their time than a few spots of tobacco on the ground.

"Look, in '60, they'd had a horrible season in San Francisco. I was going to make '61 a 'changing attitude' sort of year. Let's get our minds focused on winning pennants and not individual achievements."

Toward that aim, Alvin implemented a series of unconventional—and controversial—steps designed to break up the cliques that had divided the Giants the year before. "There were three factions on the ballclub—white, black, and Latin. During spring training, I asked [equipment manager] Eddie Logan to change all the lockers around and mix the ballplayers up so they could get to know each other better. No two black guys together, no two whites, no two Latins. It went over like a lead balloon. In a short period of time, the players went to Logan and told him, 'It's not that I don't like these fellas. I just want to sit by my buddies.' The more I thought about it, the more I realized it wasn't a good idea."

Alvin's second experiment brought on even more trouble. Upon arriving at spring training in Phoenix, the Latin players were surprised to discover a sign in the clubhouse that read: "Speak English, You're in America." Orlando Cepeda remembered what happened next. "Alvin called a meeting of all the Latin players behind second base and told us the rest of the team was complaining because we spoke Spanish in front of them and didn't know what we were saying. It was a joke and an insult to our language, and we refused to do it."

Felipe Alou did not react as angrily, but still disagreed with Dark's suggestion. "It was a tough call for Alvin. I never felt any resentment because we knew we weren't in Santo Domingo or San Juan or Havana—we were in the United States. But there were almost a dozen of us in camp, including [brothers] Matty and Jesus. Can you imagine talking to your own brothers in a foreign language? Our English wasn't really that good then, and we knew it wasn't going to work."

Instead of bringing the Giants together, Alvin polarized the ballclub further. He eventually understood his edict was not only impractical but unenforceable. "Our Latin players would meet guys from the other ballclubs by the cage and it was impossible for them to stand there and talk English. My intentions were good but the results were bad, so I stopped it. It just wasn't the right thing to do."

Dark's maneuvers weren't limited solely to improving clubhouse relations. San Francisco ballgames became a test laboratory for myriad offbeat, unconventional moves by the rookie skipper. "He was not a 'by-the-book' manager," observed Billy O'Dell. "He had his own ideas about baseball. One thing I'll say about Alvin Dark: We didn't always agree with him, but he always had a reason for what he'd done. He thought it out and believed he was doing the right thing." Added Ed Bailey: "You wouldn't always get your way, but he'd be fair about it and listen. And he would never ask a guy to do something he couldn't do."

It was not unusual for Alvin to send in defensive replacements for .300 hitters or lift his starting pitchers early. He constantly juggled his batting orders in an era of set lineups, and benched starters for reserves who hit well against a specific opponent. Dark bluffed the other team by warming up relievers he didn't intend to use, and switched fielders' positions back and forth if he believed the Candlestick Park winds were shifting. Such ploys resulted in box scores with more characters than a Russian novel—unspooling rollcalls that routinely gobbled up column inches in the daily sports page—and bedeviled the writers who covered the Giants.

"Alvin overmanaged, but even he admitted that," said Charles Einstein. "We even took to calling him the 'mad scientist.' He was the first man since [Orioles manager] Paul Richards to bring in a relief pitcher and have him issue an intentional walk. Dark had a pet pickoff play involving a fake throw with men on first and third, and another one that tried to coax a balk off the opposing pitcher. In a vacuum, these moves can be smart as hell, but on the field they didn't always pan out."

Alvin's constant tinkering drove the *Chronicle's* Charles McCabe crazy. "[Dark] is a compulsive meddler...who feels he HAS TO DO SOMETHING. He seems to think his public is palpitating for some new stroke of strategic genius each time the club loses a ballgame. He should forget it."

Dark respectfully disagreed. "If they called me 'mad scientist,' it was only because I never felt there was just one certain way to do something. I don't think I ever managed thinking some move was the 'safe' thing to do. You've got to manage according to who's hitting, who's coming up next, what inning you're in—all those factors. My nature has always been—hey, let 'er rip. Nobody's gonna die over this situation. Let's play baseball and have some fun. But you only have fun when you win."

Because he detested losing in any competitive endeavor, Alvin labored to master whatever game he played. "Dark was a horseshit bridge player, but he was a good gin rummy player," said Einstein. "Leo Durocher taught him gin and he'd play it for a lot of money and do very well." On the fairways, Alvin was an even tougher foe.

Dark seldom had trouble rounding up opponents. "There were a lot of golfers on the ballclub then. Ed Bailey, Harvey Kuenn, Chuck Hiller, Jim Davenport. And a bunch of the pitchers—Jack Sanford, Billy Pierce, Bob Bolin. In those days I probably played a little bit better than anybody else." Golf benefitted Alvin in two respects: He usually defeated his ballplayers, enabling him to collect on small but "friendly wagers"—while also enlisting the game for punitive measures. "Whenever any of our golfers made mental errors in a ballgame—a missed sign, getting thrown out at third—I'd fine 'em in golf balls instead of money, then give the balls to their buddies or another golfer on the team, and that made 'em madder than anything else. They hated playing each other with golf balls they'd turned over for fines."

A surrendered pack of Titleists was one yardstick by which Dark kept track of on-field miscues. Alvin also concocted a formula for evaluating the intangibles of daily player performance. Getting one hit in the clutch often impressed him more than three hits piled up in a one-sided game. To determine the quality of each player's output, "the mad scientist" gave birth to another one of his creations—the plus/minus system.

"When I was still a player, Leo Durocher helped get me a raise one year when my average wasn't all that great. That made a big impression on me. I thought that if I ever got the chance to go to bat for one of my players to get more money, I'd do it. But I felt like I had to have stats to show the front office so I could argue in their behalf.

"After I became a manager, I devised the plus/minus system. A home run in the first inning might get a plus, but one in the ninth that wins the game might get four plusses. I had plusses and minuses for everything, including fielding plays and baserunning. Stealing a base in a key spot, getting a runner to third, those things got plusses. Miss a sign and it was a minus."

Some players, such as Tom Haller, appreciated Dark's grading system. "It made a lot of sense, because back then you didn't have the salary structure you have now. You had guys who gave themselves up for the sake of the ballclub, and it was a good way of finding out the value of that player to the team. He might not have knocked in a hundred runs, but he may have gotten the runner over 30 or 40 times, and even though it hurt his batting average he still helped the ballclub."

Dark's statistics were supposed to remain confidential. But during a spring training rainout, Alvin revealed to several writers both the existence of the data and the grades of several players. "We were sitting around talking about Jim Davenport," recalled Dark, "and I was telling them what a great year he'd had the year before. One of the writers asked, 'What do you mean, a great year?' Well, I said he had one of the best plus/minus records on the ballclub. And they asked me what I meant, so I started talking about it. That's how it became public knowledge, even though it was supposed to be just between me and the general manager."

Dark probably wished he had kept his mouth shut, because during the same conversation he lamented the poor ratings chalked up by Orlando Cepeda. According to Alvin, his first baseman was "terribly minus, but don't put that in the headlines." It ran anyway. An article in *Look* magazine printed this additional response from the now-beleaguered manager: "I'm answering because you asked, but Cepeda had forty more minuses than plusses, a terrible record for the last half of the season."

Cepeda was furious, making no secret of his disdain for Alvin's grading results. Orlando later filed a defamation of character lawsuit against *Look*, but lost. In truth, it was the creator of the plus/minus system, not the magazine, that had been the target of his anger.

It was but one of many confrontations that took place between Dark and Cepeda during each of their four seasons together in San Francisco. Nineteen-sixty-two's set of squabbles began in March with Orlando's protracted holdout following a brilliant '61 campaign. Cepeda demanded $60,000, while the Giants were offering considerably less. But Cepeda's absence from Phoenix was merely one of Alvin's '62 spring headaches.

* * *

The pitching, supposedly improved, was a training camp disaster. Sam Jones and Billy Loes, a pair of old-timers with fading arms, were long gone, having been shipped out to the new expansion teams. Replacing them were two more wizened vets acquired in trade: 35-year-old Billy Pierce and Don Larsen, 32. Larsen's fondness for nightlife made him appear older than his age, and Pierce's woeful spring performance was making him look positively ancient. "I couldn't get anybody out at any time," Pierce remembered. "My ERA was about 16. You wouldn't think the ball could find that many holes for base hits. I was the champion homer-giver-upper in the Cactus League." Swingman Billy O'Dell was also in camp, but still hadn't signed, and no one quite knew what to expect from the moody Jack Sanford.

A number of questions still remained concerning San Francisco's relief pitchers. Stu Miller, baseball's best fireman in 1961, was in the prime of his career. But Dark wasn't as confident about the rest of his bullpen, a relatively untested corps that included Jim Duffalo, Bob Bolin, and rookie Gaylord Perry.

A pair of young starters also gave Alvin cause for concern. Twenty-three-year-old Mike McCormick had averaged better than a dozen victories in his previous four seasons, but was experiencing throwing difficulties that team physicians couldn't diagnose. "I never was able to get going, and developed what appeared to be a shoulder problem," said McCormick. "I never got untracked in spring training and the problem just carried into the season."

The troubles facing a depressed and distracted Juan Marichal were far more serious. Juan's homeland of the Dominican Republic had been a cauldron of political unrest since the assassination of dictator Rafael Trujillo the previous year. Among those who had served in Trujillo's army was the father of Marichal's fiancée, Alma Rosa. In the spring of '62, her entire family was under constant threat of reprisals from violent anti-Trujillo extremists. "They said they were going to throw bombs through their window," admitted the worried Marichal. "I was afraid for all of them, particularly Alma, because her father was the only man in the house.

"I went to Alvin Dark and told him I should go home and marry Alma so I could bring her [to America]." Dark didn't hesitate. He stuffed a pair of plane tickets in Marichal's hands and wished him well. No one could ever remember any major leaguer being granted permission to leave spring training for the purpose of marriage.

"There was no problem at all with the ballclub sending him down there," said Dark. "It was something that had to be done. He was terribly unhappy and needed to get that gal up here. We were all for it." Once Marichal returned safely with his new bride, his entire disposition brightened. The grateful young pitcher asked Willie Mays what he thought he could do to repay Dark for his compassionate gesture. Mays' succinct reply: "Win."

At 31, he was no longer "The Say Hey Kid," but Willie was still the best all-around player in the major leagues. He was one of several veteran stars Dark could count on for skill and leadership. Ten-year pro Ed Bailey was a wise and witty tutor for younger catchers Tom Haller and John Orsino. Thirty-two-year-old Harvey Kuenn, a former batting champion who could still hit, was a respected and influential force in the San Francisco clubhouse.

Shortstop and third base were well guarded by Jose Pagan and Jim Davenport, two outstanding glovemen and clutch hitters—but Dark still considered second base to be a problem area. The 1961 starter, Joe Amalfitano, had been lost in the expansion draft, leaving second-year man Chuck Hiller as heir apparent. His shaky fielding earned him the nickname "Iron Hands." Virtually nobody in the Giants' camp thought Hiller would be the team's opening day second baseman. Trade rumors circulated almost daily.

"Finally Dark realized that no matter who he was trying to swing a deal for, Hiller was the best he had," recalled *Examiner* sportswriter Harry Jupiter. "And he spent a lot of time working with him at second...giving him a lot of personal coaching that I'm sure helped Hiller. That showed me that Dark could be a teacher, and he made Hiller into a second baseman."

"Dark told me I wouldn't lose my job in spring training and that no matter how bad I looked, I'd start the season at second base," revealed the grateful Hiller. "To know the manager thought that much of me gave me a lift and kept me going."

The problem at first base was one of too many good players. On hitting ability alone, Willie McCovey deserved to start every day, but when Cepeda finally ended his holdout the job belonged to him. Dark now faced the pleasant task of populating his outfield with older stars Mays and Kuenn, along with McCovey and the two gifted Alou brothers, Felipe and Matty.

No team in baseball boasted a greater abundance of dangerous hitters, and if the pitching staff could perform to its potential, then Alvin Dark's Giants would remain in the pennant race to the finish.

Back in Phoenix, team trainer Frank "Doc" Bowman had first issued the challenge when he posted this sign in the clubhouse: "Work hard this year—and eat corn on the cob all winter." A bumper crop of ripening homegrown talent was about to make 1962 the season of San Francisco's most bountiful baseball harvest ever.

8
HOMEGROWN FOR CANDLESTICK

Raucous laughter resounded through the lobby of the Francisco Grande Motel, headquarters of the Giants' minor league complex in Arizona. A captive group of Hispanic players roared in delight, absorbing the tall tales and good-natured kidding of Allesandro (Alex) Pompez, team personnel director for the Negro and Latin American leagues.

Every player in the room—from established big leaguers Juan Marichal and Jose Pagan to rookie Manny Mota and fledgling Double-A players Dan Rivas and Jose Cardenal—owed much of their good fortune to the longtime Giants' scout. Few could have been signed without Pompez' approval, and none would have endured the culture shock of the United States without his guidance.

"As a Spanish-speaking Cuban he had become judge advocate and adviser to all Negroes and Latinos," wrote Art Rosenbaum and Bob Stevens in *The Giants of San Francisco.* "He helped with contracts, told them about haircuts, manicures, neckties and shoeshines…he explained wages and work rights."

Pompez incorporated his concern for young players in a sales pitch to parents of prospects from the Latin countries. "Every team has money to offer," he proclaimed, "but no team has a man like me! Your boy go with the Giants, and I look after him. Your boy get sick, I see he get better. With the other clubs no one speak Spanish. He might die, and no one give him a tumble! So the mother says, 'I want my boy to go with the Giants because I know that Pompez will take care of him.'" More often than not, Alex got his man.

Although nearing his 70th birthday, Pompez still cut a dashing figure. Despite a receding hairline, he retained the distinguished good looks of his youth, including a tall yet still-thin frame. "He was a very respected man among the Latin players," recalled Felipe Alou. "He was very relaxed, but had a great sense of humor and dressed very well—he was a 'dandy.'"

"Back in Melbourne, Florida, when we first broke in with the

Giants, he'd get the Latin kids together after dinner. He'd bring his car around and we'd all go for ice cream. Then he'd tell us stories about his younger days in the Negro Leagues."

Not all of those yarns dealt strictly with fun and games. Much of Pompez' earlier life was spent with bootleggers as well as ballplayers. The native of Key West, Florida, was a pioneer black baseball executive with the New York Cubans, and helped inaugurate the first Black World Series in 1924. During the winter he barnstormed Latin America with an all-star team of Cuban players. The roster almost always included a *brujo* (witch doctor) to ward off the evil spirits of *nanigo*, the dreaded Haitian voodoo.

By 1930, Pompez ran his successful New York baseball and business operations with financial assistance from gangster Arthur "Dutch" Schultz, otherwise known as "The Beer Baron of the Bronx." In return, Pompez supervised Schultz' enormously profitable Harlem numbers rackets.

The arrangement was lucrative for both sides. Schultz consolidated his political and mob power base while Pompez became one of Harlem's wealthiest, most respected figures. For many years Alex owned and operated Dyckman's Oval, a successful Harlem amusement park and baseball field. Even after Schultz was murdered in an underworld war with rival Charles "Lucky" Luciano, Pompez continued to prosper.

Unfortunately for Alex, New York special prosecutor Thomas E. Dewey was anxious to put Pompez and his numbers games out of business. In addition to racket-busting, Dewey had his eye on the governor's office, and a Pompez arrest would garner the right kind of headlines for the ambitious attorney in an election year.

In 1937, Alex narrowly escaped law enforcement agents and fled the country for Mexico, avoiding extradition despite fevered efforts by Dewey. Pompez toyed with the idea of running his businesses from south of the border, but finally decided to return to the United States—on the condition that he be granted immunity to turn state's evidence. Dewey reluctantly agreed and Alex testified. It was highly unusual that no gangland hit was ever ordered on Pompez. Observed Negro League pitching star Leon Day, "He became the only guy who ever snitched on the mob and lived to tell about it."

Pompez was permitted to keep his baseball team, which rapidly became the preeminent power of the National Negro Leagues during the 1940s. Home games were played at the Polo Grounds, an arrangement that nurtured a cordial friendship between Pompez and Giants owner Horace Stoneham. Ultimately, Alex became one of Stoneham's most valued baseball allies.

After Jackie Robinson broke the color barrier with the Dodgers in 1947, the Giants responded quickly to thwart their crosstown rivals from signing the best athletes still available in the Negro Leagues. This aggressive policy also extended to the scouting of players from the burgeoning talent pool in Latin America. And their point man in the Caribbean was Alex Pompez.

Few understood the people or the territory better than Pompez. He spent his career cultivating relationships and professional connections with such influential local figures as Horacio Martinez and Pedro Zorilla, both who eventually became Giants scouts. The Senators and Pirates were New York's primary competitors for Latin talent, but neither boasted anyone with Pompez' wealth of contacts.

By the early 1960s, no team in baseball listed more minority players on its major league roster—or within its farm system—than the Giants. Heading their minor league program was Hall-of-Fame pitcher Carl Hubbell, a loyal Stoneham soldier, and scouting secretary Jack Schwarz. Both green-lighted many of Pompez' most celebrated signings.

It is undeniable that the presence of Latins and blacks both changed and improved the quality of the sport. Their inclusion eventually enabled the more racially mixed National League to reach a level of superiority over the slower-to-integrate American League. But there were still many within the game and among the fans who loathed the presence of nonwhites in baseball, even in the allegedly liberal bastion of San Francisco.

Such racial intolerance was reflected in "poison pen" letters directed to Bill Rigney, Tom Sheehan and Alvin Dark, the three men who piloted the Giants after their move west in '58. Initially, the team was derisively labelled "Rig's Jigs"—then "Sheehan's Shines"—and finally "Dark's Darkies." During their first season in the Bay Area, the Giants' roster included minority players Leon Wagner, Willie Kirkland, Bill White, Ruben Gomez, Sam Jones, Ray Monzant, Andre Rodgers, and Valmy Thomas. All eventually moved to other clubs, but others in the system soon followed in their place. By 1962, 25 percent of the Giants spring training roster was African American or Latin.

Despite the vile bleatings of a few bigots, most fans warmly welcomed, even adored the minority players. And no one, before or since, was more deified than Orlando Cepeda, whose Bay Area arrival coincided with the Giants' team debut in '58.

* * *

In his (and San Francisco's) very first major league game, Cepeda thrilled the Seals Stadium crowd by belting a mammoth home run. From that moment, a town and an athlete fell head over heels in love. Cepeda's exuberance, temper, and booming bat captivated the city. With 25 home runs, 96 RBI and .312 average, Orlando outpolled Willie Mays for team MVP honors, while also being named National League Rookie of the Year.

The charismatic 21-year-old Puerto Rico native with the infectious grin was the toast of San Francisco, and baseball's newest star. It was almost incomprehensible that just three years earlier, the same Orlando Cepeda was a frightened, overmatched kid on the verge of being dropped from organized baseball.

Few burdens in this world weigh more heavily than being the child of a famous parent. Such was the lot of Manuel Orlando Cepeda Pennes, the son of Pedro "Perucho" Cepeda, the king of Puerto Rican baseball during the 1920s and '30s. Often called "The Babe Ruth of the Caribbean," Perucho was renowned for both his long home runs and short fuse. It was not unusual for Perucho to deliberately spike the opposition while running the basepaths, or climb into the stands to punch a taunting heckler. Orlando recognized that his dad's volatile disposition likely kept the senior Cepeda from playing in America.

"Father never came to the States because of the race problem. Negroes were having a tough time [when he played]. Father had a bad temper. He would get mad. He would fight. He would have been thrown in jail if he came here to play."

Perucho was the head of two different households (his own, as well as that of his mistress and her six children). The financial burden of supporting two families forced him to supplement his limited baseball income as a municipal water tester. Time spent with his offspring became a precious commodity.

Orlando was known as "Peruchin," which meant Little Perucho, an appropriate tag for the most athletically gifted of the Cepeda children. He was also called the "Baby Bull," a nickname that followed him to the Giants. One of his warmest memories was sharing meals with his father's ballplaying peers, including Negro League stars Satchel Paige and Josh Gibson. By the time he was 15, it was evident

Peruchin might have the talent to be as good as any of his childhood dinner partners.

Cepeda Senior coached his prodigy with a vengeance, even if it meant causing a public spectacle. "Everywhere I played my father followed. He once came out of the stands and stopped the game and bawled me out for making a play wrong. I used to be crazy about basketball, but one day my father said, 'Baseball or nothing!' I had to throw away all my basketball stuff."

Pedro, Jr., the oldest of the clan, couldn't abide his father's tirades and quit the game to become an accountant. Orlando was made of sterner stuff. He survived, even prospered under Perucho's demanding tutelage, exhibiting talents that would eventually put him in the major leagues.

Sadly, Orlando's father would not live to see that day, for hard living had made him old before his time. Before he died, Perucho requested a favor of his former employer, Pedro Zorrilla, owner of the Santurce baseball team, to look after his son. Zorrilla, already aware of the younger Cepeda's talents, took Orlando to the Giants' Florida tryout camp in the spring of '55. He was signed for $500 and assigned to the farm team at Salem, Virginia, in the Appalachian League.

The day before his first professional game, Zorrilla called Cepeda and informed him that malaria was about to claim his father. "When I got home, I saw him in the hospital and he was in a coma. He had not been able to speak or even give a sign that he was aware that someone was there, but when I said hello to him, he answered me. I could not understand what he said, but I knew he had waited for me to come home before he died. He had wanted to see me play professional baseball, and that was no longer possible. But at least I could live his dream for him."

Orlando used the $500 bonus from the Giants to pay for his father's funeral. Perucho was only 48 years old, and his death had a crippling effect on his son. For several days Peruchin was too shaken to leave Puerto Rico, and when he finally returned to America, Orlando faced a number of other difficulties. Cepeda spoke almost no English. His manager berated him constantly. Jim Crow laws throughout the South barred him from eating in restaurants or sleeping in motels where his teammates stayed. Scared and lonely, Cepeda's on-field performance suffered accordingly, and the Giants gave serious thought to releasing him.

When Zorrilla and Alex Pompez heard of the team's plans, both spoke out in Cepeda's behalf. Pompez, a longtime friend of Perucho's, was especially convincing. He explained to the front office why Orlando was unhappy playing in the South and how a move to a different club might make all the difference. The Giants reconsidered and shipped Cepeda off to their team in Kokomo, Indiana. In the North, under the guidance of a more sympathetic manager, Orlando revived. In just 92 games he drove in 91 runs with a batting average of .393. His second season in the minors was nearly as impressive.

By his third year, he was wearing out Triple-A pitchers in Minneapolis, and the Giants were convinced he was ready for the big leagues. The Baby Bull arrived at spring training with a genuine chance to make the club. Incumbent first baseman Bill White was in military service and backup Whitey Lockman was nearing the end of his career. Bill Rigney instructed Lockman to work out with the youngster and evaluate his abilities. A few days later, Lockman informed the Giants' skipper, "Too bad, but the kid's about three years away." Rigney's heart sank. "Three years away? From what?" Lockman's face broke out into a grin. "From the Hall of Fame."

The Baby Bull followed his brilliant rookie campaign with two more all-star seasons, spiraling his Bay Area popularity higher. "I can't believe how lucky I was to be in San Francisco in those days," said a grateful Cepeda. "It seemed to me then like a small New York. It had the same music, the same entertainment. It was just easier to get around. Everything there was a perfect fit for me."

Local night spots such as the Copacabana, Jazz Workshop, and Blackhawk became second homes for Cepeda, who cherished music as much, if not more than baseball. He counted Miles Davis, Max Roach, Art Farmer, and the members of the Modern Jazz Quartet among his friends. Another crony, bossa nova artist Cal Tjader, honored the Giant by composing a song called "Viva Cepeda."

When Orlando couldn't get to jazz joints at home or on the road, he brought his music with him, lugging a record player and albums alongside his baggage. "Franklin Mieuli, who produced the Giants radio broadcasts, also had connections with the local jazz station," recalled Cepeda, "and he'd get me a lot of records."

Orlando was also collecting advice from Dark when Alvin took over the team in '61. First, Dark spent hours improving Orlando's one weakness at first, his infield throwing. Alvin also worked to keep Cepeda's flaring temper in check. During one midseason brawl, Dark tackled the charging Baby Bull as he attempted to storm the pitcher's mound, a takedown that probably avoided injury and certainly saved Orlando some money. And when Cepeda responded angrily to sportswriters after reading unflattering quotes attributed to Bill Rigney, Dark did his best to soothe the hurt feelings.

Dark's advice was simple. "We had a preacher back home when I was growing up who always said, 'Never back a man into a corner. Always leave him some room to come out.' After what you said, it'd be hard for [Rigney] to say [he was misquoted]. I don't want to see you worrying about what somebody else said. That's past and done with."

Cepeda took Dark's advice and went on to the most productive season of his career. In '61 he led the league with 46 home runs and 142 RBI while batting .311, yet finished an embarrassing 100 votes behind pennant-winning Cincinnati's Frank Robinson in the MVP balloting. Cepeda was obviously stung by the results, but was even more infuriated when Dark surprised local reporters by agreeing that Robinson absolutely was the correct choice for the honor.

Orlando may have been miffed, but he was not completely shocked when his manager didn't stick up for him. Early in the season, the relationship between the two began to sour. Cepeda believed the southern-born Dark was offended by his occasionally dating white women. Cepeda also recalled a cutting comment made by Alvin during a clubhouse meeting—"I'm sick and tired of people leading the league in home runs and runs batted in and not helping us any!" Undoubtedly, Orlando's plus/minus scores were not tabulating to the manager's satisfaction.

Dark also refused to allow Orlando to bring his music into the clubhouse, a ban Cepeda believed was targeted specifically against him. He was still smoldering over Alvin's shortsighted "no-Spanish" rule from spring training. And Cepeda was well aware that Dark disapproved of his playing winter ball in Puerto Rico. The manager believed those extra games exhausted his first baseman and kept him from performing at peak efficiency over a full major league season. Even so, Cepeda, the son of the famed Perucho, felt an obligation to perform in his homeland. Orlando revelled in his Latin roots, and responded angrily when his attachment to his heritage was questioned.

During a game against the Reds, Cepeda was conversing in his mother tongue with Jose Pagan when pitcher Joey Jay stepped off the mound and barked, "Don't you know how to talk English?" "Kiss my ass, you cocksucker," sneered Cepeda. "Is that English enough for you?"

There were probably times that Orlando would have wanted to respond as graphically to Alvin Dark, but he restrained himself — until their long-simmering feud reached the boiling point during an explosive incident at Milwaukee on August 19, 1962.

After splitting the first pair of a four-game series, the Giants arose on Sunday morning at the Pfister Hotel for an afternoon matchup, with Billy O'Dell scheduled to start against Braves righthander Tony Cloninger. Around 10:30 A.M., the team bus pulled up to the entrance, where the players would board in time for an 11:15 departure to County Stadium. A few minutes before the hour, most of the players, including Cepeda, were already on the bus, as were Dark and his coaches.

During Orlando's last minor league season in Minneapolis, he lived with a Puerto Rican family, close friends with whom he still stayed in touch. The family, including their teenaged daughter, had flown down to Wisconsin for a reunion with the Baby Bull. "Somebody said that my friends were looking for me in the lobby," Cepeda recalled in his autobiography, *High and Inside*. "I got out to say goodbye to them."

What happened next is not completely clear. Like the Japanese film classic *Rashomon*, the same event apparently produced varying persectives on what actually took place. According to Cepeda, he hopped off the bus, embraced his friends, and kissed their daughter—a woman with a light complexion—in full view of Dark. "When Dark saw a white girl kissing a black guy, he got so mad that he said to the bus driver, 'let's go,' and they took off. It was only eleven o'clock," wrote Cepeda, who also added that he was forced to take a cab to the ballpark.

Not all of Cepeda's narrative squares with that of a member of the Giants' travelling party, who wasn't certain if Cepeda had yet gotten on the bus before seeing his friends. "I don't think anybody on board knew these people had flown in to see Cepeda and that they were friends of his," according to the eyewitness. "So when this happened, people were peeking out the window and wondering what the hell was going on and probably took it the wrong way. At that point, Dark says, 'Let's go, bussy.' The driver cranks up the motor and that's when Willie Mays spoke up.

"Mays says, 'It's not time to leave yet. It's still early.' So the driver cut the engine, and Cepeda finally got back on. Most of the people on that bus didn't even notice what happened."

Alvin Dark denied such incidents ever took place. "I don't remember anything like that. I'd never send a bus away from the hotel early. You set a time and when the time comes, you leave. You don't decide to leave five minutes early because someone isn't there that you don't want to get on the bus. I didn't do anything like that. But I'm not saying [Orlando] was lying. It's what he believed, or he wouldn't have said it. He's too big a man."

One thing Dark clearly did that afternoon was scratch Cepeda from the lineup card and start Willie McCovey at first base (who, for the record, hit two home runs). It was one of only five games all season in which Orlando did not play the position. Cepeda believed he had been benched because Dark was offended by what he had seen at the hotel. "That wasn't true," said Dark. "I have never benched a ballplayer for anything they've ever done off the field unless it was something like being out all night long. I sat him down because his leg was sore."

It was a fact that Cepeda's knees were a source of chronic pain throughout his career. A 1961 home plate collision with the Dodgers' John Roseboro reinjured the same knee that had been operated on when Orlando was 15. "My knees were in bad shape so many times, but I didn't tell anybody, and [Dark] jumped on me for not playing hard. He thought I was faking." Cepeda kept the injury a secret because "I was afraid to say I was hurt. They always say I did not want to play, so I was afraid." If Dark knew about the seriousness of the injury, he did not publicly acknowledge it. When the writers asked Alvin why Cepeda had been benched in the Sunday Milwaukee game, they were told Orlando was tired and needed a rest. Knee problems were not mentioned.

The Braves exploded quickly that afternoon, and took a 10-6 lead into the top of the seventh when the Giants mounted a comeback. Dark could have called on Cepeda to pinch-hit, but chose seldom-used rookie Carl Boles instead. Boles grounded into a forceout to kill the rally. By the ninth inning, Milwaukee led, 13-8, and the game was all but decided when Dark ordered Orlando to grab a bat.

Cepeda snapped. "He had a chance to use me when it meant something, and now he was trying to humiliate me. I went up there not caring. I just wanted to get out of there. I hit the first pitch on the ground to the second baseman, threw my bat away and walked back to the bench."

Dark was apoplectic. "That'll cost you fifty dollars for not running that ball out!" "You can fine me two thousand dollars, you son of a bitch!" spat the sobbing Cepeda, who stormed into the clubhouse.

While categorically denying any of his actions were racially motivated, Dark obviously ignored the advice he had once given Orlando about not backing someone into a corner. "I treated him very badly that day. I didn't realize his knee was hurting him that much. It was a horrible thing and I apologized to him afterwards. I knew his leg was sore, but not that bad. Otherwise I never would have gotten on him like that."

Bad knee or not, Cepeda was back in the lineup the next day for the series finale, and belted two home runs. Later that week in a three-game set in Philadelphia, Orlando collected nine hits, four home runs, and eight RBI— and the normally restrained Alvin Dark went out of his way to praise the first baseman to the sportswriters.

A few days after the Milwaukee incident, columnist Art Rosenbaum wrote: "Orlando Cepeda is not the elected leader of the Latins, but his father was once the greatest player in his homeland. [Cepeda] would be proud to become the Stan Musial of his group, and to do so, he must muffle his instinct to heat up in times of stress."

Cepeda finished the year with 35 home runs, 114 RBI, and a .306 average, excellent numbers, but still a dropoff from his '61 totals. Mindful of his hefty $47,000 salary, club management bemoaned the "subpar" performance, but several teammates defended Orlando. Charles Einstein remembered Willie Mays saying to him, "If a guy hits .300 and knocks in a hundred, how can he be hurting the club?"

Added Felipe Alou: "I think Orlando had more problems with [management] than the rest of us because he was more vocal. He was a better player and kind of the leader of the Latins, so the confrontation was there."

* * *

Conciliation was more in keeping with Alou's style. "Felipe was a very classy person," recalled Billy Pierce, "and a good team ballplayer. He led a great life and carried himself well. He would try to work with the guys. If some of the Latin fellows got a little excited, he would be the man to calm them down. I don't know if Felipe would ever swear about anything." Ed Bailey remembered that "Felipe always had his Bible with him on the bus, plane, train, whatever. He was a very sincere guy and very interested in religion."

A strong belief in God did not mean Alou was also a shrinking violet. He spoke up to the writers when he wished to express his views. And while he did not angrily challenge Dark as Cepeda did, Felipe let the manager know when he disagreed with his actions. On occasions when Alvin lost his temper, kicking over the postgame food table, Juan Marichal observed that "Felipe would bend over and pick some of the food and eat it off of the floor, looking Dark in the eye as he did so…it was almost as though it was a challenge in philosophies between the two men, with Dark saying, *If you worked harder, you would not have lost*; and Felipe saying, *Win or lose, you do not kick food on the floor.*"

Waste was anathema to Alou, who was born into poverty in the Dominican fishing village of Haina in 1935. He was the oldest of four sons (three of whom eventually made it to the Giants) to a blacksmith and carpenter named Rojas. His father hand-carved the first bats for each of his boys. They practiced hitting by swinging at lemons.

In high school, Felipe concentrated on track and field, playing baseball only in summer leagues. At 16 he worked in a concrete mixing factory, and gained renown for his ability to wrestle sharks with his bare hands. Alou's parents had loftier ambitions for their eldest, and the family agreed he would study medicine at the University of Santo Domingo.

Between anatomy classes, Felipe found time for the school baseball team, coached by Horacio Martinez, who doubled as a bird dog for the Giants. When Alou's father lost his job and large family debt began to mount, Felipe realized he would have to help by quitting school and signing a professional contract. Martinez got his star player a $200 bonus, then sent him off to the Evangeline League in Lake Charles, Louisiana.

Alou was promptly banned from Lake Charles simply for being black, but Felipe fared better at his second stop at Cocoa, leading the Florida State League with a .380 average. Always a self-motivator, Felipe overcame American cultural barriers by studying a bilingual dictionary and taking a correspondence language course. By the middle of '58, Alou's English was much improved and his bat was speaking in line drives against Triple-A competition. The Giants promoted him to the major leagues.

Alou fought for playing time during his first four years in San Francisco, finally nailing down a starting spot in 1961. But his wide batting stance offered an open invitation for pitchers to jam him with inside stuff. "On the first day of spring training, 1962, Alou assumed a different stance at the plate," reported Bob Stevens. "He 'closed up,' with his left foot pointing more toward the pitcher…and it has provided him with a freer swing."

The new stance made Felipe a star. After batting almost .500 in the

Cactus League, Alou kept up the pace into the regular season. Moved from leadoff to the number five slot in the lineup, he hit safely in his first 12 games, including a towering shot that shattered the letters in an advertisement atop the scoreboard in Cincinnati. After Alou demolished Dodger pitching during an April series, a disgruntled L.A. fan dispatched the following telegram to the Giants' office: "Roses are red, violets are blue…we'll give our team for Felipe Alou." Alou continued his torrid hitting throughout the summer, carrying the team during its annual "June swoon" slide, while earning his first trip to the All-Star Game. During one surreal stretch, Alou collected hits over nine consecutive at-bats. Felipe's importance was underscored when he missed a week with an elbow injury. The Giants lost six of eight games in his absence. When Alou returned, San Francisco won eight in a row. By season's end, he had 25 home runs and 98 RBI to go with a .316 average, the best on the ballclub.

Alou's greatest contribution to the Giants may well have taken place the previous winter in the Dominican Republic, when he was skin diving with Juan Marichal off the coast of Haina. On this particular day, Marichal spotted a shark and panicked. "I swam much too hard and too fast, and I got cramps and I knew I was sinking." Fortunately, Felipe was with him and pulled Juan to safety. The modest Alou played down the incident. "If he wants to think of me as a hero, fine, but he had a more narrow escape that same winter. We were spearfishing with a young boy who accidentally fired his speargun and just missed Marichal's belly. That could have killed him."

National League bats were nowhere near as threatening to Marichal during the '62 season, his third in the majors. Juan won 18 games and led the staff with a 3.35 ERA, a breakout performance that permanently erased any lingering doubts concerning his pitching abilities.

Ed Bailey, who'd handled some of the best during his career, knew Marichal was something special. "You could call just about anything you'd want and Juan was gonna be awful close to a strike. He was the best pitcher I ever caught." Pitching coach Larry Jansen marvelled at Marichal's repertoire. "He could throw it sidearm or over the top, with a screwball, fastball, slider, curve, a changeup you couldn't hit— with deception—he had everything. Every spring the sportswriters asked me what work I was going to do with Marichal. My answer was always the same—just get him in shape and stay out of his way."

It was advice entirely appropriate for Marichal, a self-made man in the truest sense of the word. The Dominican native, the youngest of five children, lost his father at age three. As a boy, he cultivated the legendary Marichal control by continuously hurling rocks at oranges and pineapples until he could knock the fruit off the vine with nary a miss. At 13 his brother Gonzalo taught him to throw a curve, but otherwise Juan educated himself in the craft by practicing endlessly and studying photographs of top pitchers.

A few years later he starred for the local club owned by United Fruit and beat the Dominican Air Force varsity to make it to the national finals. At the end of the season, the impressed Air Force brass drafted him into service. Eventually, he was ordered to play for dictator Rafael Trujillo's personal winter league team. After another brilliant showing, it was evident to Horacio Martinez that he had an uncommon pitching prospect for the Giants. Martinez informed Pompez, who eventually gave the go-ahead to sign Marichal to a contract.

Marichal won 21 games in his first minor league season, then was transferred to Springfield in the Eastern League. It was in Springfield where Juan was tutored by manager Andy Gilbert in the high-kick delivery, the distinctive pitching motion that was to become his trademark.

Gilbert was in awe of Marichal's talents and maturity. In a written report to the Giants, Gilbert was overflowing with praise. "This is an eighteen-year-old who acts like he's been a pro for ten years…in a year he'll be winning for the Big Club, I honestly believe."

Gilbert's words were prophetic. After a half season at Triple-A Tacoma, Marichal was called up to the Giants in July 1960, starting his initial game against the Phillies. He retired the first 19 batters he faced, allowed only one hit, and struck out 12 in a 2-0 major league debut.

Other pitchers in the past, notably Carl Hubbell, Dazzy Vance, and Lefty Grove, employed the high kick, but theirs was not as towering as Marichal's. Gilbert had recommended the motion because it helped reduce arm strain, but there were other benefits. "Juan liked it because it was easy for him to do," said Larry Jansen. "And he felt he was hiding the pitch from the batter a lot longer. They had trouble finding the ball and that had to be pretty intimidating if you were hitting against him."

Marichal impressed the league with his skills and charmed the public with his affability. The media called him "Laughing Boy" and eventually "The Dominican Dandy." Juan was nearly as religious as Felipe Alou: He neither drank nor smoked and was a dedicated pitching student who kept copious handwritten notes, in Spanish, on every batter in the league.

A heel injury limited Marichal to a 13-10 sophomore season, but he pledged to do better in '62. After securing his wife's exit from the politically dangerous Dominican Republic that spring, Marichal appeared ready to take on the world. Dark granted him the honor of pitching on opening day and Juan responded with a three-hit, 10-strikeout, 6-0 win against the Braves. As a bonus, Marichal added two hits and a pair of RBI.

An early season bout with the mumps was virtually the only foe capable of knocking Juan out of any game. There would be another injury that caused a dispute with Dark, but that was still several months away. In the meantime, Marichal became the acknowledged staff ace, then made the National League roster and earned the victory in his very first All-Star appearance.

* * *

Joining Marichal on the All-Star team was another first-time selection, Jim Davenport. The honor held special significance for the Giants' infielder, who had been plagued by injuries in each of his first four years in the majors. The prevailing view had always been that Davenport was the best-fielding third baseman in the league, but bad medical luck was preventing him from becoming a star. "He's been hit from the tips of his toes to the top of his head," bemoaned team trainer Doc Bowman. One sportswriter quipped that, "It seemed as though the rubbing table and Davenport were going steady," while another dubbed the jinxed infielder "a man for all lesions."

Curiously, Davenport never incurred serious injury while playing quarterback and safety in college. Jim had been offered a scholarship to the University of Alabama, but it was rescinded when the school discovered he was married, a violation of their grant-in-aid regulations. Davenport enrolled at Mississippi Southern instead, leading them to successive upsets over the Crimson Tide in his sophomore and junior seasons. The losing quarterback in both games was Bart Starr, the future Green Bay Packer and Pro Football Hall of Fame enshrinee.

Davenport left school during his senior year to sign with the Giants, and made it to the majors in 1958. Almost immediately his health troubles began. In his rookie season, Jim suffered rib and ankle injuries. An eye infection knocked him out for part of '59. When he finally returned, Jim marked his 26th birthday by tearing up a knee in a home plate collision with Reds catcher (and future teammate) Ed

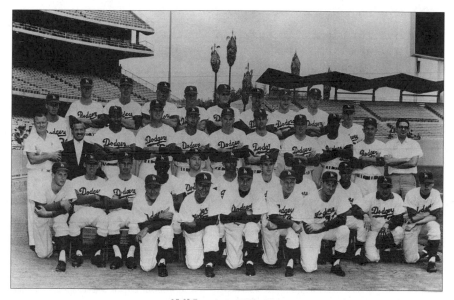

1962 Los Angeles Dodgers

Front Row—L to R: Coach Greg Mulleavy, Coach Pete Reiser, Manager Walt Alston, Coach Leo Durocher, Coach Joe Becker.
First Row—L to R: Ballboy Rene Lachemann, Wally Moon, Sandy Koufax, Jim Gilliam, Stan Williams, Phil Ortega, Tim Harkness, John Roseboro, Maury Wills, Ed Roebuck, Batboy Jim Reynolds.
Second Row—L to R: Trainer Wayne Anderson, Traveling Secretary Lee Scott, Tommy Davis, Don Drysdale, Lee Walls, Daryl Spencer, Larry Sherry, Ron Perranoski, Willie Davis, Batting Practice Pitcher Carroll Beringer, Trainer Bill Buhler.
Third Row—L to R: Joe Moeller, Larry Burright, Andy Carey, Duke Snider, Ron Fairly, Pete Richert, Norm Sherry, Doug Camilli, Johny Podres, Frank Howard. (Courtesy of Los Angeles Dodgers)

Dodgers owner Walter O'Malley—"Public Enemy Number One" in Brooklyn and "Baseball Visionary" of Los Angeles. O'Malley was the primary force behind the major leagues' migration to California. (Courtesy of Los Angeles Dodgers)

Dodger Stadium— the first privately owned ballpark to be constructed since 1923, and the architectural model for virtually every baseball facility built in the latter half of the century. (Courtesy of the Los Angeles Dodgers)

The dedication plaque marking the inaugural season of the ballpark the press jokingly called "The Taj O'Malley." The all-time single-season major league attendance record was broken in 1962, Dodger Stadium's very first year of existence. (Courtesy of the Los Angeles Dodgers)

Walter "Smokey" Alston—the quiet, conscientious manager of the Dodgers, who endured the most trying season of his career in 1962. (Courtesy of the Los Angeles Dodgers)

Leo "The Lip" Durocher—L.A.'s flamboyant third base coach, whose marked contrast with Alston in personality and managing style created tension and divisiveness in the Dodger clubhouse. (Courtesy of the Los Angeles Dodgers)

Below: Maury "Mousey" Wills—1962 league MVP and baseball's "Prince of Thieves," the man who permanently changed the way the game was played by stealing a record 104 bases. (Courtesy of the Los Angeles Dodgers)

Jim "Junior" Gilliam—the
Dodgers' "team player" who
sacrificed his own statistics to
protect the larcenous Wills until
late in the season when he finally
grew weary of acting the role of
"good Samaritan." (Courtesy of
the Los Angeles Dodgers)

Tommy Davis—notorious "Giant Killer"
and the National League batting (.346)
and RBI champion (153). No major
leaguer has driven in 150 or more runs
since Davis did it in 1962. (Courtesy of
the Los Angeles Dodgers)

Frank "Hondo" Howard—the largest man in baseball, with frightening home run power and one of the best throwing arms in the National League. Howard's affable nature and enormous size thrust him into the role of Dodger locker room peacemaker in '62. (Courtesy of the Los Angeles Dodgers)

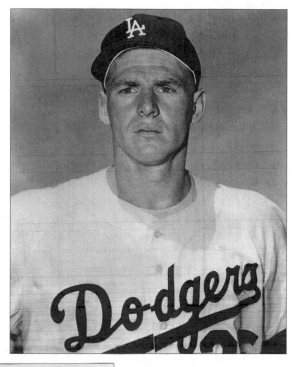

John "Gabby" Roseboro—the quiet yet cerebral presence behind the plate who guided the talented '62 Dodger pitching staff. No other catcher in baseball ran the bases with as much speed and skill. (Courtesy of the Los Angeles Dodgers)

Don "Big D" Drysdale—
deserving Cy Young Award
winner, the major league leader
in both wins and strikeouts—
and the undeniable ace of the
'62 Dodger staff. (Courtesy of
the Los Angeles Dodgers)

Sandy Koufax—National League
ERA king and author of a no-
hitter whose mysterious
circulatory ailment at midseason
changed the entire complexion of
the '62 pennant race. (Courtesy
of the Los Angeles Dodgers)

Johnny "The Point" Podres—
a 15-game winner for the '62
Dodgers, and the man
regarded by general manager
Buzzie Bavasi as the pitcher
he would choose over all
others if L.A. had to win one
ballgame. (Courtesy of the
Los Angeles Dodgers)

Stan "The Big Hurt" Williams—
the hardest-throwing—and
possibly the wildest pitcher in Los
Angeles. His disastrous ninth
inning against the Giants in the
deciding game of the '62 playoffs
marked Williams' final appearance
in a Dodger uniform. (Courtesy of
the Los Angeles Dodgers)

1962 San Francisco Giants

Seated Front: Batboy Ernie Reddick. Front Row (Seated): Billy Pierce, Ernie Bowman, Jose Pagan, Matty Alou, Willie Mays, Coach Wes Westrum, Coach Whitey Lockman, Manager Alvin Dark, Coach Larry Jansen, Felipe Alou, Jim Davenport, Juan Marichal, Chuck Hiller, Jack Sanford, Billy O'Dell. Second Row (Standing): Equipment Manager Eddie Logan, Stu Miller, Carl Boles, Bob Garibaldi, Tom Haller, Harvey Kuenn, Bob Nieman, Ed Bailey, Willie McCovey, Cap Peterson, Dick LeMay, Bob Bolin, Orlando Cepeda, Jim Duffalo, Mike McCormick, Gaylord Perry, Jerry Robinson, Don Larsen, Trainer Frank Bowman. (Courtesy of the San Francisco Giants)

Horace Stoneham—the ebullient owner of the Giants, whose acts of personal kindness and ardor for elbow-bending were both well-documented. (Courtesy of the San Francisco Giants)

Candlestick Park—the Giants' home field, whose ill-advised geographic location and architectural shortcomings made it the most despised stadium in the major leagues by player and fan alike. (Courtesy of Dick Dobbins)

Alvin Dark—San Francisco's devoutly religious but intensely competitive manager, whose unconventional strategies and personnel moves earned him the nickname "Mad Scientist." (Courtesy of the San Francisco Giants)

Orlando "Baby Bull" Cepeda—hard-hitting and hot-tempered Giants first baseman who feuded all season with San Francisco management. (Courtesy of the San Francisco Giants)

Willie Mays, posing for photographers, was the Giant most in the public eye in '62. Despite serious personal problems and tepid fan support, the Giant outfielder led the majors with 49 home runs to go along with 141 RBI. (Courtesy of the San Francisco Giants)

Giant Sluggers (Left to Right): Willie Mays, Harvey Kuenn, Matty Alou, and Felipe Alou—four key hitters on the '62 Giants, the most prolific run-scoring major league team since 1953. (Courtesy of the San Francisco Giants)

Ed "Mr. Clean" Bailey—salty-tongued veteran Giants catcher, whose leadership, good humor and clutch hits were welcomed assets in the Giants' clubhouse. (Courtesy of Dick Dobbins)

Tom Haller—former Big Ten quarterback and the younger member of the '62 Giants' catching duo, which combined for 35 home runs and 100 RBI. (Courtesy of Dick Dobbins)

Jack Sanford—moody, often irritable ace of the Giants' pitching staff who overcame circulation problems in his shoulder to win 24 games. During one stretch, Sanford won 16 consecutive times, three short of the major league record. (Courtesy of the San Francisco Giants)

Billy "Digger" O'Dell—previously labelled the "composer of unfinished symphonies"—but the team leader in complete games in '62. Given the chance to become a full-time starter, O'Dell responded with 19 victories. (Courtesy of Dick Dobbins)

Juan "The Dominican Dandy" Marichal—high-kicking power pitcher who posted 18 wins before a foot injury sent him to the sidelines—and into Alvin Dark's doghouse. (Courtesy of the San Francisco Giants)

Billy Pierce—the most popular of the Giants' pitchers, a former White Sox all-star who prospered after being traded to the National League. Pierce won 16 games in 1962, including 12 victories without a defeat at Candlestick. (Courtesy of Dick Dobbins)

Stu "Killer Moth" Miller— the deceptive junkballer of the Giants' relief corps, who possessed, according to L.A.'s Ron Fairly, "the best changeup in baseball." By his own admission, Miller's fastball seldom travelled faster than 85 miles per hour. (Courtesy of the San Francisco Giants)

Don Larsen—a valued member of the Giants' bullpen, and one of baseball's great eccentrics. Larsen limited his pub-crawling in '62, spending more off-field time gigging for frogs in northern California marshlands. (Courtesy of Dick Dobbins)

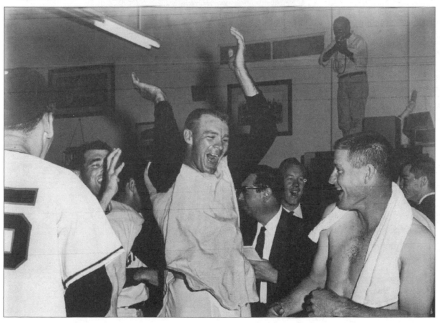

Locker room Jubilation: Harvey Kuenn (center) and Billy O'Dell (right) celebrate following the Giants' dramatic 6-4 comeback victory against Los Angeles in the decisive game of the National League playoffs. (Courtesy of Dick Dobbins)

Three Happy Giants: A trio of San Francisco stars smile for the cameras after beating the Dodgers in Playoff Game 3 From left: Billy Pierce, Orlando Cepeda, and Willie McCovey. (Courtesy of the San Francisco Giants)

Giants first baseman Orlando Cepeda (left) and Dodger shortstop Maury Wills (right) bask in the Hollywood spotlight with television personality Steve Allen. (Courtesy of Dick Dobbins)

Bailey. Many still believe it was Davenport's absence that ultimately cost the Giants the pennant that season.

A year later a pitch from the Cardinals' Larry Jackson cracked his collarbone. Then an attack of bleeding ulcers sent him to the emergency room of a Milwaukee hospital, where he was administered a three-quart transfusion. Less than a month later, he returned to the lineup, but the episode clearly affected his stamina and Jim tailed off at the end of the season. In '61, a groin injury cost him more playing time, but Davenport recovered and posted the best numbers of his career. Nineteen-sixty-two proved to be even better (despite still another injury): 14 home runs, 58 RBI, and a .297 average.

Jim led all N.L. third basemen in fielding from 1959 through '61, but had no tangible reward to show for his efforts. That was rectified in '62 with a long-overdue Gold Glove and a spot on the All-Star team. "Here was a guy who was so quiet, and he never sought out publicity," said Bob Stevens, "but he is still the best fielding third baseman I ever saw."

Few would have ventured a similar opinion to describe the leatherwork of Chuck Hiller. No second baseman in the major leagues committed as many errors in '62, a dubious distinction that saddled him with an unflattering nickname. Tom Haller was present at its creation. "One time in Cincinnati, we went to see the very first James Bond movie. At the end of the picture, it was discovered that the bad guy, Dr. No, had iron hands. So poor Charlie got nailed with 'Dr. No' for a while."

Ironically, Hiller led two different leagues in fielding while playing in the minors. Signed by the same Cleveland scout who discovered Bob Feller, Chuck toiled in the Indians' organization until the Giants drafted him in 1959. He batted well over .300 during his next two seasons, earning an opportunity with San Francisco in '61.

Hiller arrived at spring training brimming with confidence (Cepeda remembered teammates calling him " 'Abner,' as in Abner Doubleday, because he talked like he invented the game"). Unfortunately, Chuck hit a wall against big league pitching and booted more than his share of fielding chances. "I made a couple of errors my first year as a regular and the sportswriters began writing about it. The next thing I know I had this reputation for having bad hands. That was pressure. All I could think of when a ball was hit to me was 'Don't blow it. Don't blow it.' It's very hard to play baseball that way."

He spent most of the rest of '61 in Triple-A, and it seemed unlikely

Chuck would regain the position in '62, but once Dark told him the job was his, Hiller's attitude changed dramatically. One sportswriter shook his head in disbelief over the transformation. "He was in a shell all spring. Suddenly the season started and he was walking around the field as if he owned the joint."

Chuck played in nearly every game, batting a credible .276. And despite his alarming errors total, only Pirates fielding wizard Bill Mazeroski turned more double plays at second base than Hiller. Chuck was quick to thank shortstop Jose Pagan for his improvement. "Pagan has been making me look good on double plays...When [he] gained confidence in me, we started to function as a combination. We're at ease with each other now."

Cepeda was another Pagan booster. "With big stars like Mays, Marichal and so many other players, it's too bad Jose never really got the recognition he deserved. He was there every day, made all the plays and he could hit." Added Billy O'Dell, "You didn't have to worry about Pagan at all. He was in the right place all the time. Some of the other guys, you might have wanted to move them a little bit, but not Jose." Beat writer Bob Stevens called him "a Phi Beta Kappa shortstop."

Pagan and fellow Puerto Rican Cepeda were signed at the same time by Pedro Zorrilla, but it took Jose a bit longer to make it to San Francisco. He got his first audition after five minor league seasons, but couldn't hit his way into the lineup. After a demotion to Tacoma, Pagan was given a second chance in 1961 and beat out incumbent Ed Bressoud, who eventually ended up with the Red Sox.

Teammates began calling Jose "Humphrey" (as in Bogart) because of his deadpan expression and offbeat sense of humor. In early May of '62, the Giants' charter jet lost an engine while flying to Chicago. The pilot clicked on the intercom and informed the team they would be forced to make an emergency landing in Salt Lake City. The Giants were badly shaken. Not a sound could be heard within the cabin.

Then the usually taciturn Pagan stood up. "I say we should take a vote. I'm for taking the bus." The unexpected quip broke up the players and eased the tension. Even after the plane landed safely, several Giants were still chuckling over Jose's remark.

Those same teammates also marvelled over Pagan's productive bat. Even though he hit eighth throughout the season, Jose still had 57 RBI. "He was probably the biggest surprise on the club," said Hiller. "He drove in a lot of big runs for us and had as good a year as anyone."

Pagan also posted the highest fielding percentage of any National League shortstop, and played in 164 of 165 games, which remains the all-time Giants' record.

Willie McCovey would eventually hold more than a half-dozen team records himself, but in 1962 he was still struggling to find himself as San Francisco's slugger without portfolio. In seasons past, the former Rookie of the Year had split time at first base with Cepeda, an awkward situation that pleased no one. The Baby Bull's prodigious 1961 campaign all but guaranteed him exclusive rights to the position, and forced the weak-fielding McCovey to the Giants' already crowded outfield. It prompted one Giant to quip, "Don't give [Willie] a glove. Give him a cigarette and a blindfold."

When "Stretch" did play, most N.L. pitchers must have felt as if they were attending their own execution. A dead-pull left-handed slugger, McCovey probably had the most powerful swing in the major leagues. His at-bats-to-home runs ratio was unequalled by anyone in baseball, starters included. In just 229 seasonal at-bats, he belted 20 home runs, 54 RBI and a .293 average. But with the Giants' surplus of talent, the soft-spoken and painfully shy Willie had to sit and wait his turn.

Like most of the farm system graduates on the '62 roster, McCovey was still a young Giant. In fact, none in the "homegrown-for-Candlestick" crop was older than 28. Alongside this youthful presence, there was a collection of "over-30" Giants—ballplayers with experience and refined skills essential to San Francisco's pennant hopes. Virtually all of them had come to California via trade, viewed by their previous employers as damaged goods or athletes past their prime. In 1962, each of these veterans proved to their former teams just how wrong they were.

9
GOLDEN GATE IMPORTS

At the end of May, the first-place San Francisco Giants boasted a 35-15 record, the best in baseball, but recent history warned of trouble ahead. In a cover story in *The Sporting News*, beat writer Jack McDonald queried, "Will the Giants, carving out a whirlwind, pell mell early pace, as usual in the first month of the season, go *kerplunk* in June, as has been their pattern the last five seasons, or are they going to prove the bona-fide Yankees of the National League?" A sidebar cartoon ominously wondered, "June Brides Happy—What About Giants?"

The '62 version of the "June Swoon" arrived punctually on the sixth. Holding a two-game lead over the Dodgers, San Francisco proceeded to lose six straight, then half of its next dozen to fall out of first place. Cackled *Los Angeles Times* columnist Jim Murray: "a business executive is standing in his office looking down over the city and dictating to his secretary. Suddenly, a falling figure shoots past the window. 'Uh oh,' the man says, glancing at his chronometer. 'It must be June. There go the Giants.'"

On June 12, the Giants temporarily halted their slide by sweeping a doubleheader in Cincinnati. That same day, back in San Francisco, three criminals serving long sentences for robbery used spoons to dig their way out of Alcatraz Federal Prison. It was the first escape from the island penitentiary in its history, and fugitives Frank L. Morris and brothers John and Clarence Anglin were never found.

The three convicts were likely intent on fleeing the Bay Area after the jailbreak, in stark contrast with other recent arrivals who were delighted to be staying in San Francisco—June Swoon notwithstanding. The grateful transplants included six players on the Giants who had been acquired by trade over the previous three years. They were men with considerable mileage on their major league odometers, but team management viewed such experience as a badly needed asset. The homegrown farm system players were fundamentally skilled but still young and not quite ready to lead. "We didn't really have vocal, take-charge guys," said pitcher Mike McCormick, "until we got Harvey Kuenn and Ed Bailey."

Both came to San Francisco in 1961 via separate trades. Kuenn was a former American League batting champion who failed to hit .300 only once in nine previous seasons. Bailey had been an all-star catcher with a penchant for belting clutch home runs. But each man brought much more to San Francisco than simply impressive baseball résumés.

Right from the start, Harvey Kuenn proved he was cut from a different cloth than most ballplayers. In 1952, after completing studies at the University of Wisconsin, Kuenn announced he would only accept sealed bids for his major league services, an unheard-of practice at the time. Amazingly, the interested parties complied, and the Tigers won their prize for $55,000.

Detroit inherited an already polished player. The young shortstop spent only 63 games in the minors before the Tigers recalled him in September of '52. The next season, Kuenn was named American League Rookie of the Year, then celebrated by inviting his Tiger teammates to a lavish party at a local hotel. The 21-year-old picked up the entire tab. Wrote author Paul Gregory, "This was unusual for a rookie, even in modern times. In the old days a freshman not only could never have financed such a party, he wouldn't even have been allowed to attend."

Harvey routinely batted over .300 during his next six seasons in Detroit, even after switching to the outfield. He made seven straight All-Star teams and became the Tigers' captain. His .353 average in 1959 won him the batting crown, an event which may have been the catalyst for one of the most controversial trades in baseball history.

In April 1960, Kuenn was sent to the Indians in exchange for Rocky Colavito, a home run hitter who had ascended to godlike status in the city of Cleveland. Ohio baseball fans roasted the Indians' front office for the deal and booed Kuenn unmercifully, even though Harvey batted a solid .308. The swap didn't seem to adversely affect Kuenn's new teammates, who voted him to be their representative in the player's union.

Cleveland fell from second place to below .500, and to ease public pressure, general manager Frank Lane (in what proved to be his last trade with the Tribe) dealt Kuenn to San Francisco for outfielder Willie Kirkland and pitcher John Antonelli.

The Giants gained more than simply a skilled ballplayer; Kuenn was a commanding presence. Rare was the moment when Harvey did not have a chaw of Red Man bulging in his cheek, or a foot-long cigar within his grasp. Ever gregarious, Kuenn simply made the team club-house a more enjoyable place. *Sports Illustrated*'s Tex Maule referred to Harvey as "a tobacco-chewing gentleman with a penchant for four-let-ter words, earthy humor and locker-room hijinks...his great contri-bution to the Giants has been to entertain them, and thus relax them, and thus finally to help unite them."

"He was the team leader, no question about it," insisted Billy Pierce. "There are some guys that can mix with people well and others who have a tough time with it—and people take it the wrong way. Harvey could tell somebody something and there was never a prob-lem, whether he was kidding them or making fun of them or whatever it was. I don't think there was anyone on the club who enjoyed life or playing in the big leagues more than Harvey."

Willie Mays was the victim of a classic Kuenn prank. One day Mays arrived at the ballpark and found a present in his cubicle. He opened the gift and was delighted to see he'd gotten a box of candy. Mays removed the lid only to find the contents were two dozen decora-tively wrapped pieces of horse manure. The entire team, including the victim, roared over the practical joke. "You done it. I know you done it," giggled Mays as he pointed an accusatory finger at Kuenn. Har-vey's gleeful laughter offered ironclad proof of his guilt.

It took Kuenn a full year to adjust to the National League, but by '62 he was as good as ever, posting a .304 mark to go with 10 home runs and 68 RBI. Even the midseason death of his father did not seemingly affect his performance. And Kuenn was always willing to share his baseball knowledge. "He taught the younger players about hitting, volunteering his own time which was something Mays didn't do," recalled Bob Stevens. "He also became very close to Stoneham. He loved drinking martinis with Horace during spring training."

Harvey's capacity for liquor only added to his bigger-than-life per-sona. Observed Charles Einstein: "Kuenn was well-respected because drunk or sober, he could play baseball.

"But a guy who could really *talk* was Bailey. Only about twenty percent of it had anything to do with baseball. He'd talk about women, food, golf, anything you want. He was garrulous and outgoing, and not everybody on the club was." The players reveled in the earthy lan-guage and cracker-barrel philosophy of their new catcher. His spicy verbiage earned him such nicknames as "Words" and "Mr. Clean."

"Ed was a practical joker," according to Mike McCormick. "He loved to give guys the hot foot. Wes Westrum was one of Bailey's favorite victims, because Wes used to fall asleep on the team bus. He sometimes even lit guys up in the dugout." "He kept us loose and made everybody laugh," said Billy O'Dell. "I don't think he ever got mad at anybody in his life."

The native of Strawberry Plains, Tennessee, first broke into the major leagues with the Reds in 1953, and made the All-Star team three times as their catcher. In April 1961, after Cincinnati recognized their need for a second baseman, Bailey was sent to the Giants for veteran infielder Don Blasingame, catcher Bob Schmidt, and pitcher Sherman "Roadblock" Jones. The Reds went on to win the pennant, and Bailey began to wonder if he would ever play on a championship team. "Naturally, you start to have thoughts like that, but I was happy to be in San Francisco. These guys really went out there to win, and I liked that atmosphere."

Despite his jovial nature, Bailey was a fierce competitor, no matter what the contest. "I won the National League cow-milking championship four years in a row. I learned how to do it on my dad's farm. But there were plenty of country boys around the league who gave me a battle."

In 1962 Bailey had his hands full battling Tom Haller for playing time behind the plate. The 24-year-old Haller, a former quarterback at the University of Illinois, caught only sparingly as a rookie in '61. But it was evident that Tom had the better throwing arm and would likely hit for a higher average than the 31-year-old Bailey. And Haller's approach to catching was much more serious than the seldom-rattled, fun-loving Bailey. "Alvin told us we were both going to play," Ed recalled, "but it's only natural for them to want to go with the youngest guy they've got and look to the future. And Dark liked having me available to come off the bench."

Perhaps Bailey's most memorable blow occurred on the evening of April 25th against the Pirates in Forbes Field. "Cepeda had just hit a home run and [pitcher] Bob Friend threw the ball behind my head. I started out after him and got tackled by [catcher] Don Leppert." Both benches emptied, while Bailey and Friend continued to shout threats at each other. Order was finally restored and two pitches later, Bailey smacked a 400-foot shot into the right-center field seats. The Giants prevailed, 8-3, giving rookie pitcher Gaylord Perry his first major league victory. Bailey's defiant poke was also the spark that began a 10-game winning streak, the Giants' longest of 1962.

Dark's Bailey/Haller platooning strategy proved to be a successful one. They combined to hit 35 home runs and 100 RBI, and because their personalities and catching styles were so different, each earned individual followings among the pitching staff. Billy O'Dell's relationship with Bailey bordered on the telepathic. "Lonas (Bailey's given first name) has the quickest hands I've ever seen on a catcher…[he] can catch anything, even if he doesn't know what's coming.

"Lots of times you wonder if maybe [the opposition] is stealing your signs…so I won't shake off Bailey's sign, but I'll just go ahead and throw what I want to throw. Ain't no way they're gonna steal signs on me that way."

O'Dell admitted that he and Bailey ignored using signals more than 90 percent of the time he pitched during the '62 season. "I have no idea how it started, but it happened, and I was the only pitcher on the team who did this. We must've been on the same wavelength."

Like Bailey, O'Dell grew up below the Mason-Dixon Line, hailing from Newberry, South Carolina. The gaunt lefthander starred at Clemson College, then was immediately signed by the Baltimore Orioles, never pitching a day in the minors. He became known as "Digger," the same name as the undertaker character on the popular comedy program, *The Life of Riley*.

In 1957, after two years of military service, a beefier Billy reported back to Baltimore where he both started and relieved. This "neither-fish-nor-fowl" status continued over the next four seasons and became a major bone of contention throughout his career. "I never really had just one job. I just wanted the opportunity to do one or the other."

Digger pitched well enough to make the '58 All-Star team, and dazzled the hometown Baltimore crowd with three perfect innings of relief to preserve a 4-3 American League victory. But a back injury the following year forced him to wear a supportive corset. "That's when I got the reputation for being a seven-inning pitcher. That darn brace kept binding and rubbing until my skin was raw. By the time I got to the fifth or sixth inning of a game I could hardly stand it." After another losing season, O'Dell and Billy Loes were traded to the Giants for outfielder Jackie Brandt and two other players.

Unfortunately, O'Dell's reputation for early exits followed him to San Francisco. He seldom started games and finished even fewer, working conditions that Digger found intolerable. Once when Dark lifted him from a game in 1961, O'Dell kicked the rosin bag and was fined $250. During the same year the two had to be separated during a clubhouse shoving match. Despite a handful of promising starts that

September, the Giants thought so little of Billy that he was originally left unprotected in the league expansion draft. Only at Horace Stoneham's behest was O'Dell's name finally removed from the pool at the 11th hour.

The disgruntled O'Dell came to spring training in '62 without a guaranteed job or a signed contract. But a pitching staff riddled with question marks opened the door for Digger. "Alvin came up to me and said, 'You'll pitch every fourth day until you show me you can't do it.' I just wanted that chance." Billy allowed only one earned run the entire spring, by far the best performance on the team. He started the second game of the season and threw a four-hitter against the Braves. After years of frustration, O'Dell finally became a permanent fixture in the starting rotation.

Billy's 1962 statistics silenced his critics. "I won 19 ballgames, led the team in innings and strikeouts, and was second in the league in complete games, so I think that settled the question about whether I could finish what I started." And always working with Billy from start to finish was Ed Bailey.

"He never really got credit for being a good catcher, but I thought he was a great receiver. He'd always say just to throw whatever I wanted and he'd catch it." O'Dell's endorsement all but guaranteed Bailey would be in the lineup on the days he pitched, but such was not the case when Jack Sanford drew the starting assignment.

"Haller caught him most of the time," admitted Bailey. "Jack and I just couldn't get it going. He was terribly set in his ways. He had a good fastball and he was gonna win or lose with it. When he pitched, he was off in another world."

Tom Haller probably understood the moody righthander as well as any of the Giants. "Jack wasn't the easiest guy to know. He was born on the 'wrong side of the tracks' in a rough neighborhood near Boston and had to battle for everything in his life. He was always leery of being too trusting of people."

By his own admission, Sanford didn't display big league potential in high school, and was summarily rejected at a Red Sox tryout camp in 1948. "But I just happened to see this fella from the Phillies there...I walked over to him and asked if he'd give me a chance to play, which he did." Philadelphia's newest prospect signed for $125 a month and was promptly shipped to the bush leagues. For the next eight years, Sanford toiled in the minors, struggling to find himself. During one difficult season in Dover, Delaware, Jack agreed to both pitch and drive the team bus.

Each spring Sanford was clearly the hardest thrower in the Phillies' camp, yet failed to make the club. Once Jack nearly punched a club official after being told he'd be going back to the minors. When Phils traveling secretary Johnny Wise brought the bad news to him again a year later, Jack asked, "Why was I sent down? Did I have a curveball? Did I have a fastball?"

"You did, indeed, have these things," admitted Wise. "You also have the reddest neck in baseball."

Sanford's mercurial temperament was keeping him from the big leagues, but it didn't stop Uncle Sam from drafting him into the Army. Jack reported for his tour of duty and pitched well for service teams, but was also involved in an incident that would forever plague him with the dubious tag of "six-inning pitcher."

According to Sanford in an interview with author Mike Mandel, a clot formed in his arm after a fight during an Army game in 1955, a condition that retarded the flow of blood into his hand. "When they discharged me from the service, they sent me to a hospital in Pennsylvania and they diagnosed it then, and they wanted to cut down into my clavicle. And I just put my clothes on and left, I wasn't going to let them."

Despite the obvious medical problems of such a condition, Sanford pitched through the pain and continued his odyssey through the Phillies' farm system. In 1957, Jack was finally given the opportunity to start in the majors and he did not blow his chance, winning 19 games to go with a 3.08 ERA. At the age of 28, John Stanley Sanford became the oldest player ever to win the Rookie of the Year Award.

The next season, Philadelphia finished in last place and Sanford was dragged down with them, posting a losing record and a prohibitive 4.45 ERA. In a moment of panic, the Phils sent Jack to San Francisco for pitcher Ruben Gomez and catcher Valmy Thomas. It remains one of the most lopsided trades in Giants history, although it took a while before Sanford made it so.

During his first three seasons in the Bay Area, Jack pitched steady if unspectacular baseball, winning 40 and losing 35. Each winter guaranteed a bitter feud between the dour pitcher and stubborn front office over contract negotiations, followed by summers of Sanford's scowlings.

Jack seldom slept the night before he pitched, and his behavior on game day was difficult to endure. "Wife and kids run for the storm shelters as No. 33 quietly has his breakfast," wrote Bob Stevens. "His ride to the park is a silent one…He undresses slowly, never uttering a word, only glaring around him as though expecting a fight at any minute…He warms up in silence, works in silence, returns to the clubhouse in silence." Although his demeanor between starts was far more sociable, Stu Miller was always trying to get Sanford "to relax a little more. He was too tense, too tight, more so than other pitchers."

"He always wanted me to go out and have a beer with him after the ballgame," said Larry Jansen, "and I couldn't do that because I didn't think it was appropriate for a coach to drink with the ballplayers. I think he held that against me, because Jack had trouble expressing his emotions and this was probably his way of reaching out to me and saying I was an okay guy."

"Jack was a loner, and I never really got to know him," recalled O'Dell, who occasionally roomed with him on the road. "He wasn't a guy who'd jump up and down when he won, and when he lost he'd get depressed. He wouldn't get mad at anybody, but he would get mad at himself and he was the type of guy who'd turn things over and throw things."

Like O'Dell, Sanford was known as "a composer of unfinished symphonies." But few were aware of the real reason why Jack was seldom around for the late innings. "The clot just grew over the nine years until finally it just shut off completely," Sanford told Mike Mandel. "Nobody knew about it on the Giants. I didn't think it was any of their business. As long as I could go six, seven, or eight, that was fine…There were just a few blood vessels on top of the shoulder feeding what little blood I was getting to my fingers and forearm. And as long as it was warm, which it wasn't very much at Candlestick Park, I was OK, but I would definitely get tired toward the end of the game, because it just wouldn't pump the blood."

Despite continuing circulatory woes, Sanford overcame the problem and became one of baseball's best pitchers in 1962, leading the team in victories. Haller remembered a meeting during spring training "with Jack, Dark, and myself, where Alvin told him exactly how he wanted him to pitch. He convinced him that he could be successful pitching a certain way and he told me how he wanted me to catch him. And that's the way it went for the year."

Sanford, a highball hurler who savored his strikeouts, now worked to keep his pitches down and the strategy produced, at age 33, the finest season of his career, 24 wins against only seven defeats. From the middle of June until early September, Jack could not lose. He won 16 consecutive decisions, three shy of the all-time major league record.

True to his nature, Sanford did not celebrate. "This is ridiculous. No one wins 16 in a row…I don't care who you are or how lucky you are, you don't do it…I have no idea who won 19 in a row, and I don't care. A record doesn't mean anything to me." After all Jack Sanford had endured to reach this point, such an accomplishment clearly must have meant more to him than he would ever allow anyone to know.

*   *   *

While Sanford grimaced, Billy Pierce grinned. Billy O'Dell was but one of a legion of Pierce's admirers. "Bill was a real easy-going guy. He'd go out and do his job, give you his best effort and wasn't ashamed of anything. If he didn't win, it didn't quite cut him as bad as it did people like Sanford. And everybody liked him. Billy was the type of guy who'd listen to anyone's problems, either on or off the field." "Class on the mound," added Dark. "A gentleman pitcher," according to Ed Bailey. "Never a bad word about anybody—the nicest man you'd ever want to meet," in Larry Jansen's estimation.

He was also one of the best at his trade during the 1950s. For 13 seasons, backed by light-hitting White Sox teams, Pierce was Chicago's undeniable ace. In only one of those years did he fail to win in double figures. Twice he won 20 games, along with individual league ERA and strikeout titles. Seven times he made the All-Star team. In 1958 against the Senators, he allowed no baserunners for eight and two-thirds innings until pinch-hitter Ed FitzGerald doubled to ruin his perfect game. A year later he won 14 games as the Sox claimed their first pennant since the end of World War I. But by the end of '61, Chicago management believed his career was heading on a downward cycle. "I was about 35 at that time, and without any question, my more productive years seemed to be behind me. But I still thought I could pitch."

The Giants agreed, and acquired Pierce and Don Larsen, another aging hurler, in late November for four younger players. Upon arriving in San Francisco, Billy asked equipment manager Eddie Logan if he could wear uniform number 19—Dark's old number when he played on the championship teams of '51 and '54. "Go ahead and give Pierce the number he wants," Alvin advised Logan.

Dark might have had second thoughts about his generosity the following March when Pierce was routinely torched by every Cactus League batter he faced. "During that spring training, everything was hit hard or into a hole somewhere. But then the regular season started and I won eight in a row and everything went right."

A good deal of Billy's success could be credited to the Giants' coaching staff. They were certain his productivity would be enhanced—if Pierce were used properly. Jansen believed "Billy might've worn out if he'd had to keep pitching in Chicago's heat. In Candlestick Park he stayed much stronger. He liked the cool weather." Dark made sure to "have him ready for a home stand. We were gonna get him into as many games there as we could. But he always had his four of five days rest, too."

Candlestick may have been a house of horrors for some players, but for Pierce it was heaven on earth. "Psychologically, the cooler air makes you feel stronger and throw better. I could pitch the ball where I wanted it with something on it. And the results were about as good as I could expect because I won 13 in a row at home."

The man the White Sox believed was washed up finished the season at 16-6, despite missing a month from a spike wound. Even that setback was viewed as an advantage by the always-upbeat Pierce. "Being out also was getting a rest. So in September, for the playoffs and everything I may have been a little stronger."

Sobriety, not stamina, was the critical issue concerning Don Larsen, the other pitcher the Giants obtained in their '61 trade with the White Sox. In an era when alcoholism in baseball was papered over by the media and all but unknown to the general public, Larsen was one player whose reputation for nightlife was well documented.

"At the time we played baseball, there was a lot of drinking," disclosed Mike McCormick. "There were no drugs, there was a lot of free time and a lot of boredom in that free time. I think as a result, the players overall probably drank more than they do today. To single out one player from then is probably unfair. I can say in all honesty I was around [Larsen] a couple times when even I marvelled at how much he could consume, but I never saw it deter his performance. Maybe it shortened his career, but that's something that nobody will ever really know."

Larsen's career had been a rollercoaster ride of emotional highs and lows. In 1954, his second year in the majors, Don won only three of 24 decisions for the Orioles, but just two years later with the Yankees, he became the first (and still only) man in baseball history to pitch a perfect game in the World Series. Despite four consecutive winning campaigns in New York, Larsen was eventually peddled to the lowly Athletics, bottoming out at 1-10 in 1960. That was poor even by Kansas City's subterranean standards, and the A's demoted the one-time Series hero to the minor leagues.

In good times and bad, Larsen was a creature of the night. As a Yankee he celebrated championships with fellow revelers Billy Martin, Mickey Mantle, and Whitey Ford, who called their fun-loving drinking companion "Goony Bird." But in losing venues such as Baltimore or Kansas City, Larsen's nocturnal forays were primarily for the drowning of sorrows.

A lifeline was thrown to Larsen in '61. An eight-player trade between the A's and White Sox sent him to Chicago, where he went 7-2, despite a high ERA. It was enough to indicate to the Giants that Don could still pitch, and they insisted upon his inclusion in the Billy Pierce deal that winter.

Catcher Joe Pignatano was one of Larsen's biggest boosters at the Giants' camp the following spring. "He likes to feel wanted. I roomed with him at Kansas City last year. I know how he thinks. He wants to work. When he pitches, he's all right. Sometimes he has a bad day. Then they forget him for a while. He starts to get down on himself. He figures if they don't want him to pitch he might as well go out and have a good time. If this club lets him work, I think he can be a winner."

Bob Bolin ("The hardest thrower on the staff," according to Ed Bailey) was expected to increase his bullpen work load, but 1962 would be only his second major league season. All along, the Giants publicly stated their desire for a veteran middle-inning relief pitcher, and told Don the job was his from the first day of spring training. The vote of confidence was all the motivation Larsen needed. "Don wasn't a teetotaler, but he was not a heavy drinker that year," said Billy O'Dell. "In fact, he and I started doing some exercises together. He got real excited about it and it took off about three inches from his waist."

The new and improved Larsen won five games and saved 11 others, often punctuating his performances with the same potent finishing kick of the cocktails he so dearly loved. "He came in against Pittsburgh one night with the bases loaded," recalled Ed Bailey, "and struck out the side on nine pitches. When he went out there, you knew you were gonna get a pretty good effort."

Larsen was capable of legendary deeds even on days he did not pitch. Bullpen eyewitness Tom Haller remembered Don "saving a huge aluminum ball. He collected everyone's gum wrappers and by the end of the year that thing was over 18 inches in diameter." Don was even more prolific when it came to bringing home the spoils of the great outdoors.

Mike McCormick was familiar with Larsen's routine. "He used

to go up north to what they call the Delta near the town of Williams and go 'gigging' for frogs. He'd get into a boat, ride along the edge of the river with a flashlight and a stick that had prongs on it—and he'd catch lots of frogs and bring 'em home. Then he'd clean 'em and cook up the frogs' legs. They were a real delicacy. If he heard you really liked them, he'd bring some to the ballpark and you could take the legs home to eat."

Don endeared himself to San Francisco's clubhouse gourmands, and even more so to the starters who fattened their win totals by entrusting a lead in his hands. But in the late innings of close ballgames, the Giants' nonpareil relief pitcher was baseball's most notorious junk peddler—Stu Miller.

"I don't think my fastball got up to 85 miles an hour," he confessed. "I made my living off deception. Look, I didn't throw anything anybody else didn't throw—but my off-speed pitches were better than anybody else's. I could see hitters trying to wait on my pitches and look for them—and they still couldn't hit it."

According to the Dodgers' Ron Fairly, "Stu had the best off-speed pitch of anybody in the history of baseball. Miller made more great hitters look bad at the plate than any pitcher I've ever seen. He could throw just hard enough that you had to respect his fastball or he'd throw it by you. Then by the time you think you had his slow stuff down, he'd throw one a little slower and you'd still be out in front of it." One strikeout victim, Phillies catcher Choo Choo Coleman whined, "He threw me three pitches, I swung three times, I missed three times. But what you don't understand is this: the ball was THERE! I swung where it was. How could I miss it?"

Because of his fluttering changeup, the press nicknamed Stu "The Killer Moth." The Giants called him indispensable—and perhaps he was too valuable. In 1961, his best season in San Francisco, "It seemed like Miller was always coming into the ballgame," lamented Alvin Dark, "and our pitchers were depending on him too much." During a three-game series in Philadelphia, Dark told each of his starters, "We've got no bullpen tonight. You need to work, you need to get after it." Dark then instructed Miller not to dress and to sit up in the stands because, "If you stick around in uniform I know I'm going to use you."

Stu was busy again in '62, leading the staff in appearances and saves. Yet in another way, Miller was as baffling to his pitching coach as he was to opposing hitters. Larry Jansen remembered "Stu getting on the team bus early during road trips, then hopping off the bus 10 minutes before it was supposed to leave to do something—then just making it back on about a minute before it left. It happened more than once and why he did this I don't know."

Billy O'Dell had the answer. "That was Stu—always working a crossword puzzle. He'd be the last one in the clubhouse and he'd be the last one dressed, just sitting there doing them puzzles." "I liked crosswords—the hard ones, not the easy ones," confessed Miller. "And playing bridge too, because I enjoyed games that tested your brain."

Like the other veteran pitchers on the San Francisco staff, Stu began his career someplace else. After breaking in with St. Louis in 1952, Miller also pitched with the Phillies before being traded to the Giants in '57. He flip-flopped between the rotation and relieving until 1961 when Dark decided to use him exclusively out of the bullpen. From that time on, Stu never started another game in the major leagues.

Miller and Mike McCormick were two of only three former *New York* Giants still playing for the San Francisco Giants by 1962. The only other Polo Grounds alumnus still on the roster was outfielder Willie Mays.

10
A-MAYS-ING GRACE

Nineteen-sixty-two was Carl Boles' only year in the major leagues. He was recalled from El Paso in midsummer to give the Giants another right-handed hitting outfielder on their bench, but the bench was primarily where Boles resided. Despite a .375 average, he appeared in only 19 games. Aside from a subsequent career in Japanese baseball, Boles' only other claim to fame was his uncanny physical resemblance to Willie Mays.

"It was really noticeable when we made a trip back to the Polo Grounds. Willie would get these huge ovations there. That night I came out through the center-field bleachers before he did and the crowd thought I was Mays. They gave me a standing ovation and I wasn't sure why, but thought to myself, 'Wow, this is great for a rookie.' But when I got to the dugout and they saw my [number] 14 instead of 24 they started booing me. That same night when I went up to pinch-hit, they booed me out of the park.

"After games, if I left the stadium before Mays, I would be mobbed by fans wanting autographs. When I wrote my own name, they'd get upset, so sometimes as a joke I'd sign Willie's instead. In hotels I'd get service you wouldn't believe. I knew this couldn't be normal treatment. And since I roomed with McCovey, they must have figured I had to be Mays."

Even with a look-alike on his own team, there was no mistaking Willie Howard Mays for anyone else when he took the field. In 1962, Mays was still universally regarded as the best all-around player in the game. On Opening Day, he hit the first pitch Milwaukee's Warren Spahn threw to him for a home run, one of 49 that would lead the major leagues. He set a career high with 141 RBI and batted over .300 for the sixth straight season. At 31 he was still a dangerous baserunner, and no other outfielder successfully handled more chances. Mays' $90,000 annual salary ranked among baseball's highest, and fan polls consistently listed him as the most recognizable figure in his sport.

Accordingly, 1962 should have been Willie's happiest season as a San Francisco Giant. In reality, it was probably the most demanding, tumultuous year of his life. That same summer, Mays recorded a single entitled "My Sad Heart," a ballad that accurately mirrored his doleful disposition.

Despite a sizeable paycheck, Mays' personal finances were in a shambles. A bitter and very public divorce was still titillating fodder for the local press, and he got into his first major league baseball fight. Dwarfing all these episodes was the strain of the grueling pennant race, a daily grind that pushed him to the brink of exhaustion.

"He was so intense," noted Orlando Cepeda. "He played so hard in every game that he just wore out." Alvin Dark agreed: "I thought the pressure was greater on Mays that year than ever before in his career, even more than 1954 when we won the pennant. I don't think he felt like he was under as much pressure then. We had other [leaders] on the club and he was much younger. But in 1962 he's a more mature guy, and now he's expected to carry the ballclub, and I think that had a lot to do with his getting tired."

In order to get his vitally needed rest, Mays became a virtual recluse. Such isolation also suited an obsessive desire for solitude. "He wouldn't talk about his business—period," according to Boles. "Even if you tried to help him, it was no use. He had very few real close friends, and he fought his own battles."

One such conflict was his ongoing struggle for acceptance by the San Francisco fans. From the moment he came to the Bay Area in 1958, Mays was respected, but not loved. Regional provincialism and northern California baseball history were two forces working against him.

The roots of San Francisco baseball extended back to amateur leagues in the 1850s (where the widely used term *sandlot* first originated). In 1903 the Pacific Coast League was born, and the Bay Area was eventually awarded not one, but two local teams—the San Francisco Seals and Oakland Oaks. Both were thriving franchises well into the 1950s. San Franciscans were equally proud of the many native sons who became major league stars: Lefty O'Doul, Mark Koenig, Harry Heilmann, Earl Averill, Paul and Lloyd Waner, Ernie Lombardi, Billy Martin, and the greatest center fielder of them all— Joe DiMaggio.

Charles Einstein believed, "The fundamental trouble Mays had out here was that he took DiMaggio's place. And this town wasn't ready to accept an import who was going to take DiMaggio's place. San Francisco was an enormously chauvinistic town, and these guys came from New York. And Mays was the symbol of New York being thrust down San Francisco's throat."

"I can understand the fans' reluctance to accept me," Mays told sportswriter Jack McDonald. "This is Joe's hometown. He's their idol. He was mine too...I didn't come to San Francisco to show Joe up. I only wanted to prove that I, too, could play baseball."

The legend of Willie Mays had been recanted endlessly to the locals long before his West Coast arrival. They heard ad nauseum of his rookie year in '51 when he sparked the Giants to the greatest comeback charge in baseball history...how the "Say Hey Kid" blasted home runs by day and played stickball with neighborhood youngsters by twilight...of the deluxe MVP season of '54, complete with World Series circus catch and accompanying championship ring.

None of this made much difference to the northern California crowds, who were more eager to embrace the region's newer, younger *San Francisco* Giants. In '58, Willie hit .347 and led the league in runs and stolen bases, yet was booed for the first time in his career. At season's end, the fans voted for Cepeda, not Mays, as club MVP. "The Baby Bull was no Polo Grounds transplant," noted McDonald. "Fans tolerated Cepeda's shortcomings but demanded perfection from Mays' every move." No matter what Mays accomplished, however herculean, it was never quite enough. In 1959, after Soviet premier Nikita Krushchev completed his tour of San Francisco, veteran newspaper editor Frank Coniff cracked, "It's the damnedest city I ever saw in my life! They cheer Krushchev and boo Willie Mays!"

Others carried their dislike for Mays to further extremes. Willie faced tremendous obstacles while attempting to buy a house in exclusive, segregated Miraloma. For the first year and a half after moving in, not one white neighbor ever uttered even a word to his wife Marghuerite. In the summer of '59, a bottle shattered their bedroom windowpane in the middle of the night. Its contents: a virulently racist note. Eventually, Mays sold the property and moved out.

Despite his arms-length relationship with the city, Mays pressed on, even while playing in despised Candlestick Park—the concrete wind tunnel that chipped away at the strongest skills of his game. His morale improved when ex-teammate Alvin Dark was named Giants manager at the end of 1960. Two days after the announcement, Alvin sent the following letter to Mays: *Just a note to say that knowing you will be playing for me is the greatest privilege any manager could ever hope to have.*

"When we played together, we had a great relationship," said Dark. "I loved Willie as a player and as a friend. When I became his manager, I felt I had to build him up to the public and with the writers to let them know the type of player he really was. He wasn't as popular as I felt he should have been. I was trying to give him the credit he deserved and wake San Francisco up to the facts of life."

Even if the fans were slow to heed the gospel according to Alvin, such confidence boosting was a rejuvenating tonic to Mays, who proceeded to hit .308 with 123 RBI and 40 home runs. Four of his homers came in one game against the Braves, even though Mays was sick that day with an upset stomach. Even greater production was anticipated in the expansion season of '62. "If Mays can take advantage of the league's pitching dearth—the way he riddled Milwaukee's in '61—" predicted writer Ray Robinson, "we may see the kind of year always latent in Mays, but until now never fully evident."

Off-field distractions, not National League pitchers, were the source of Willie's most vexing problems in 1962. It began with money; Mays didn't have any. He owed the Giants more than $65,000 for salary advances and nearly $9,000 more in federal back taxes. "If, when you speak of foolish investments," Mays wrote in one autobiography, "you mean buying a new car bigger or sooner than you have to, or having 20 tailor-made suits instead of half a dozen you could buy off the rack, or going out on a whim and paying retail for the most expensive pool table you ever saw, or getting married and throwing thousands into drapes and carpets and even wallpaper—all right. That was me."

Expenses soared higher when Willie's marriage to Marghuerite disintegrated. The Mays' debt meter kept clicking: Alimony payments, a second home in New York, lawyers' fees, private detectives, and income taxes on his '62 salary of $90,000, even though he would actually net but a third of that amount.

April 17th was probably his worst day of '62. That morning, Willie arrived at San Francisco Superior Court with his lawyer, Bergen van Brunt, to contest numerous expenses levied against him by his estranged wife's attorney. Mays had already lost custody of his adopted son, Michael, age three. Now, he faced more humiliation. One by one, each fee was scrutinized—then recorded in excruciating detail by the *San Francisco Chronicle* for next day's front-page story, "Mays' Long, Long Day in Court."

The Giants were scheduled to play the Dodgers that same afternoon at Candlestick, but Willie was still in the thick of legal entanglements as the game began. By the time Mays arrived at the ballpark, the Giants were losing. Knowing how upset Willie was over his legal troubles, Dark held him out of the game until pinch-hitting him in the seventh inning. Mays struck out with two runners aboard. Then, with two out in the ninth and the Dodgers ahead, 8-7, Mays batted with the tying run on base, but popped out to end the game. The Candlestick crowd added to the day's misery by booing him unmercifully.

The same fans who jeered Willie may have also been the ones who constantly pestered him away from the park. Because of his celebrity and charisma, Mays drew crowds without even trying. "He's under tremendous strain," said Dark. "Wherever he goes, people want his autograph. He has to eat in his room, because he can't go out. The phone rings all the time, and he's not like other guys. He doesn't shut it off."

Right after Mays' nightmarish day in court, the Giants left town for a road trip that began in Milwaukee. Willie did not usually burden others with his problems, but that evening, alone in his hotel room, the pressure was too much to bear. "That night I couldn't sleep," he recalled. "I had the shakes. I found myself, for no real reason I knew, on the verge of tears. I called Dark on the phone. I said, 'I don't know what's wrong with me.' "

Alvin invited Willie up to his room, then called trainer Doc Bowman for some sedatives. "Sleep in here with me," Mays recalled Dark saying, as he pointed to the other bed in his room. Then Alvin listened sympathetically as the two ex-teammates talked for almost an hour before the pills finally helped Mays doze off.

Because of his importance to the team, Willie was seldom given a day off, but in other ways Dark did whatever he could to look after his star. "We usually rotated players in and out of first class on the plane," recalled Mike McCormick, "but Mays was the exception. The rest of us had roommates, but Willie always roomed alone. Still, because it was him, I don't think any of the other players resented it."

Nearly every Giant liked Mays. Most called him "Buck," an abbreviated version of a childhood nickname, "Buckduck." That label was itself a bastardized derivative of "Duck-butt" ("He always had a high behind," noted Mays' Aunt Ernestine). In the clubhouse, he could be loose and convivial. "Once he got to know you, he was a terrific guy," said Billy Pierce. "Baseball was fun for him, the game was his release. He just blocked everything else out."

Although Mays was no social butterfly, he would occasionally invite some of the Giants to his home. "I just like to have a few friends over for a game of cards—four-handed whist, bridge or gin rummy. Poker? I play a little. Stu Miller, Harvey Kuenn, Jim Davenport, and me like to play pinochle together." Mays also kept a full liquor cabinet for his guests, but never touched a drop of his stock—or anyone else's.

According to Larry Jansen, "Willie really took care of himself. He didn't drink, he didn't smoke, he didn't carouse—because he knew he was going to play every day."

Mays had girlfriends, but mostly he kept to himself. Solitary meals and clothes shopping on the road, TV shoot 'em ups, and billiards at home. "This is more than loneliness," wrote Arnold Hano. "It is withdrawal. Mays slipping out of the group and into his own cocoon-like environment, where he is by himself, with himself, and the rest of the world is neatly shut out."

By living in isolation, Mays created a self-sustaining existence. He counted on no one, so nobody could let him down. Such fears were understandable; Willie's parents split up before he was six. His mother passed away in his early 20s, and then his aunt Sarah, who raised him after the divorce, died shortly thereafter. From then on, Mays was reluctant to depend on blood ties. When he initially separated from Marghuerite and left New York for his hometown of Birmingham, Alabama, Willie moved into a motel and lived by himself rather than stay with family.

Ultimately, his work was his salvation. "For nine innings," Mays confessed, "I can play just baseball. But after the game, I've got a lot to think about." But personal problems were not the only issues on his mind.

During a '62 series in Houston, Willie was approached by a man named Eldrewey Stevens, who identified himself as the president of the Progressive Youth Association, a local civil rights organization. He observed Mays, McCovey, and Cepeda walking up to the box office of a segregated movie house. Stevens went over to Mays and asked him not to buy tickets at that theatre. Willie, politely but firmly, declined. Both McCovey and Cepeda later told the *Chronicle* that they would have honored Stevens' request if Mays had done so first. But confrontation and controversy were situations Willie preferred to avoid.

There was one instance when Mays did not back down from a fight. For 11 years, he had played in the major leagues without once getting into a brawl, but that ended on the afternoon of May 27th.

The Giants were hosting the Mets in the opening game of a double-header. The trouble began in the first inning when New York's Roger Craig twice buzzed knockdown pitches past Willie. In the seventh, Cepeda fielded a grounder and his throw accidentally hit baserunner Joe Christopher in the head. Craig took note, and in the bottom of the inning, after Mays singled, the Met pitcher plunked Cepeda in the shoulder.

Orlando trotted to first, then heard a remark from Craig that infuriated him. Cepeda charged the mound, but Alvin Dark bolted from the dugout in time to restrain his first baseman from attacking. Both benches emptied, but, like most baseball donnybrooks, there was more posturing than punching. Order was soon restored and the game resumed.

With Mays dancing off second, Craig twice tried to pick him off with throws to shortstop Elio Chacon ("Why?" Dark asked later. "No one *ever* picked Willie off second"). The year before, when he was with Cincinnati, Chacon had been spiked in the knee by Mays on a play at second base. The wound required 10 stitches and put the injured Reds' infielder on the disabled list for two weeks. It was an incident Chacon had obviously not forgotten.

After Craig's second pickoff throw, Chacon began punching the sliding Mays on the back of his head. Willie, more surprised than hurt, arose and, as sportswriter Dick Friendlich described it, "picked up his foe as though he were a sack of cement, hurled him to the ground and began to belt him."

Both benches cleared a second time as Cepeda sought to resume his earlier feud with Craig. More blows were exchanged before intervening parties separated the two. Meanwhile, Mays ended his fracas with Chacon and rushed to help Cepeda. When the dust finally settled, the umpires, for some reason, decided to eject only Chacon and not Cepeda, Craig, or Mays. The Giants went on to win the opener, 7-1, then the nightcap, 6-5.

After the game, Chacon was surrounded by reporters. "He spike me," pointing to a slight wound on his left shin. "He try the first time he slide back and he spike me the second time. Last year he spike me, too." A skeptical Charles Einstein later wrote, "How does a guy coming back head first go about spiking somebody?"

Mays escaped with a bruise on his forehead and a cleat-torn pair of white sanitary socks—armor that, according to Doc Bowman, was Willie's last line of defense. "If that spike had gone through, it could've ended Mays' career," insisted the Giants' trainer. "A little deeper and his achilles tendon could have been severed."

Elio Chacon was still bearing some emotional scars himself that evening as the Mets boarded their jet to return home. The club was about to open a seven-game homestand with the Dodgers and Giants, each team's first regular-season appearance in New York since their abrupt departure in 1957. A sullen Chacon balefully stared out the plane window. He knew his scuffle had been televised back east to a large viewing audience—and that said audience was still enormously fond of prodigal son Willie Mays.

Finally, the diminutive Venezeulan spoke. "Will they boo?" he wondered. Chacon did not say another word for the rest of the flight.

* * *

It was evident simply by looking at their uniforms. The same shade of blue adorned by the Dodgers…the identical orange trim of the Giants…the curling "NY" cap logo, the exact lettering once worn by the previous Polo Grounds tenants. The '62 Mets dressed the part—and even created themselves in the image—of the two dearly departed teams.

The New York roster included former Dodgers Gil Hodges, Charlie Neal, Don Zimmer, Clem Labine, Roger Craig, and ex-Giants Hobie Landrith and Jim Marshall. Even with this lofty pedigree, none of the above could prevent the Mets from losing the most games, 120, in a modern baseball season.

Still, the New York fans turned out, even if only in morbid curiosity, to watch their new team try—and almost always, fail. "They've shown me ways to lose I never knew existed," groaned manager Casey Stengel.

Through their first 15 home dates, the Mets' total attendance was just under 156,000, or slightly better than 10,000 fans per game. But for the five May and June dates against the Dodgers and Giants, the Polo Grounds took in almost 198,000 customers. "The fans came out in droves that week, and I think that's when the Mets really became popular," said the Dodgers' Daryl Spencer, who had also once roamed the Polo Grounds as a Giant. "Everybody was so pissed off at the Giants and Dodgers for moving that they just jumped on the Mets' bandwagon. When they booed us, you got cold chills because you felt like these were your fans, it hadn't been that long since we were there, and now they were rooting against you."

The Dodgers were the initial arrivals, playing their first New York-based game on May 30th. By seven in the morning, fans were already lined up at the ticket windows to assure their presence at the Dodgers' welcome home party. "Are crowds always like this here?" wondered catcher John Roseboro. "In Los Angeles they're quiet, but they've been buzzing here ever since we arrived." As an added attraction, ex-Bums Don Newcombe and Ralph Branca were brought in to pitch batting practice against their former mates. In the hitting cage, Ebbets Field icon Duke Snider thrilled the locals by launching a ball into the outfield seats.

Before the largest Polo Grounds crowd since 1942 (a Dodger-Giant game, to no one's surprise), L.A. swept the Memorial Day twin bill, 13-6 and 6-5. Brooklyn-born Sandy Koufax won the opener, helped by two home runs from an unlikely power source, Maury Wills. In the second game, the Mets executed a triple play and got a pair of homers from ex-Dodger Gil Hodges (giving him three for the doubleheader). Still, New York lost in the ninth when Willie Davis hit the seventh L.A. home run of the afternoon to snap a 5-5 tie. Los Angeles completed their series sweep the next night, winning, 6-3.

Despite the three Mets' losses, the Dodgers' homecoming was considered a smashing success. "Perhaps a new tradition, a new rivalry was born yesterday," said *The New York Times*. "[The Dodgers] yanked the customers through the turnstiles with the same magnetic power they exerted when, to get here, they merely had to cross a bridge from Brooklyn, instead of a continent."

The Giants made an even more emotional return to their former home when they arrived a day later. "I think we were all very nostalgic," recalled team vice president Chub Feeney. "I loved the Polo Grounds—a place Horace Stoneham and myself had left very reluctantly. It was a great old park, and I had grown up there from the time I was a kid coming to watch the games. It was funny being the visiting team in the ballpark that meant so much to all of us." Added Whitey Lockman, "I'm surprised that some of the old Giants didn't go to the wrong dugout from force of habit."

One former Polo Grounds' regular actually was a bit disoriented. The afternoon of the series opener, Doc Bowman carried his trainer's kit into the home team clubhouse. Surprised Mets attendants straightened him out and directed Doc to the appropriate quarters. Willie Mays later disclosed that he had never even seen the visitors' dressing room.

San Francisco swept all four games of the weekend series, but New

York fans did not appear too agitated over the results. Most were simply pleased to welcome back the old tenants, particularly Mays. Many of the local sportswriters who knew him were struck by the aura of maturity Mays seemingly had acquired since moving west. When one newspaperman asked Willie if he could speak with him, a puzzled Mays wasn't sure what he meant.

"I used to have to ask Durocher if it was all right to ask you a question," the reporter clarified. The older and wiser Mays answered, "I can talk for myself now."

"This was Willie's moment and it was fantastic," recalled Billy Pierce. "The press people were clamoring for him in the clubhouse. He was their lost hero." Columnist Arthur Daley later wrote, "The center field turf at the Polo Grounds looks normal this weekend for the first time in almost five years. Willie Mays has come home."

More than 43,000 turned out for the Friday night series opener. Many arrived early to watch Mays bash some fat batting practice offerings into the cheap seats. As he jogged towards the bleachers for fielding warmups, hundreds of screaming fans called his name. One eager follower leaned over so far that his cigar fell onto the turf. "Willie fielded it on the big hop and tossed it back into the stands," reported the *Times*.

To mark the occasion, each of the Giants was introduced over the public address system before the game began. Mays was accorded the most deafening ovation, a salute that lasted nearly two minutes. In theatrical fashion, Willie responded to the love-laden outpouring by bashing a home run off Roger Craig in the fifth inning. The next day, another Mays homer hit the base of the left-field light tower.

His homecoming was not perfect. In the first game of the Saturday doubleheader, Mays committed one of his only fielding miscues of the entire season, allowing a Richie Ashburn liner to skid through his legs for a three-base error. During game two, Willie struck out in his final three at-bats. In the Sunday finale, pitcher Bob Miller fanned Mays two more times in the first and third innings. But Willie refused to allow the memorable weekend to end on a sour note. In the sixth, he socked Miller's first pitch against the left-field roof facade for his third home run in as many days.

* * *

When Duke Snider made his initial pilgrimage back to New York earlier that week, he was asked how it felt to be playing once more in the Polo Grounds. "This place is full of ghosts," replied the former Duke of Flatbush.

"Dead ghosts?" followed up the reporter.

Snider shook his head. "Live ghosts. I keep looking up and seeing Willie catching a long one."

For four summers, these Polo Grounds spirits had remained largely undisturbed. They were resurrected with the birth of the Mets in '62. The void created by the Dodgers/Giants departure was finally filled; the old ballclubs had been replaced, and, in time, would be displaced as well. In effect, 1962, not 1957, would be the final chapter of the Dodgers-Giants era in New York City baseball.

Confronted with the humbling reality of an actual successor to their National League identity, both the Giants and Dodgers were emboldened to mount one last *mano a mano* pennant race, an attempt to claim the immortality of their New York rivalry.

THE PENNANT RACE

11
LIKE BACK IN
THE BOROUGHS

By midsummer, San Francisco and Los Angeles had effectively distanced themselves from the rest of the National League. The other eight teams became little more than supporting characters in the drama between the California clubs, playing out their schedules, then receding into the background when the two leaders met face to face.

The Dodgers and Giants battled 18 times during the regular season, and split the series with nine wins apiece. The competitive course could usually be charted simply by noting where the games were contested. San Francisco beat writer Joe King put it best: "It seems to be an incontrovertible fact that neither team can play well in the other chaps' ballpark. The Giants are sad sacks in L.A.; nobody may ever see a team drop dead like the Dodgers in Candlestick."

"We would go up to San Francisco with our great pitching staff," recalled Ron Perranoski, "and there were games where we'd get blown out, 12-3 or whatever. Then they'd come down to Dodger Stadium and we'd win low-scoring games by a run. The two ballparks dictated the action."

The local weather and stadium architecture weren't the only factors determining the temper of the games. Each city's groundskeeping staff added their own gardening "touches" to cater to the strengths of the home team. The power-laden Giants preferred tall greenery and a slow infield. They prevailed upon their groundsmen to muddy the basepaths and dampen the grass. Not so the Dodgers. "We played to our speed," admitted Ron Fairly. "Our crews used to slope the third base line at Dodger Stadium so that when we'd bunt the ball down the line it would stay fair. We kept the infield hard and the grass short. The more things we could do to piss [the Giants] off, the better chance we felt we had to win ballgames."

Alvin Dark was more than a little dismayed when he arrived early one afternoon at Chavez Ravine. "I got out there and saw these heavy rollers on the infield rolling down the basepaths. I'd never seen that done on dirt before. Those rollers packed that dirt down like asphalt. I went out there on the infield and dribbled a baseball and said, 'Holy smoke, I hope no one catches a spike in this.' Now, I didn't blame the Dodgers, because they needed that fast track to score runs. That was their home-field advantage. But I felt when they came to our park, we'd handle things a little differently."

Any payback against Los Angeles would be sweet revenge after what the Giants endured in their first two visits to southern California. In May, the Dodgers easily won both games of an abbreviated series. In late July, prior to the second All-Star break, the Giants returned, with L.A. holding a one-game lead in the standings. More than 162,000 fans poured in that weekend, creating traffic congestion so severe that comedian Milton Berle jokingly told Walter O'Malley he was going to avoid the crowds and fly to San Francisco where he could "watch the games on TV."

The Giants probably wished Uncle Miltie had taken Frank Howard with him. Hondo crashed three home runs and drove in 12 as the Dodgers swept the series, 3-1, 8-6, and 11-1. The trifecta gave L.A. a perfect 5-0 home record against San Francisco. Although the results weren't quite as impressive at Candlestick, the Dodgers were reasonably satisfied to have split their first six games on the Giants' field.

The '62 pennant race took on a virtual life of its own—often competing for front-page headlines with major news stories. The worst stock market drop since the 1929 Crash, Israel's execution of Nazi war criminal Adolf Eichmann, Project Mercury space flights, and the opening of the Seattle World's Fair all shared equal billing with Dodger-Giant fortunes—at least in the California newspapers.

On August 4th, the Giants staged their first-ever "Old-Timer's Day" since moving west, and even the retired legends of baseball in attendance were caught up in the excitement. "Miracle at Coogan's Bluff" heroes Bobby Thomson, Monte Irvin, and Eddie Stanky were already drawing comparisons to the storied race of '51. San Francisco native Joe DiMaggio announced he'd be taking in all three games that week when the Dodgers came into Candlestick. Sadly, Joe abruptly had to change his plans when his ex-wife, film actress Marilyn Monroe, died of a drug overdose on the night of August 5th. DiMaggio flew to Los Angeles to take personal charge of the funeral arrangements, and never saw any of the Dodger-Giant games that weekend.

* * *

The Dodgers arrived in the Bay Area for their series on August

10th, the last scheduled road games of '62 with the Giants. By now, Los Angeles had increased its lead to five and a half games, the widest margin of the season. The Giants, still reeling from the three Chavez Ravine losses, could ill afford to fall further behind in the standings. The Candlestick Park grounds crew was enlisted to make sure that would not happen.

Since the end of World War II, every blade of grass and granule of infield sand at Giants home games had been tended by chief groundskeeper Matty Schwab. Matty liked to be close to his work, so much so that in New York, he convinced management to build him his own apartment right in the Polo Grounds. Joined by wife Rose and son Jerry, the Schwabs lived under the left-field grandstand. "Bobby Thomson's home run landed on my roof," he often boasted.

Eleven years later at Candlestick Park, Matty was given an opportunity to help the Giants in another pennant race. In early July, Schwab had hosed down the basepaths during a home series against Los Angeles, but that spray was literally "a drop in the bucket" compared to the horticultural sabotage planned for the August games. The night before that series was to begin, Dark called the groundskeeper into his office. "I told Matty, 'This is our diamond. Let's cut down that Dodger speed. I want this infield slow, I want it watered, and I want it soft.'"

At 5:30 the next morning Schwab went to work. He dug a pit around the first base area, dumped in a gloppy soufflé of water, sand, and peat moss, then covered it with a thin veil of camouflaging topsoil. When the Dodgers took infield that night, it didn't take long to notice something was wrong. Umpire Tom Gorman was informed of the irregularities and, upon closer examination, insisted that Schwab remove his homemade dirt mix. The crew promptly filled up three wheelbarrows and carted the contents off to storage under the stands.

Matty then ordered son Jerry to sprinkle the area. "Put enough water on it so that you can see it," he instructed. "And don't miss. If you do, you're fired." Soon the entire area was completely flooded. The Dodgers were not pleased, nor was Gorman, who demanded the puddles be dried out.

Billy O'Dell, the Giants starting pitcher that night, recalled what happened next. "I saw Matty coming in with a wheelbarrow full of sand and wondered what was going on because he never did that himself. Matty always had someone else do it. So he pushes it out and dumps the whole thing out at first base, and that made it worse than it was before." Schwab redeposited the original mixture of goo he had removed just 10 minutes earlier.

The entire episode completely unglued the Dodgers. "If the Giants wanted to shake us up they couldn't have picked a better way to do it," admitted Maury Wills. "We were really demoralized. It even affected our hitting because we were so angry over the mud we couldn't concentrate properly at the plate." Neither Wills, Willie Davis—nor any other Dodger—came close to stealing a base. Pitcher Johnny Podres lost his cool on a disputed call and was eventually knocked out of the game. A livid Leo Durocher was ejected for arguing in the sixth inning. Meanwhile, the gleeful Giants, on the strength of four RBI from Willie Mays, cruised to an 11-2 victory.

The following afternoon Schwab's crew was at it again, vigorously washing down the Candlestick infield. "If they put more water around first base, I'll catch pneumonia," snickered Ron Fairly. Out in center field during batting practice, Duke Snider lay on his stomach and flailed his arms in a mock breaststroke.

In a retaliatory measure reminiscent of Ebbets Field and Polo Grounds daffiness, an unknown Dodger stole San Francisco's leaded practice bat. A light-fingered Giant promptly responded by swiping L.A.'s practice bat. Other Dodgers were more preoccupied with the groundskeeping mischief, accusing the Giants of continuing their basepath tampering. With an absolutely straight face, Dark demurred. "You have to water down that infield because along about three o'clock the wind blows the dust in everyone's eyes, including the fans."

Burdened with the prospects of another Candlestick quagmire, the Dodgers countered with their own weapon of intimidation, ace starter Don Drysdale. Big D, unbeaten in his last 11 decisions, would not be reluctant to throw inside against San Francisco's hitters if conditions warranted.

Before the game was 10 minutes old, Giant-killer Tommy Davis (season's average vs. San Francisco: .452) continued tormenting his hosts with a three-run home run off starter Billy Pierce. Drysdale followed with two strong shutout innings, and the Dodgers appeared to be regaining their equilibrium. That all changed in the top of the third.

Wills, still furious over the soggy playing conditions, was the lead-off hitter. In an apparent act of protest, Maury continuously stepped out of the box just as Pierce was about to pitch. Plate umpire Al Forman cautioned Wills three times to get back in and hit. After the third warning, Maury blew his stack. "You didn't do anything about this field. You ain't got no freaking guts."

"What did you say?" asked the riled Forman. Wills repeated his charge verbatim. "I didn't hear you," replied the ump. This time, Maury was shouting: "YOU AIN'T GOT NO FREAKING GUTS!"

Forman threw off his mask and promptly thumbed Wills out of the game. Now it wouldn't matter if the basepaths had been bone-dry; L.A.'s offensive sparkplug was done for the day. When the Giants roared back with two runs in the bottom of the fourth, it was clear the Dodgers were in trouble. "During that second game Larry Jansen and I were standing in the dugout talking," recalled Dark, "and both of us noticed the change in their attitude. Those guys were still more worried about the infield than they were about playing baseball."

As Alvin predicted, the Candlestick Park winds began to pick up by the sixth inning, causing even the dampened dirt to blow in the eyes of the players and umpires. Play was frequently halted until the gusts died down, but all the delays did was heighten the tension of what was, to that point, the most suspenseful inning of the season.

Nursing a 3-2 lead, Drysdale faced leadoff hitter Felipe Alou, who blooped a double down the right-field line. Tom Haller struck out, bringing Jim Davenport to the plate. Big D promptly uncorked a fastball that struck Davenport in the left hand. The Giant infielder fell to the ground, writhing in pain with a hairline fracture of his finger. But this was no knockdown. The last thing the Dodgers wanted was to put the go-ahead run on base. An obviously concerned Drysdale raced quickly to home plate. "I'm really sorry," Don later said. "Jimmy's one of the nicest guys I've ever met." Drysdale even called Davenport at his home the next morning to apologize again.

The injury would cost the snake-bit third baseman more than two weeks of playing time. Davenport was led off the field as Billy O'Dell went in to pinch-run, but Drysdale quickly regained his composure, retiring Jose Pagan on a called third strike. One more out would wrap up the inning, and Pierce was the scheduled batter. But the Giants' pitcher remained on the bench as left-handed pinch-hitter Willie McCovey, himself hampered by a muscle pull, limped to the plate. Immediately, Walter Alston made a visit to the pitcher's mound.

The reason for Alston's concern was obvious. As John Roseboro wrote in his autobiography, "[McCovey] became the only batter who could consistently destroy Drysdale. Willie wasn't intimidated by Don's inside pitches, and he had the size and strength to reach out and rap Don's outside pitches." Added *Sports Illustrated*: "The very sight of Drysdale turns McCovey from an erratic power hitter into Paul Bunyan with a baseball bat."

In a previous confrontation the month before, McCovey nicked Big D for a home run and a single. In 1961, Stretch hit a 475-foot blast off Drysdale, the longest home run in Candlestick Park history. Despite this dubious résumé—and even with left-handed fireman Ron Perranoski ready in the bullpen—Alston decided to stick with his ace.

Drysdale worked the count to 3-2, then got his next pitch up high. *Chronicle* sportswriter Bob Stevens described what happened next: "McCovey uncoiled, and the collision of bat and ball was almost deafening. The ball sailed in a majestic arc into the right field bleachers, three quarters of the way up, for what has to be one of the most dramatic home runs in San Francisco's big league history."

Stu Miller pitched the final three innings and preserved the 5-4 win, the 200th career victory for Billy Pierce. The Dodgers lost another game of their lead, Drysdale's 11-game winning streak was over, and the ejected Maury Wills owed the National League $50.

L.A.'s weekend of water torture ended quietly on Sunday afternoon with Juan Marichal limiting the visitors to four hits in a 5-1 Giants' victory. After the game, the angry and soggy Dodgers exploded. Buzzie Bavasi insisted he'd be filing a formal protest with the league. "It was a very bush league thing to do," sputtered vice president Fresco Thompson. "It is the only time, to my knowledge, where a major league team has tampered in such a manner with its infield." Added a scolding Walter Alston: "Willie Mays could have broken a leg as easily as Maury Wills. That would be a bad thing for baseball."

Reaction from the Los Angeles media ranged from bemusement to outrage. Vin Scully proclaimed that Alvin Dark would now be known as "The Swamp Fox." Quipped *Times* columnist Jim Murray: "One more squirt and the Red Cross would have declared a disaster area and begun to evacuate the Dodgers by rowboat…an aircraft carrier wouldn't have run aground…they found two abalone under second base." Colleague Sid Ziff took a more truculent stance, labeling the series, "The most disgraceful case of poor sportsmanship since major league baseball came to the coast."

Such a view was shared by Maury Wills, who maintained his ejection was unfair, given the circumstances. The unrepentant shortstop reluctantly paid his fine in person the next week when the Dodgers were in Cincinnati, site of the league headquarters. Maury went to a local bank and obtained $50 in pennies, then dragged the 80-pound sack to the office of N.L. president Warren Giles. "I hoisted it onto his desk and turned it upside down. Pennies cascaded everywhere," Wills recalled. "Mr. Giles, here's your fine," he said to the startled league boss. "Could you count it for me, please? I'd like a receipt."

*   *   *

The Dodgers' collapse at Candlestick convinced Walter Alston he would have to make two essential changes within his ballclub. Even before the Giant series the team had fallen into a hitting slump, so Alston decided to bench struggling Daryl Spencer, replace him at third with Tommy Davis, and put Wally Moon in left field. It would be a risky gamble; Davis was not terribly comfortable playing third base and his presence would weaken an already porous L.A. defense. In 1962, only the woeful Mets committed more errors and had a worse fielding average than the Dodgers—and no team turned fewer double plays.

Walter's second decision was to shorten the long leash he had granted Leo Durocher. Since the July injury to Sandy Koufax, Leo had made up his mind to disregard Alston's instructions while relaying signals from the third base coach's box. "Forget the signs. Speed overcomes everything. Let them run," Durocher wrote in *Nice Guys Finish Last*. "We had a manager who sat back and played everything conservatively. To hell with it. Alston would give me the take sign, I'd flash the hit sign. Alston would signal to bunt, I'd call for the hit-and-run."

Durocher's low regard for Walter was also apparent in private conversation. He often referred to Alston as "the farmer" when he was out of earshot. "Leo could be overbearing at times," said Stan Williams. "He nearly created some real dissension with himself and the manager by putting a wedge between the players."

The line of demarcation separating the Alston and Durocher camps could be charted in two ways. According to Joe Moeller, "There was clearly a division on the club: Guys that weren't playing were on Leo's side and the guys who were playing were on Walter's side." Loyalties also seemed divided by age group. To a man, every Dodger liked and respected Alston as a person, but a coterie of the veteran players—including Roseboro, Williams, Carey, Gilliam, Drysdale, and Snider—questioned some of Walter's managerial moves. Daryl Spencer backed Durocher because "Alston could never make a decision and left himself open to a lot of second guessing by the older guys. He never gave you a feeling of confidence. I liked a guy who would speak up, and Durocher—right or wrong—would make a decision while Walter was kinda wishy-washy."

Some of those decisions were ill-advised, such as the time Leo verbally badgered Cubs third baseman Ron Santo during a game at Wrigley Field. According to Cubs general manager John Holland, Durocher yelled constantly at Santo from his coaching box, claiming that Ron would soon be traded to the Dodgers. "That comes close to tampering, and I won't stand for any more of it," said Holland. Buzzie Bavasi assured the Cub GM that if the charges were true he would talk to Durocher personally, "and you can bet it won't happen again."

Alston could have forgiven Durocher simply for being overzealous in this instance, but Leo continued to overstep the boundaries of his job by regularly ignoring the manager's signals and instructions. After losing their second game to the Giants in the waterlogged August series, Walter decided he'd had enough.

With the entire team present, Alston made the folllowing pronouncement: "Starting with this ballgame, I will take complete charge of this ballclub. And Leo, that means you. If I give you the bunt sign, that's what I want. The bunt. And if I give you the take sign, I want the hitter to take. Any sign that I give and you miss, I will fine you two hundred dollars and the player at bat two hundred dollars."

With that edict, Alston felt the issue was finally resolved, but just five days later in Pittsburgh, Durocher became embroiled in another controversy. First, Tommy Davis ran into his own bunt, and then Ron Fairly missed a sign during a double steal. As Leo returned to the dugout he screamed, "Somebody oughta take some money from these kids."

Alston rushed towards Leo and stared him coldly in the eye, his temper rising to a boil. "I guess you mean me, because I'm the only one who can take money from them." Now Walter was shouting. "I don't need any advice from you. You do the coaching, Durocher, and I'll do the chewing out and fining." The manager finished the tirade by reminding his coach that he was still missing signs given from the bench, and that Alston had to whistle three times simply to get Leo's attention.

Later, when a sportswriter criticized Alston for castigating Durocher in front of the players, Walter gave the newspaperman an earful. "You're pretty sensitive about Durocher's feelings, but you don't seem to care much about mine. What about the times he has shown me up in front of the players? How much of this do I have to take?"

In the early months of the season, Durocher invariably dressed by the locker located next to Alston's. And Leo always made it a point to sit beside the manager on the team bus during road trips. By the final weeks of '62, Leo had switched to a different locker and made sure he sat in the rear of the bus, as far removed from Alston as possible.

Leo's summer of discontent did not end there. On August 24th in New York, Durocher suffered a serious reaction from a penicillin injection. Leo was talking to a reporter in the Dodger clubhouse prior to a night game with the Mets when he suddenly grabbed his chest and fell. The writer and one of the team trainers hastily lifted him on to a table. Durocher, certain the Grim Reaper was hovering nearby, asked the writer to find Alston. When Walter arrived, Leo staged a death scene that would have been right at home in the corniest Hollywood sports biopic. "I think this is it, Walt," he gasped. "Go get them."

It could have been a classic baseball farewell, but the opportunity was lost when Durocher did not die. Sustained dosages of vitamin B were administered which eventually returned him to full health. Still, Leo was absent from the club for almost two weeks. Right after his misadventure, the Dodgers promptly won seven of their next eight games, giving them a three-and-a-half-game lead over the Giants by Labor Day.

That holiday afternoon, Los Angeles hosted San Francisco in the first of a four-game series in Chavez Ravine, their final head-to-head competition remaining on the schedule. This time, the Dodgers were determined to avenge their embarrassing series in Candlestick by exploiting every benefit of the home-field advantage.

As expected, the diamond dirt was packed down to brickyard consistency, as hard and "as dry as a Pharaoh's tomb," according to the *Chronicle*'s Charles McCabe. The largest crowd in Dodger Stadium history, 54,418, came out to cheer their heroes and boo the Giants. Still mindful of the August "water follies" games, the vengeance-craving fans arrived at the ballpark wearing feathers and toting duck calls. More than 3,000 calls were sold that afternoon at two dollars apiece by the shrewd-minded stadium concessions department. For some diehards, the calls weren't authentic enough: Two of them carted in a real duck and chicken and threw both on the field during the game. In each instance, Dodger batboy Rene Lachemann speedily chased down the livestock and removed them from danger.

When the Giants emerged from the clubhouse for batting practice, they were greeted by a chorus of quacking customers and a special gift resting on the steps of their dugout. It was a spouted canister colored in shocking pink with the following inscription: *Ed Bailey's Chavez Ravine 1st Base Watering Can.* When the din of duck calls died down, the public address system blared this mocking verse from Danny Kaye's "D-O-D-G-E-R-S Song:"

> Cepeda runs to field the ball
> And Hiller covers first
> Haller runs to back up Hiller
> Hiller crashes into Miller
> Haller hollers "Hiller!"
> Hiller hollers "Miller!"
> Haller hollers "Hiller," points to Miller
>   with his fist
> And that's the Miller-Hiller-Haller-
>   Holler-lujah twist!

The Giants had not won in Los Angeles since August of 1961—a drought of 10 straight games—but the dry spell was about to end. Dark shook up his batting order, moving Felipe Alou to third and sliding Willie Mays to fifth (the first time he'd batted in that slot since 1954). Mays responded by clubbing a three-run homer in the fourth to chase starter Stan Williams. It staked San Francisco to an early lead and provided more than enough support for Jack Sanford, who won his 20th game by a 7-3 score. Sanford went the distance, and did not walk a batter for the first time all season.

After the game, the Giants celebrated the win as guests at actress Jayne Mansfield's Hollywood mansion—a party that included cocktails and a buffet dinner by her swimming pool. "She wasn't anything at all like her image on the screen," admitted a surprised Billy Pierce. "She was pleasant, but very businesslike and proper. We knew she was a big baseball fan, but I think there was also some kind of promotion or commercial involved. To the ballplayers, this was a big deal. We went because we wanted to see Jayne Mansfield, her house, and that heart-shaped swimming pool."

The fantasy world of Hollywood evaporated the next night as Los Angeles gave the Giants a harsh dose of reality, defeating them, 5-4. The recognizable trademarks of Dodger baseball were evident throughout: Willie Davis scored all the way from first on a single, John Roseboro stole home, and the L.A. pitching staff was miserly when it had to be.

After rookie starter Pete Richert tired in the fifth, Ron Perranoski came in for four and one-third innings of gritty relief to preserve the win. Trailing 5-2 in the ninth, the Giants narrowed the lead with Jose Pagan's two-run homer, the first home run Perranoski had allowed all year. But the Dodger fireman came back strongly by striking out both Mays and Cepeda to end the game.

The Giants rebounded with even better pitching to win the next night, although it was to be a pyrrhic victory. Two Mays doubles and a single accounted for the scoring in the 3-0 decision, but the pivotal character of the evening was Juan Marichal. For six innings, he completely baffled the Dodgers, but on a play at first against Willie Davis, Juan jammed his foot while making the putout. Eerily, it was almost a year to the day since Duke Snider had ended Marichal's 1961 season when he spiked him at the Coliseum. "I thought of what happened last year and I was scared," confessed Doc Bowman as he ran to attend to the wounded pitcher.

Subsequent X-rays showed no fracture, and the doctors diagnosed the injury as a sprained or twisted ankle. Juan would be sidelined for about a week, they said, but ultimately, he would miss considerably more time than that.

Bob Bolin sewed up the victory with three innings of shutout relief, preserving the 18th—and ultimately last—win of the season for Marichal. The injury would eventually become the flashpoint of a serious rift between Marichal and Alvin Dark.

For the moment, Dark was distracted by other matters. Prior to the final match of the series, Alvin watched with curiosity as Walter Alston gave a pregame interview. This was not your normal Q & A; for the first time in history, a live radio sportscast was being beamed via the new Telstar communications satellite to U.S. armed forces personnel worldwide. While an Army sergeant asked questions from West Germany, Alston gave his responses from Los Angeles and Yankees manager Ralph Houk chimed in from New York City. Both skippers had been selected because their clubs were in first place, "But if they're going to talk about the World Series," noted Dark, "they may have picked the wrong man." He wasn't referring to Houk.

The Giants went out and backed up their manager's supposition with a Hollywood-tailored cliffhanger whose ending would have been preposterous even by Tinseltown standards. It began as soon as Alvin filled out his lineup card. Dodger starter Don Drysdale felt a wave of dread when he spotted Willie McCovey's name in the batting order.

By the fourth inning, McCovey had already singled in one run, then doubled and scored another. The Giants were cruising, 4-0, but L.A. roared back to tie the game on a clutch Tommy Davis single and Frank Howard's home run.

Drysdale, perhaps encouraged by the Dodger comeback and wary of the Willies, immediately proceeded to knock down both McCovey and Mays with high and tight fastballs. The very next inning, Giants starter Billy O'Dell retaliated by buzzing a heater past Drysdale himself.

Umpire Ed Vargo had seen enough, stopping the game to call both managers out to home plate. Alston sprinted out, but Dark remained in the dugout. "If you don't come out right now, you're out of the game," bellowed crew chief Al Barlick to the Giants' manager. Alvin angrily relented, storming onto the field for a volatile exchange with the umpires and Alston.

After several minutes of heated discussion, Vargo warned both managers that, "The next pitcher who throws another bean ball is gone." There would be no more knockdowns, but the evening's drama had far from played itself out. The Giants retook the lead in the eighth, but Tommy Davis tied the score with a solo home run in the bottom of the inning.

It came down to the last inning of the last scheduled Dodger-Giant game of 1962—and if this was to be their final confrontation, then both teams were going to ride this endurance test of a baseball game to its logically tumultuous conclusion. The 54,263 fans packed into Chavez Ravine were about to witness a denouement that captured the intensity of the Dodger-Giant rivalry at its most sublime.

The Dodgers entrusted matters to Ron Perranoski, the pitching hero of game two, but the ace reliever quickly dug himself into a hole. Chuck Hiller started the inning by singling off Perranoski's glove. Jim Davenport, still sore from his August hand injury but in the lineup nonetheless, laid down a sacrifice bunt. Perranoski fielded it and tried to get Hiller at second, but his throw sailed over Maury Wills' head into center field. Both runners advanced into scoring position, forcing the Dodgers to intentionally walk Felipe Alou, loading the bases with none out.

Bob Bolin was due to bat next, but Dark lifted the reliever for Carl Boles, who fouled out behind home plate. The next hitter was Mays. He had been the offensive hero of the two earlier Giant wins, but not tonight. Willie tapped weakly to Jim Gilliam who threw home for a forceout of pinch-runner Ernie Bowman. The bases remained loaded, but with two out, it appeared Perranoski might be out of trouble.

Ron worked a full count on Orlando Cepeda, then just missed on ball four to walk in the go-ahead run. "It took something out of the stricken [Perranoski]," wrote Bob Stevens. "He seemed to sag and his face was a mask of misery." Then Harvey Kuenn added to the Dodgers' woes by ripping a dramatic double to left-center that cleared the bases, increasing the San Francisco lead to 9-5. "Certainly, it was the biggest hit of my career," proclaimed Kuenn after the game.

Many of the local fans beat a hasty retreat to the Chavez Ravine parking lot, but they would soon come to regret their decision. Dark called on Don Larsen to finish the game, but the Giant reliever ran into trouble when pinch-hitter Tim Harkness singled and Wills drew a walk. Stu Miller replaced Larsen and got one out, but then Willie Davis singled to load the bases. The remaining Dodger fans exploded with the most deafening cheer of the series.

Up strode Tommy Davis, bane of the Giants' existence, and already the author of two hits and two RBI for the night. Miller fluttered his junk at the league batting leader, but Tommy was not fooled. Davis smoked a drive deep to left that had home run written all over it. Kuenn, who'd previously made a hitting contribution, was about to save the Giants' season with his glove. Harvey raced to the fence and speared the liner with his back against the wall. In the Giant dugout, a spent Alvin Dark dropped to his knees.

A run scored, but now there were two outs. The next hitter was Frank Howard, who always dreaded facing Miller. During one stretch in their personal rivalry, Hondo struck out four straight times, and was badly fooled on each occasion. "Frank was a big, strong, powerful hitter, but he had one flaw," disclosed The Killer Moth. "He strided too fast, hit off the right foot, and gave himself away too quickly, which will kill you against off-speed pitching—and that was my forte."

True to form, Frank flailed badly at Miller's first offering for strike one, but the next pitch was slow, straight, and easy to pick up. Hondo got all of it and the Chavez Ravine crowd jumped to its feet. The ball soared into the left-field stands, curving foul only at the last moment. By now, Dark was covering his eyes, but two pitches later he looked up as Howard barely made contact, looping a soft foul towards third which Davenport gloved for the final out.

"It was the most important game I've ever managed," the sweat-soaked Dark confessed later in the clubhouse. In point of fact, it had been the critical series of '62, because it shattered the Dodgers' aura of home-field invincibility against San Francisco.

The Giants flew home that night, exhausted but thrilled to be only a game and a half behind Los Angeles. From now on, the two rivals would have to wage their battles against other adversaries while constantly checking the out-of-town scoreboard. Little more than three weeks remained on the schedule, but not even the most prescient souls on either ballclub could have foreseen the debilitating and rancorous events that were about to dominate a turbulent September.

12
SEPTEMBER SWOON

Felipe Alou gratefully acknowledged the polite applause as he stood before the Palo Alto congregation of the Peninsula Bible Church. "I gave basically the same talk that I had given in other churches," he later recalled, "presenting my Christian testimony and explaining what the Lord meant to me." Seated among the crowd of nearly 2,000 parishioners was a sanguine Alvin Dark, who most assuredly added a demonstrative "Amen!" when Felipe spoke of the blessings he had received.

Alou had just hit safely in seven straight plate appearances against the Cubs, a string he would continue with two more hits the following afternoon against the Pirates. In fact, the entire San Francisco team was as torrid as the church's guest speaker. Coming off the successful series in Los Angeles, the Giants extended their winning streak to seven by sweeping Chicago and Pittsburgh at Candlestick Park.

To the Cubs and Pirates, their journey to the coast must have seemed more like a California quake, because both ballclubs received the same rude treatment when they played at Chavez Ravine. The Dodgers regained some momentum lost during the Giants series by taking four of five from the two visitors. However, that one defeat meant L.A.'s lead over San Francisco was only a half-game as both contenders departed for their final road trips of 1962—10 away dates for the Dodgers, 11 for the Giants.

A muggy midwestern heat wave greeted the Giants when they arrived in Cincinnati on September 12th. "The trip from the West Coast was a jolt for everyone used to playing in the cooler air of San Francisco and Los Angeles," observed rookie Gaylord Perry. "I had to change shirts twice that night. The sweat was pouring off me just sitting in the dugout before going out to the bullpen."

The weather was also bothering Willie Mays, who shortened his normal batting practice routine to only a few swings before heading into the clubhouse. His first time up, Mays struck out. There would be no second plate appearance.

As the third inning began, Willie suddenly staggered and fell with a thud to the dugout floor. For several minutes, he remained unconscious, even as trainer Doc Bowman attempted to revive him. Bowman feverishly waved smelling salts under Willie's nose until the outfielder eventually came around.

"Take it easy, Buck, take it easy," implored Bowman.

"What happened? What's wrong with me?" asked the bewildered Mays.

"Nothing's wrong, with you. You just passed out. That's all."

Larry Jansen leaned over his former teammate. "What do you say, Buck? Feeling better?"

"I don't know. I just don't feel like I want to have to move. I can. I just don't feel like it."

Doc Bowman had heard enough. Turning to the gathering of players he barked, "Get that damn stretcher!"

Mays was carried into the locker room where he was examined by Reds team physician George Ballou. Initially, the doctor thought Mays would be all right if he merely went back to his hotel room and rested, but when Willie complained of stomach pains, Ballou changed his mind and called for an ambulance to take the stricken Giant to nearby Christ Hospital.

"I was sitting right next to him In the dugout when he collapsed and it was scary," recalled Carl Boles. "He'd eaten a hamburger and french fries and a whole bunch of junk food a couple of hours before the game. I think the combination of the heat and that food did it."

The hospital staff conducted a thorough battery of tests, but could find nothing physically wrong with Mays. By the next morning, Willie felt better and asked if he could rejoin the team. Rather than take any unnecessary risks, the doctors urged that he stay at least another 24 hours for additional observation.

Back in San Francisco, the local papers were rife with rumors as to the cause of the collapse: a squabble in the dugout, venereal disease, heart attack, epilepsy. The most outrageous theory was that Kentucky gamblers had slipped a Mickey Finn into Willie's drink to improve the odds on their wagers.

"I knew then what it was and I know now what it was," Mays admitted later. "I was exhausted. Mentally, physically, emotionally, every other way."

Without Mays, the Giants lost both of their games in Cincinnati. He was dressed for the next series in Pittsburgh, but Dark had no intention of writing Willie's name on the lineup card. "Nobody wants to win a pennant more than I," said Alvin, "but I'm not going to do it at the risk of shattering somebody's nerves, perhaps permanently.

"The tests taken of Willie in Cincinnati didn't show anything wrong with him, and yet I won't let him play. How can tests tell what goes on inside [a man]? These players are human beings."

A wirephoto circulating around the country pictured a dejected Mays sitting in the Forbes Field dugout with the caption: "Aching to Play." Even if the sentiments were accurate, the portrait was not. The wire service cameraman had filmed Willie's look-alike, Carl Boles, by mistake.

Alvin held Mays out of action for the first two Pittsburgh games, watching helplessly as the team extended its losing string to four. Since 1951, Mays had missed a total of 19 games in which he could have played; the Giants' record in those games was 0-19.

The circumstances of the Pittsburgh defeats were especially galling for San Francisco. In the opener, the Giants led, 2-1, until the ninth inning, when Pirate pitcher Earl Francis hit the first home run of his career to help win the game. The following evening, with Mays still resting, the Pirates broke an eighth-inning tie when rookie Bob Bailey socked his first-ever big league extra-base hit, a two-run triple.

Mays finally returned in the third game and homered to send the contest into extra innings, but another home run by Bucs catcher Smoky Burgess in the bottom of the 10th handed the Giants their fifth straight loss. Pittsburgh completed the sweep the following night when a rookie named Elmo Plaskett collected the first hit of his major league career, a three-run home run off Mike McCormick. After the game, a furious Dark hurled several dozen hard-boiled eggs throughout the locker room. The next morning's sarcastic *Chronicle* headline read: "A Tisket, a Tasket, SF Sunk by Plaskett." The Giants, only a half-game from first place a week ago, found themselves trailing the Dodgers by four as they limped out of Pittsburgh for their next series in St. Louis.

The deficit could actually have been worse, but the Dodgers were also struggling. After winning seven straight, Alston started Stan Williams against the Cubs at Wrigley Field on September 16th. "I'd pitched against the Cubs at Dodger Stadium the week before, and as I remember it, I'd allowed only a couple of hits and had maybe a dozen strikeouts. Four days later I'm pitching in Chicago and I gave up a grand slam home run in the first inning to a rookie named Nelson Mathews and we ended up losing the ballgame.

"Subsequently, I was taken out of the starting rotation permanently and didn't pitch even once during the final week of the season.

Neither Alston or [pitching coach] Joe Becker ever explained why they pulled me. Here I'd been one of the four starters all year long and then, all of a sudden, I'm not pitching. It really hurt my pride that they felt I wasn't good enough to do the job."

L.A. proceeded to drop two of the next three in Milwaukee, then flew to St. Louis, checked into the Chase Hotel, and took a scheduled day off prior to their series with the Cardinals. But it was not a time of rest for all of the Dodgers.

Few members of the team were aware that Walter O'Malley had flown into town at the same time and taken a suite at the nearby Park Plaza. On the morning of Thursday, September 20th, travelling secretary Lee Scott assembled a select group in O'Malley's suite for a confidential meeting. Among those attending were Alston, the coaches, and team captain Duke Snider.

O'Malley quickly got down to business. From his vantage point, it appeared as if the team was falling apart and that Alston was being too lenient with the players. "Get tough, Walter," O'Malley sternly commanded. "You've got to ride herd on 'em. They're going to blow this thing, sure as hell, unless you can light a fire under them. Warn them that if they blow this pennant, they'll lose more than just the World Series money. It will be reflected in their salaries next year."

Alston listened quietly, then responded. A vote of confidence, not angry threats was the best strategy, he believed. "They feel bad enough as it is... They're just kids and they might blow sky high."

This was not what O'Malley wanted to hear. "Walter, these are not high school kids—they're professionals. I want you to ride herd on them, and it's all right with me if you make me the heavy."

Again, Alston respectfully but firmly insisted his approach was the best course of action. O'Malley grudgingly acquiesced but got in a parting shot. "All right, but if we blow this thing, some heads will roll."

Snider, who remained silent through most of the meeting, found it difficult to understand why the owner was so concerned. The players were still confident of victory and believed the front office should have felt the same. "Don't worry, Mr. O'Malley. We're going to win it," Duke assured.

A few hours later, events at Busch Stadium at least temporarily soothed some of O'Malley's fears. Because of a quirk in the schedule, the Giants were also in town, completing an abbreviated two-game set against the Cardinals. The day before, San Francisco had snapped its six-game losing streak by beating St. Louis on the strength of two Tom

Haller home runs. But that night, with many of the Dodgers in attendance, the Giants took another step backward, enduring perhaps their strangest loss of the season.

Leading, 4-3, in the bottom of the ninth with a Cardinal runner on third, Dark was forced to stay with little-used reliever Dick LeMay, recently recalled from the Tacoma farm team. Giants vice president Chub Feeney was there for the inglorious finish: "LeMay was set to pitch, then dropped the ball for a balk, which scored the tying run for the Cardinals. I have never seen that happen in baseball before or since." Ken Boyer followed with an RBI single off Don Larsen, and the Cardinals won, 5-4. "After that," added Feeney, "we pretty much resigned ourselves to the fact that we weren't going to win."

Earlier, Felipe Alou had run into Ron Perranoski in the lobby of the Chase Hotel. According to Alou, the Dodger reliever greeted him cordially and said, "We'll see you guys next year."

"I don't think he meant to say it in a bad way," Alou explained later, "but to me it sounded like he was saying he felt sorry for us because we were so far behind them. At least that's the way I understood it at the time. As it turned out, he wasn't going to have to wait till next season before we saw each other again."

* * *

On September 7th, Maury Wills broke the National League record for stolen bases in a season by swiping four in a game against the Pirates. It gave him 82, eclipsing the mark of 80 set by Cincinnati's Bob Bescher in 1911. "My sincere congratulations," wired league president Warren Giles. "Now go all the way and break the record held by the great Ty Cobb."

Cobb's major league mark of 96 stolen bases had been accomplished over 156 games, since his Tigers team was involved in two ties during the 1915 season. With better than two weeks to go before the Dodgers reached their number 156, Wills was reasonably sure he could break the record. But on the day before L.A. was to play their 154th game, Commissioner Ford Frick shocked Maury with a startling proclamation.

Wills, claimed the commissioner, was going to have to set the standard in 154, not 156 games, since that was the official length of Cobb's record-breaking season. With a total of 94 stolen bases, Wills would need to steal three in their September 21st game with St. Louis in order for major league baseball to officially recognize him as the new stolen base champion.

Maury was devastated by the announcement. "I wouldn't have minded so much had Frick made his ruling earlier. But why did he wait until the last day? If I'd known this a week or two weeks ago, I would've broken the record by then. There were games where I'd already stolen three bases by the sixth inning and the guys were crying on the other side of the field, so I stopped. Cobb got 156 games to set his record and I thought I would, too."

Game number 154 essayed enough storylines to transform the event from baseball to soap opera. The drama began with the scheduled starting pitchers. Since July 17th, the injured Sandy Koufax had not made a single appearance. Alston, perhaps with the voices of the O'Malley meeting still echoing in his mind, elected to go with the left-hander. The Cardinals countered with their intimidating power pitcher, Bob Gibson, but Gibby fractured a bone in his ankle during batting practice, ending his season.

"There was a tremendous sigh of relief from the Dodgers because they hadn't been hitting, and now they wouldn't have to face this [future] Hall-of-Famer," recalled Vin Scully. "Curt Simmons, who was very much nearing the end of his career, was rushed into the breach to pitch for Gibson." When Wills heard what happened, he, too, was delighted. "I could get out of bed in the middle of December and steal two off Simmons. He didn't like to throw the ball over to first."

The night began badly for the Dodgers. Koufax, showing definite signs of rust, walked the first two Cardinal batters. After striking out Stan Musial and popping up Ken Boyer, it looked as if Sandy might slip out of trouble, but then Bill White walked to load the bases. The next batter, Charley James, ripped a shot that barely cleared the pavillion roof for a grand slam home run. "It would have been an easy out in Dodger Stadium," Alston said later, but after Sandy walked the next batter, Walter had seen enough and removed Koufax from the game.

Meanwhile, Simmons held the Dodgers in check and kept Wills off the basepaths until the sixth inning. Trailing 4-1, Maury coaxed a walk, then, with Jim Gilliam at bat, swiped second for steal number 95. Sensing his opportunities were dwindling and mindful of Frick's declaration, Wills danced off second with a covetous gaze towards third.

Gilliam was still at the plate as action resumed. Like all the other Dodgers, Junior had heard the commissioner's announcement and understood its implications. All season long, he had sacrificed his own statistical well-being so Wills could run. Now Gilliam had the opportunity to help Maury make baseball history, but for whatever reason—

jealousy, disgust, or perhaps simply fatigue—Jim apparently decided he had grown weary of playing the good Samaritan's role.

Just before Simmons' next pitch, Wills took off like a rocket. He appeared to have third base stolen easily, which would have tied Cobb's record. Gilliam, who could clearly see Maury was going to make it safely, surprised everyone by laying down a bunt. The Cardinals fielded the ball and threw Junior out at first. Although Wills made it to third, the official scorer had little choice but to rule the play a sacrifice. No stolen base could be credited.

Wills would not get another chance to run that night as Simmons pitched a complete game and beat the Dodgers, 11-2. Afterwards, in the L.A. dressing room, *Long Beach Independent Press-Telegram* sportswriter George Lederer asked Maury if Alston had signalled Gilliam to bunt in the sixth.

"Why don't you ask him?" sneered Wills as he pointed across the room to Gilliam. Lederer approached Junior's locker and repeated his question. If looks could kill, Gilliam's expression would have struck the man dead. "Mind your own goddamn business," he spat.

"You must have seen that Wills had the base stolen," Lederer continued. "What was going through your mind?"

By now, The Devil had had a bellyful. "If you don't get away from me, I'll punch you in the nose." Wisely, Lederer retreated.

Privately, Wills was seething, but elected not to air his dirty linen in the press. "If Gilliam had taken one more pitch before he bunted, I'd have tried for 96," he told Frank Finch of the *Times*. Continuing the Dodger damage control, Wills added, "Jim was bunting for a base hit, and I haven't asked anybody to sacrifice himself for me all season, and I'm not about to now."

The evening's disappointments were all but forgotten the next night when Johnny Podres and Larry Sherry combined to beat St. Louis for L.A.'s 100th win of the season. It was the first time a National League club had reached the century mark in victories since the pennant-winning Brooklyn team of '53. However, Wills failed to steal a base and would have to face his nemesis, veteran righthander Larry Jackson, the following afternoon. It was game number 156 on the Dodger schedule.

"Jackson was the toughest guy in the league for me to steal against," Wills later disclosed. "And I don't think I'd ever gotten more than four or five hits off him in my career." After grounding out in his first at-bat, Maury singled in the third inning. With the St. Louis crowd cheering him on, Wills broke for second and slid in safely ahead of the throw from catcher Carl Sawatski.

The Cardinals broke the game open two innings later, and led, 11-2, as L.A. batted in the top of the seventh. Baseball protocol dictates that teams losing by wide margins usually don't try to steal bases. But this was no ordinary situation. Just before Maury stepped into the on-deck circle Alston told him, "Even though we're getting beat, if you get on base, take off."

With a Cardinal victory assured, the Busch Stadium crowd shifted its allegiance to Wills. They booed vociferously when Jackson jumped ahead with two quick strikes. Maury continued to battle, fouling off several pitches before he finally poked one between first and second for a base hit.

Now the grandstands were thundering. In both dugouts, every player was off the bench and standing on top of the steps. Gilliam was the next batter, but Jackson could not have cared less. Wills was the only man that mattered. The Cardinal pitcher threw over to first more than a half dozen times, and each time first baseman Bill White slapped a hard tag across Wills' skull as he scrambled back to the bag.

While White's "love taps" were ringing in his ears, a thought suddenly crossed Maury's mind. Earlier, scouting director Al Campanis suggested that since Jackson gave him so much trouble, a delayed steal might be an effective countermove. The play's essence is surprise over speed, but was seldom used in the early '60s. It was a stealing strategy Wills never needed, but perhaps this was the moment to try it.

Wills shortened his lead, giving the impression "that Jackson had me buffaloed and I had given up." The pitcher threw home and Maury stood still. As the ball crossed the plate, the infielders reacted to Gilliam's next move and momentarily took their eye off the deceiving Dodger. Maury sprinted for second to the complete shock of Sawatski, whose throw bounced harmlessly past converging shortstop Dal Maxvill. Wills slid in head-first, clutching the bag like a newborn baby. Ty Cobb's record was broken.

In the ninth inning, Maury came to bat and received a standing ovation. The game was stopped as Wills was presented the second base bag. "And you won't have to steal this one," joked the stadium public address announcer.

That night, even Ford Frick avoided his customary role of wet blanket when he seemingly backed down on his edict. "It's a record," he proclaimed. "Whether we say it's a record in 162 games or not, there's no question. It's a new record, the most bases ever stolen in a season."

His legs were swollen, his thighs a mass of bruises, but the pain no longer mattered. Maurice Morning Wills was baseball's reigning prince of thieves.

* * *

While Wills was swiping bases in St. Louis, the Giants were swatting horseflies—and a few baseballs—in Houston's humid hotbox, Colt Stadium. San Francisco won the series opener, 11-5, on Friday night, September 21st, but fell apart on Saturday when reliever Stu Miller suffered an uncharacteristic fit of wildness. After his string of walks loaded the bases in the bottom of the ninth, Jack Sanford was brought in (for his only relief appearance of the season) to face Houston outfielder Roman Mejias. Mejias promptly stroked a pitch past the drawn-in infield for the winning run, and the Giants found themselves four games behind Los Angeles with only seven remaining. San Francisco regained a glimmer of hope when they salvaged their Sunday getaway game, bringing the otherwise disastrous 3-8 road trip to its conclusion. Heading into the final week, with six games to play, the standings read:

	W	L	GB
Dodgers	100	56	...
Giants	97	59	3

On Monday, September 24th, both L.A. and San Francisco took a scheduled off-day before beginning their final homestands of the season. Many of the Giants relaxed in the backyard of team booster Bud Levitas, who threw a party in their honor. "It seemed more like a farewell gathering at the time," observed Billy Pierce, "because we were going to have to win just about every game while the Dodgers were going to have to lose nearly all of theirs."

Several Giants players viewed Alvin Dark as a rock of stability as the team entered its final week. "At that time we were a team that really didn't know how to win," recalled Felipe Alou, "and he gave a speech in St. Louis about not quitting that made a big impression." Chuck Hiller was another player who saw the manager as "a guy who kept our confidence up through that entire last month." Added Carl Boles: "Everybody thought he was nuts, but Alvin made a statement in front of the entire team. He said, 'We're gonna catch those damn Dodgers and we'll beat 'em in the playoffs.'"

Others remember a different Dark. In their respective autobiographies, both Juan Marichal and Orlando Cepeda wrote of a "bitter clubhouse meeting, in which [Alvin] told us that if we didn't finish second, he would not support us in salary talks in the following winter. In other words, he had given up." In rebuttal, Dark claimed, "I can't recall if that's true or not, but it's almost impossible for me to believe I would have made a speech like that as long as we had any mathematical chance to win." A second incident involving Billy O'Dell illustrated that even if Alvin had not yet packed it in, his confidence wasn't as unswerving as it appeared to the public.

"I sure thought we were out of it," admitted O'Dell, "and then Alvin told me, 'Billy, you've pitched enough this year, and as soon as we're out of this thing, you should go on home.' So I called San Francisco Airport and made reservations, but then we won and the Dodgers lost, so I called to change my flight for the day after. Then we won again and I had to change the tickets again. By the third or fourth time I called, the airline lady said, 'Oh, hello, Mr. O'Dell. I guess you're calling to cancel your reservations again.'"

*   *   *

The Giants began the final week strongly, taking the first two games against the Cardinals, while the Dodgers split at home with Houston. But on Thursday afternoon, catcher Gene Oliver socked a three-run homer to help St. Louis salvage their final game at Candlestick, 7-4.

It was another rough day in a rough September for Willie Mays. In the bottom of the sixth with Mays at third and one out, Orlando Cepeda swung at a third strike. Willie lost track of the number of outs and casually walked off the bag. Third baseman Ken Boyer snared the relay and quickly tagged the stunned Mays to end the inning. In the ninth, Willie was given a chance to wipe out his baserunning blunder. He came to bat with two men on and two away, but struck out to end the game, amid a fierce chorus of booing fans.

A Dodger win that night would clinch at least a tie for first, but once again, L.A. failed to deliver. Koufax was entrusted with his second start since returning from injury, a contest he believed "may well have been the key game of the season for us. I had great stuff for four innings," he wrote in his autobiography. "The first eleven batters went down in a row, four of them on strikes."

In the fifth, Koufax ran into trouble, but escaped the inning still ahead, 4-2. Even so, the cautious Alston was taking no chances and went to his bullpen. Ed Roebuck, Larry Sherry, and Ron Perranoski were all shelled and L.A. lost, 8-6. The Dodger lead remained at two with three games left. "That loss was the turnaround game," Perranoski said later. "I think we all realized that the burden of Koufax' injury had finally caught up with the team." Added broadcaster Jerry Doggett, "By that time we really began to hear the 'footsteps of doom' behind us."

* * *

Every season, the St. Louis Cardinals circled their scheduled games in Los Angeles with a red pencil. Few National League teams took better advantage of L.A.'s "attractions" than St. Louis, and their late-night escapades must have done them good; the Cards were the only visiting club to post a winning record at Chavez Ravine in 1962.

"When I was with the Cardinals [in 1961]," disclosed Daryl Spencer, "a lot of guys had a lot of fun in L.A. There was quite a bit of chasin' around out there with some gals." The practice apparently continued after St. Louis arrived for the final series of the year against the Dodgers.

"You could tell they were loose," observed Joe Moeller. Their season was over and they weren't feeling any pressure. You go into our clubhouse and you could have cut the tension with a knife."

"[The Cardinals] were staying out till three or four o'clock in the morning for day games and they didn't care," claimed Ron Fairly. "Then they'd go out to play and everything they did was right and everything we did was wrong. They were as free and easy as you please. They made pitches that they might not have thrown if they'd gotten a good night's rest. They were thinking, 'What the heck, go ahead and throw that pitch—I haven't thrown him this all year and maybe it'll fool him.' And that's how they got us out."

The series opener set the tone for the entire weekend as the Dodgers lost, 3-2, in 10 innings against Larry Jackson. "All year long we'd been getting the necessary runs to win," said Perranoski, "and it just wasn't coming the last weekend. We couldn't score. It became a joke in the clubhouse. It seemed like every play was a ground ball to the shortstop, so we started saying the Cardinals didn't need to have any other players except the pitcher, the catcher, the shortstop, and the first baseman."

The Giants gained a half-game even though they did not play. The only rainout at Candlestick Park all season washed away their Friday match with Houston, forcing a doubleheader the next afternoon.

Before the first game, former Giant and then-current Colt infielder Joe Amalfitano sidled up to Mays and asked him, "Can you guys score a run?" Willie wasn't sure he understood the question. Sensing his puzzlement, Amalfitano continued. "If you can score, you got the pennant. [The Dodgers] are never going to score another run."

San Francisco pushed 11 of their own across the plate to win the opener, with home runs from Cepeda, McCovey, and Haller backing the pitching of Sanford and Miller. A twin bill sweep would trim the margin to a half-game, circumstances the Dodgers would be aware of when they took the field later that night in their second meeting with St. Louis.

Juan Marichal had not started a game since San Francisco's Labor Day series in Los Angeles. Although his twisted foot still bothered him, X-rays continued to show no existing fracture. In fact, four full years would pass before such a break finally did appear on the screen, but in late September of '62, the injury was not evident. This lack of medical "proof" clearly concerned Marichal. The pain affected his ability to pitch, but he wasn't sure Dark believed him. "He said very little," Marichal wrote later, "but the look in his eye told me that he thought I was trying to quit under pressure."

Because of the rain-forced doubleheader with Houston, Alvin had little recourse but to start Juan in the second game. "My broken foot was still broken, but Dark had run out of pitchers," stated Marichal, "and I could not claim I had a broken foot because the X-rays didn't show a break."

Marichal tried his best, but barely lasted into the fifth inning, allowing four runs, two on a homer from ex-Dodger Norm Larker. It was more than enough support for Houston starter Bob Bruce, who beat San Francisco, 4-2. In the clubhouse after the game, the Latin players gathered around Juan's locker to console him. Soon the dialogue grew more heated, and the players began shooting wrathful glances over at Dark and the coaching staff. Any bystander fluent in Spanish might have been able to discern from the conversation that the angered group (which included Felipe Alou and Cepeda) believed the Giants had risked permanent injury to Marichal by starting him that day.

Maybe it was because a righthander would be pitching for Houston on Sunday and Dark preferred having two left-handed bats in the batting order. Perhaps their late-season hitting tailspin was a factor. It is also possible that the bitter feelings stemming from Marichal's rough outing may have had some influence. Whatever the reason, Alvin decided that neither Alou or Cepeda, two of his most productive sluggers all season long, would be in the starting lineup for San Francisco's most pivotal game of the year.

The players finally cleared out of the clubhouse and went home to listen to the Dodger-Cardinal broadcast, a telegraph wire re-creation by Giants announcers Russ Hodges and Lon Simmons. Don Drysdale pitched superbly for L.A. but was trumped by a hard-throwing Card named Ernie Broglio. Broglio, a native of Berkeley, gladdened the hearts of his Bay Area brethren by tossing a two-hit shutout. "He was throwing 2-0 and 3-2 curveballs for strikes, for crying out loud," moaned Perranoski. "That had to be the best game he ever pitched in his life." Broglio's offensive support wasn't much mightier than the Dodgers'. The only Cardinal scores occurred when Frank Howard misplayed a flyball that allowed two unearned runs to cross the plate.

The next morning, the cynical *Times* jeered, "Should O'Malley tempt fate by ordering champagne for the Dodger clubhouse today, he'd best order it on consignment." L.A.'s lead was down to one game heading into the final day of the season, and their slumping hitters were making Joey Amalfitano look like a prophet.

* * *

On September 30, 1962, a season-long battle between traditional baseball rivals reached its climax, but the rest of the nation drew its attention to a far more serious conflict. Two thousand miles east of California in the southern university town of Oxford, Mississippi, a student named James Meredith was attempting to become the first black ever to enroll at segregated Ole Miss. For weeks, local politicians and the federal government had feuded bitterly over Meredith's fate, and on the final weekend in September, their confrontation reached its flashpoint.

President Kennedy ordered the National Guard into Oxford to escort Meredith to class, but the guardsmen were met by hordes of angry rioters. The rabble threw rocks, overturned vehicles, torched property, and attacked the soldiers. Additional federal troops were sent in to restore order, but the price of peace was high: 160 marshals were injured, 28 more had been shot, and two men died. By the end of the rioting, nearly 200 people had been arrested. The president characterized the day of bloodshed as "the worst thing" he had seen in his life.

Amidst Oxford's smoke and rubble, the heavily guarded Meredith attended his first day of school without further violence. It proved to be a crucial victory for the civil rights movement, and the beginning of the end for educational discrimination in one of the last remaining bastions of enforced segregation.

The bloody Mississippi riots were still several hours from exploding when the Giants took the field at Candlestick for their afternoon game with Houston. The headlines from Oxford had to be especially disturbing to all of San Francisco's minority players, who had endured the sting of racial prejudice throughout their lives. But the events would have to be blocked out for the next few hours; the Giants needed a win, then some more help from St. Louis simply to force a tie for first.

Dark chose Billy O'Dell to start, while the Colts countered with hard-throwing ex-Dodger Turk Farrell. Farrell had already beaten his former team earlier that week and was confident of similar results against the Giants. "I don't intend to lose," he told reporters.

Farrell was nearly untouchable for most of the afternoon, making one of his only mistakes in the fourth inning. Ed Bailey socked one of Turk's offerings into the right-field seats that curved just foul, then hit the next one in virtually the same location. This time it landed over the fence for a solo home run. "He threw me the same pitch again," Bailey later disclosed. "Needless to say, I was grateful."

In the bottom of the eighth with the score tied at one, Mays, hitless in his last 10 at-bats, led off and was once again greeted by a smattering of boos. Rushing to Willie's defense, Candlestick organist Lloyd Fox tapped out a few sprightly bars of the Giants' fight song, "Bye Bye Baby." Fox' musical selection turned out to be remarkably prescient. Farrell delivered his first pitch, a breaking ball that Mays fouled off into the right-field corner. The next pitch was a fastball that Willie sent into the 14th row of the left-field seats.

"It became a blur of white, smashed through the noise of roaring throats, sailing high into the blue," wrote the *Chronicle's* Bob Stevens, "and it gave San Francisco the best shot it has ever had at the long-awaited pennant." The poke was Mays' 47th of the year, good enough to clinch the league home run title. It was also a remarkable act of symmetry on Willie's part; he had homered on the first pitch he saw on opening day and now had hit one out on his last pitch of the season.

Stu Miller maintained the lead to the end, fanning pinch-hitter Billy Goodman for the final out of the 2-1 victory. The rest of the

Giants ran onto the field and mobbed the diminutive reliever as the crowd of 41,327 jumped to its feet. They cheered for nearly five minutes until a squad of special police escorted the team off the diamond and into the clubhouse.

The game was over, but only a few in the stands headed for the exits. There were five automobiles still to be awarded for a special "Fan Appreciation Day" promotion. More importantly, the results were still not in from the game at Los Angeles, since it had started an hour later. So Giant fans stayed put in the park, in hopes of both winning a car and tying for a pennant.

In their previous eight games before Sunday, the Dodgers had won only twice. Both times, the winning pitcher was Johnny Podres, and Los Angeles could only hope The Point's hot streak would continue for at least one more afternoon. Superstition may also have guided Alston's pitching choice: It was Podres' 30th birthday. The Cardinals countered with Curt Simmons, who had thrown so effectively the week before in the series at Busch Stadium.

For seven innings, neither team came close to cashing in—not that the Dodgers didn't have their chances. Three atrocious baserunning blunders kept L.A. off the scoreboard. In the second inning, Lee Walls was gunned down at second while attempting to stretch a single into a double. In the third, Willie Davis singled, then got fooled on a decoy play and was thrown out trying to advance after Podres popped up. Tommy Davis committed another mental error in the seventh when he drilled a leadoff single, only to be picked off by Simmons.

By now, a massive listening audience in the Bay Area was also following the action in Los Angeles. In downtown San Francisco, cars pulled up to curbs, with motors idling as drivers strained to hear Russ Hodges' updates on KSFO. Also tuning in were more than 38,000 football fans at Kezar Stadium watching the 49ers against the Vikings. Down in the clubhouse, the nervous Giants were hanging on every word. "Come on! My bleeding ulcers!" wailed Harvey Kuenn.

The results were slow to trickle in. Each play was delayed by nearly a minute as the Western Union tickertape yielded pitch-by-pitch results to an impatient Hodges. Russ also tried to pick up the Dodger broadcast from southern California on his transistor radio, only to be defeated by a steady stream of static. The slow-as-molasses wire copy would have to suffice.

For a while, the results bore a certain sameness. Podres continued to blow the Cardinals away, striking out seven and walking none, while allowing but five hits. "It was one of the greatest games I ever pitched," he said later, "even better than I did in that seventh Series game back in '55."

Johnny made only one bad pitch all day, but it cost the Dodgers dearly. With one out and the bases empty in the eighth, Gene Oliver stepped to the plate. Earlier in the week, Oliver's three-run homer at Candlestick had been the decisive blow in a win against the Giants. The Cardinal catcher was about to prove that in this pennant race, he wasn't going to play favorites.

"I threw him a low curveball," said Podres, "but it wasn't the kind of curve that could finish a hitter off. It didn't snap—it rolled. I couldn't get him to turn his hands over—he picked it up. He just did get it over the wall. He hit it into the left-field seats, about the third row back."

At the same time the home run cleared the Dodger Stadium fence, a lucky Giant fan was being handed a set of keys to his brand new automobile. Suddenly the public address announcer broke in with the news of Oliver's blast. The stadium roared in approval. Moments later, the next winning contestant was introduced, an attractive blonde who gleefully ran onto the field to claim her prize. The delighted crowd thundered again, almost as loudly as they did when the Cardinal home run was mentioned.

The Oliver home run also created a stir at Kezar Stadium. The 49ers were facing a fourth and one situation at the Vikings 18-yard line as quarterback John Brodie brought his team into the huddle. Like a tidal wave, a crescendo of cheers cascaded down from the stands. Brodie, certain the fans were urging him to gamble for the extra yard, waved his arms, calling for quiet. Only later did he discover that their boisterous response was caused by the Cardinal hit. The Niners held on to win, 21-7, but few fans had any intention of leaving the confines of Kezar. With radios glued to their ears, they, too, waited for the final outs at Chavez Ravine.

In the bottom of the ninth, the Dodgers finally ended the suspense. Pinch-hitter Ken McMullen flied to center, as did Maury Wills. The last hitter was Jim Gilliam. During his at-bat, the only sounds the KSFO audience heard was Hodges' crackling transistor radio and the footsteps of Chub Feeney, who was nervously pacing in the broadcast booth. Finally the result unspooled into the announcer's hands. "Gilliam—popup to Javier." After 162 games, the Dodgers and Giants were tied for first place. The longest season in National League history was going to run a bit longer.

Fans in both Candlestick and Kezar erupted. In the Giants' clubhouse, Willie McCovey and the Alou brothers paired off in a victory dance while Alvin Dark screamed, "Wahoo!" After accepting congratulations, the manager claimed to reporters, "This was the finest comeback of any team I was ever associated with." Before he could continue, Dark was deluged with a battery of calls and telegrams. He could barely hear the voices at the other end of the phone as a delirious Kuenn pranced around the locker room shouting, "Come on! Let's get 'em!" An anonymous voice added, "And next the Yankees!"

Nobody was talking about the Yankees in the Dodgers' dressing room. "Damn it, damn it, damn it," cursed the obviously disappointed Podres. "We had all the opportunities to win this thing," admitted Alston. "We have no excuses. We can't back into it now...We're in a hitting slump and that's all there is to it."

That was putting it mildly. The Dodgers had not been able to score a run for 21 consecutive innings, and lost 10 of their final 13 games in the bargain. But at 7-6 over the same span, the Giants didn't exactly terrorize the league, either. As *New York Times* columnist Arthur Daley wrote: "It was like two drunks having a fight in a saloon and trying to stagger to the safety of the swinging doors. Both kept falling down. The Giants, however, could crawl better than the Dodgers."

A disconsolate Podres left the clubhouse and drove home to the Mayfair Hotel, his L.A. residence during the baseball season. Unbeknownst to the birthday boy, a group of friends had gathered in his honor. "They had a big cake waiting for me when I got there. I walked in and they cut me a piece, but I wouldn't eat it. It was a sad day. And I have no idea what happened to that cake."

By prior agreement, it had been determined that the Giants would host the opening game of the best-of-three playoffs, with the series switching to Dodger Stadium for the final two contests, if necessary. Alston and Dark waited as a coin flip by league president Warren Giles settled the matter. Walter won the toss, just as he had in 1959 when Los Angeles beat Milwaukee in their extended playoff. Perhaps history would repeat itself, Alston hoped.

Alvin may have been thinking the same thing. Before the playoffs of 1951, the Dodgers had won the toss then, too. But it was Dark and his Giants teammates who won the pennant.

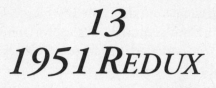

13
1951 REDUX

National League Standings, Monday, October 1, 1951

	W	L	GB
Dodgers	96	58	...
Giants	96	58	...

National League Standings, Monday, October 1, 1962

	W	L	GB
Dodgers	101	61	...
Giants	101	61	...

For Mays, Snider, Durocher, Dark, Westrum, Lockman, and Jansen there was the unmistakable feeling of *déjà vu*.

Each had been there at Ebbets Field on Monday, October 1, 1951, for the first game of the National League playoffs, a 3-1 Giants win.

And for the second game at the Polo Grounds on Tuesday, October 2nd, a 10-0 rout by Brooklyn.

And the clincher on Wednesday, October 3rd—"The Miracle at Coogan's Bluff"—when Bobby Thomson cracked the most famous home run ever to bury the Dodgers, 5-4, and give the Giants the pennant.

Eleven years later *to the day*, the same two teams were about to meet again to determine the National League champion. But this time, baseball's oldest rivalry would write its latest chapter with California, not New York City, as the backdrop.

Nineteen-fifty-one's third postseason participants were also present. The New York Yankees, American League champs of 1962, were waiting patiently for their N.L. foes to settle the matter, exactly as they had done more than a decade ago. Only a few days earlier, the '62 Bronx Bombers were scheduled to fly to Los Angeles, so certain were they of a Dodger pennant. But when L.A. collapsed in the final week, the Yanks changed their minds, jetted to northern California and checked into the posh TowneHouse Hotel. By doing so, gloated the *Chronicle*, "[The Yankees] unofficially picked the San Francisco Giants to win the playoff for the National League title."

The Giants understood it was going to take more than the Yankees' vote of confidence to defeat the Dodgers. Mindful of the psychological edge gained from their earlier water-soaked sweep of the Dodgers at Candlestick, Dark instructed Matty Schwab to weave his groundskeeping magic one more time.

Schwab had actually begun his dirty work the day before, heavily soaking the left side of the infield prior to the final game against Houston. When that game ended and the giveaway automobiles for Fan Appreciation Day were being rolled out, Schwab warned the drivers not to park the vehicles anywhere near third or short, "because the cars will sink to their hubcaps."

Sunday night, after the stadium was deserted, the grounds crew began spreading mounds of sand across the skinned portion of the infield. When the Dodgers arrived at Candlestick on Monday morning, their reaction was immediate and volatile. "It's just as bad as the last time we were here, only in a different way," complained Maury Wills.

L.A. publicity director Red Patterson began searching for league president Warren Giles to protest, but was unable to find him. Patterson finally spotted umpire Jocko Conlan and beefed, "Now they've got the sand on it and after infield practice they'll turn on the sprinklers and wet it down like it was for a water follies."

Conlan agreed to get to the bottom of the situation, and began by collaring Alvin Dark. "They've got to put this field in regulation condition," Jocko decreed.

"This is our park and we'll do whatever we want with it," retorted the Giants' skipper.

Conlan was not pleased with that response. "Get me the groundskeeper."

"You find him," answered Alvin. "You're the boss. You go get him."

Jocko finally did, then ordered Schwab to clear off the sand, pat down the infield and keep the hoses turned off. As the admonished crew began its housekeeping, Dark exploded, placing the blame on The Biggest Dodger of Them All. "Imagine an umpire coming out before a game to interfere with the ground crew's work," Alvin declared later. "That wouldn't have happened anywhere except where the Dodgers are involved. Mr. O'Malley is the most powerful man in baseball. His word is law."

Whether or not O'Malley's omnipotence was at work, his team appeared reasonably satisfied with the cleanup, and also had to be pleased with the unusually benign Candlestick weather; sunny skies, with temperatures in the mid-70s and virtually no wind.

The rest of the day was a Dodger disaster.

Their troubles began in the bottom of the first. Sandy Koufax, making only his third start since returning from injury, surrendered a two-out double to Felipe Alou. Willie Mays followed with a booming shot that cleared the right-center field fence. An inning later, Jim Davenport led off with a home run and Ed Bailey whistled a single through the box, sending Koufax to the showers. "I can't be the same after two months off," Sandy told reporters afterward. "My finger is okay, but I felt like the third week of spring training. My arm has nothing."

Meanwhile, opposing starter Billy Pierce breezed through the slump-ridden Dodger order, scattering three hits, allowing no runs and striking out six, prompting him to admit later, "It was the most satisfying game I ever pitched." It was also Billy's 12th victory of the season at Candlestick without a defeat.

The Dodgers could do nothing against Pierce, yet kept the game close until the sixth on the strength of four shutout innings of relief from Ed Roebuck. Still, none of the L.A. pitchers could shackle Mays, who didn't make an out the entire afternoon.

Not that the Dodgers didn't try. In the third, Roebuck threw behind Willie on one pitch, then knocked him down with the next. Undaunted, Mays dusted himself off and whacked Roebuck's next offering into left field for a base hit. In the sixth, Larry Sherry fired a brushback at the Giants' superstar, but Willie drove a subsequent Sherry fastball over the fence for his second home run of the game.

At that precise moment, all of the heartache, the personal problems, the unrelenting fatigue of Willie's '62 season seemed to vanish, swallowed up in a cascading crescendo of cheers. This was not the customary roar from the grandstands. Mays had never heard a Candlestick crowd respond in such fashion. "I think it was the moment where the San Francisco fans finally took him to heart," Pierce observed. "They believed he was doing something for *San Francisco*—not the Giants—but San Francisco. He was doing something to try to bring a winner to the city. Willie heard those cheers, and he liked it." Added a grinning Mays after the game, "I think the fans are starting to warm up to me."

Nearly forgotten amidst the rapture of the Mays lovefest was Orlando Cepeda's home run which immediately followed Willie's blast. That made the score 5-0, and three more runs in the eighth clinched the one-sided San Francisco victory.

An obviously disheartened Walter Alston was blunt and direct during the postgame press conference. "We haven't scored in 30 innings," he snorted while lighting a cigarette. "This club is due to go on a two-game winning streak. We're sure overdue to hit, and that goes for everybody on this club."

And who would be his starter tomorrow, queried one writer. "Stan Williams," Walter answered without hesitation. "I could go with Drysdale on two days rest, but he had a tough game last time out. Then where would we be for the third game? Stan's had plenty of rest."

Alston himself saw to that; Williams had pitched exactly one inning of relief in the last eight days, primarily because he'd fallen out of favor with his manager. But now, in the do-or-die game of the season, Stan Williams was Walter's choice to start. The anti-Alston faction on the ballclub was stunned.

"What the hell are they saving me for, the first spring intrasquad game?" bellowed an obviously disgusted Drysdale. One veteran even pleaded directly to Walter, "Let's go for broke. There's no point holding Drysdale off for the junior prom."

The issue was still being hotly debated as the Dodgers boarded the Electra II for their flight home to Los Angeles. The Giants, already a game up with ace Jack Sanford set to pitch, enjoyed a far more peaceful plane ride to southern California.

After arriving at the Ambassador Hotel that evening, most of the Giants ordered room service, then went straight to bed. A few insomniacs stayed up late to watch a young comedian named Johnny Carson make his debut as permanent host of NBC's *Tonight Show*. Some even viewed it as a good omen when one of Johnny's guests, singer Tony Bennett, performed his pop chart hit, "I Left My Heart in San Francisco."

* * *

By sunrise on October 2nd, a hazy shroud of smog was already hanging over the city of Los Angeles, weather that perfectly mirrored the mood of local baseball fans. Many had already resigned themselves to another Dodger defeat, and the traffic to the early afternoon game reflected it. One disgruntled cab driver en route to the park told a sportswriter, "Usually we're jammed up at the entrance, but not today. I tell you, this town has given up on the Dodgers. We're disgusted. It's a boycott."

Only 25,231 Angelenos paid to watch game two — nearly 30,000 short of stadium capacity and 7,000 fewer than the opening playoff game crowd at Candlestick.

Those who did attend were somewhat taken aback by the revamped Dodger batting order. Desperate to generate any offense after 30 scoreless innings, Alston started Duke Snider in left, Tommy Davis at third, and Wally Moon at first. Walter's biggest surprise was his last-minute switch of starting pitchers. The dissenting Dodger players had apparently won the argument: Drysdale, not Williams, would draw the assignment after all.

Big D, who'd worked eight full innings on Saturday, was obviously tired, but the eventual Cy Young winner battled gamely through the first five innings, allowing only one run. Several Giants claimed Drysdale's effectiveness was helped along by a doctored baseball. After numerous complaints from the San Francisco dugout, plate umpire Al Barlick finally reprimanded the Dodger righthander and cautioned him to keep his hand away from his mouth and the dirt off the baseball.

After Barlick's warning, Drysdale began to run out of steam. With one out in the sixth, he walked Tom Haller and surrendered a double to Jose Pagan. Jack Sanford laid down a bunt that Drysdale bobbled, scoring Haller from third. Back-to-back run-scoring singles from Chuck Hiller and Jim Davenport made it 4-0, and Drysdale was done. Another RBI single from Willie McCovey off Ed Roebuck upped the lead to 5-0, and Dodger pennant hopes sunk to their lowest ebb of the season. "Down in the dugout, manager Walt Alston was poring over the stagecoach schedules to Darrtown," deadpanned Jim Murray in the *Times*.

But the rally had exacted a steep price on San Francisco. Sanford began the game nursing a heavy cold, "looking like five miles of bad road," according to the *Chronicle*'s Bob Stevens. Then Jack had to expend even more of his limited energies lumbering from second to home as a baserunner. As Sanford finished his warmup tosses prior to the bottom of the sixth, Dark and Larry Jansen were keeping a close eye on their weary ace.

When leadoff hitter Jim Gilliam drew a walk, Alvin rushed to the mound. Despite pitching a two-hit shutout, Dark was certain Sanford had run out of steam, and lifted the 24-game winner for Stu Miller.

"Jack had had enough, and the lead looked pretty safe," said Miller. "So [Alvin] called on his 'ace bullpenner' to sew up the ole pennant. Needless to say, I didn't do a very good job. I was followed by O'Dell—I had a little fire started—and he threw some gas on it. And he got knocked out too, so Larsen relieved him. By the end of that inning, they were ahead and I could feel the goat horns sprouting."

Miller unwittingly began the Los Angeles resurrection by yielding a double to Snider, moving Gilliam to third. Then Tommy Davis lifted a sacrifice fly, scoring Gilliam to end the Dodgers' runless drought at 35 innings. Once Junior crossed the plate, the floodgates opened. Moon walked, then Frank Howard followed with an RBI single to chase Miller and bring in O'Dell.

The pitching change set the strategic wheels turning in the Dodger dugout, as Alston called on three straight right-handed pinch-hitters to face the San Francisco southpaw. First up was Doug Camilli, who singled to load the bases. Andy Carey was next, and he was promptly hit on the leg to force in a run, making it 5-3. Finally, Alston selected Lee Walls to bat for Roebuck.

In Walls, the Dodgers possessed baseball's best pinch-hitter. Coming off the bench, the bespectacled utility man had ravaged National League pitching at a .481 clip, including 12 pinch-hits in his last 17 at-bats. His hot streak continued when he roped an 0-2 pitch off the left-center-field wall, clearing the bases to give the Dodgers a 6-5 lead. "It was the biggest hit of my life," Walls told reporters afterward. "I was fighting the tears back when I saw those guys cross the plate."

Figuratively and literally, Walls wasn't quite finished punishing the Giants. Drifting off third with Wills at bat, Lee broke for home when Maury hit a high chopper to Orlando Cepeda. Catcher Tom Haller painfully recalled what happened next: "Cepeda's throw came in and I got the ball with plenty of time to tag him. But Walls got up high and he jumped and hit me in the forearms and drove 'em between my legs and I ended up dropping the ball. I needed six stitches in my right arm, and I didn't play the next day."

Don Larsen replaced the beleaguered O'Dell and finally retired the side, but the Dodgers had the lead, 7-5. To the Giants, the parade of runs had seemingly taken forever. The sixth-inning marathon alone took an hour and 11 minutes to play.

By contrast, the seventh inning was completed in less than 10 minutes, with neither club threatening. But in the top of the eighth, the Giants struck back to tie the game. They may well have gotten more, if not for a controversial ruling by third base umpire Jocko Conlan. After leadoff hits by Davenport and Mays, pinch-hitter Ed Bailey laced an RBI single to right-center. Tommy Davis gunned the relay to third, which the sliding Mays appeared to have beaten. Conlan began extending the "safe" sign, then changed his mind and thumbed Willie out.

The questionable call irked the Giants even more when the next batter reached safely on an error. A walk by reliever Stan Williams loaded the bases, but Alston elected to stay with the jilted would-be starter. The Big Hurt rewarded his manager's faith by retiring John Orsino on a sacrifice fly and Jose Pagan on a grounder. The Dodgers failed to score in their half, leaving the two rivals knotted at 7-7 heading into the ninth.

Williams breezed through the Giants batting order, nailing the last two hitters on strikeouts. But the Dodgers did not go gentle in their last turn at bat. After Wills drew a base on balls, Bob Bolin was lifted for lefthander Dick LeMay, who promptly walked Gilliam.

Playing the percentages, Alston sent in the right-handed Daryl Spencer to bat for Snider. Dark countered by bringing in rookie righty Gaylord Perry, then gave his young pitcher the following instructions: "Gaylord, the Dodgers will be bunting. Davenport and Cepeda will be charging the plate. If you field the ball, go to third. Pagan will be there ahead of Wills. Let's go."

As expected, Spencer did bunt, and Perry scooped it up. He glanced to third, and sure, enough, Pagan was converging towards the bag. A quick throw would have nailed Wills, but inexplicably, the rookie panicked and took the out at first, putting Dodgers at second and third.

According to Perry, the infuriated Dark ripped the dugout phone off the wall and threw it to the opposite end of the bench. Then he stormed to the mound, tore the ball from Gaylord's grasp and signalled to the bullpen for Mike McCormick. Walk Tommy Davis intentionally, Mike was told, then take your chances with Ron Fairly.

Alvin's directive made sense. Like McCormick, Fairly was a lefty—and Ron's bat was mired in a late-season 1-for-31 deep freeze. "I'd barely pitched during the last three weeks of the season, and now here I am, bases loaded, score tied, and one out in the bottom of the ninth," said McCormick. "I made a good pitch to Fairly for strike one. My next pitch was good, too, and he hits a pop fly to center field. If Mays makes his normal good 'Willie Mays throw,' he nails Wills at the plate. Turns out, he throws the ball up the line, Wills scores, and the game is over."

The jubilant Dodgers spilled onto the field, lifted Maury onto their shoulders and carried him into the clubhouse. So overwhelming was their outpouring of gratitude that the diminutive shortstop, fearing for his physical well-being, raced to the trainers' room and kept the door locked for 10 minutes. "Those guys were acting crazy," gasped Wills.

Meanwhile, the celebration continued. Raucous cheering was punctured by the piercing whistles of pitching hero Stan Williams, likely the happiest of all Dodgers. When the noise subsided, Lee Walls, his voice failing, rasped, "Let's get 'em tomorrow boys, and take it all!"

Voices of an entirely different timbre resonated from the dejected Giants' locker room. "Some of the guys thought Sanford had gotten tired a little too quick," disclosed O'Dell. "They thought he didn't give the effort he should have. One fella even said right to his face that he'd quit on us.

"But Jack hadn't done that because he'd been like that all year. That's the way he pitched, and if it hadn't been for Jack, we wouldn't have been there to begin with. But after I heard all that arguing, I thought right there that we were through."

It was a volatile end to what Walter Alston called, "the biggest scrambler I've ever seen. I've never been in a wilder, woolier one, personally." A record 42 players saw action in a contest that lasted four hours and 18 minutes—making it the longest nine-inning game in the history of major league baseball.

Its epic length proved costly to NBC, which lost nearly $300,000 in advertising revenue when the game ran into prime time back east. *The Huntley-Brinkley Report, Laramie,* and *Phil Silvers Show* were all preempted by the Dodger-Giant marathon.

Network executives may have been dismayed, but not the Dodger fans in the Hollywood community. After watching the game from a bar near Universal Studios, actor Rock Hudson declared, "We've got it made. Those Dodgers will kill [them]. The Giants won't have a chance tomorrow. They won't come close. You wait and see." Later that night at Chasen's restaurant, director Alfred Hitchcock pledged "the utmost confidence in the ultimate defeat of the Giants. The good guys always win in our fair city."

* * *

On Tuesday, a paying customer could have sat just about anywhere he wanted in Chavez Ravine. But by mid-morning Wednesday, the lines stretched endlessly from the stadium ticket windows. The deciding game of the 1962 playoffs took in 45,693 fans, including showbiz rooters Doris Day, Rosalind Russell, and Frank Sinatra. The Dodgers' improbable comeback victory had revitalized the entire city. And now that city was certain its team was ready to secure the pennant, a flag they felt rightfully belonged to L.A. in the first place.

The Dodgers themselves were loose and confident. Typical was Ron Fairly's pregame conversation with Willie Davis. "I told him, 'Three-Dog, this one is ours, and there's nothing they can do to stop us from winning this game.' That's truly the way we felt."

Ever-superstitious Leo Durocher had taken additional measures to insure victory. While chatting with writers during batting practice, Leo pointed to the T-shirt under his jersey. "I haven't worn one of these since I joined the Dodgers as coach. This is the one I had on for the 1951 playoffs." The Lip was also wearing the same shorts and socks he had on the day Bobby Thomson won him a pennant with the Giants; now Leo was certain the same apparel would work for the Dodgers. "I wore them yesterday when we won, and they have enough magic powers to work again today."

When the same writers asked Alvin Dark if he brought anything from 1951, the current Giants manager answered, "Yeah. Willie Mays."

Dark possessed something else the Dodgers did not—a well-rested (albeit still ailing) starter in Juan Marichal. By comparison, L.A. counterpart Johnny Podres, for the first time in his career, was pitching with only two days off. "Even so, I pitched pretty good," Podres remembered later. "I got us into the sixth inning before Eddie Roebuck bailed me out."

The Giants grabbed a 2-0 lead in the third, due in large measure to three Dodger errors, including one by Podres. But the Dodgers cut the lead in half in the bottom of the fourth when Duke Snider doubled and eventually scored on Frank Howard's groundout.

In the sixth inning, San Francisco threatened to break the game open. Consecutive singles by Orlando Cepeda, Ed Bailey, and Jim Davenport loaded the bases with none out. Alston strolled to the mound, patted Podres on the back, and signalled for Roebuck, even though Ed was making his sixth appearance in the last seven days. But the Giants failed to capitalize, grounding into a force at home and an inning-ending double play.

The dramatic escape appeared to adrenalize the Dodgers, who took their first lead, 3-2, in the bottom of the inning. Snider stroked his second hit of the afternoon, which preceded a 400-foot blast into the left-field bleachers by Giant-killer Tommy Davis. The cheers following the home run doubled in intensity when the stadium message board flashed the news: A successful splashdown by Mercury astronaut Walter Schirra, who had just finished orbiting the earth six times.

The Dodgers added an insurance run in the seventh when Wills lined his fourth hit of the afternoon. In Spanish, a frustrated Orlando Cepeda screamed at Jose Pagan to hit Maury between the eyes if he didn't slide in low enough on a force play. But Pagan never got the chance.

Wills stole second, and then third, his 104th theft of the season. As Maury slid towards the bag, Bailey's throw from behind the plate sailed wildly over Davenport's head into left field. "Wills ran for home," Felipe Alou later told author John Devaney, "and Durocher ran all the way down the line with Wills and slid as Maury slid home safe.

"Durocher got up laughing. Right then he thought he had the game won...I wanted to beat them after what Durocher did. Sliding. Like it was a show."

But neither the angered Alou or any other Giant could solve Roebuck's sinker in their next at-bat, and, in the bottom of the eighth, the Dodgers found themselves in position to drive the final nail into their rivals' coffin.

"We had a situation in that inning with the bases loaded," said Daryl Spencer. "Dark had put two guys on intentionally, which forced Alston to have to do something with Roebuck. Eddie had pitched his rear end off for three innings and some of us were kinda hoping Walter would put up a pinch-hitter and try to get a couple more runs. But he let Roebuck bat and he made the last out." When asked later why he did not hit for the tiring reliever, Alston replied, "I'd rather have Roebuck pitching for us with a two-run lead than anybody I've got."

According to Durocher, a number of players on the bench, including Koufax and Podres, pleaded with him to convince Alston that Roebuck was too weary to continue. Drysdale even volunteered to take his place. "You're damn right I would have liked to pitch," he later told columnist Bud Furillo. "Only they didn't ask me. I didn't think Roebuck should have started the ninth. He did enough."

Ironically, fatigue is often an ally for a sinkerball pitcher such as Roebuck. "The tireder I got, the more the ball sunk, which is probably one of the reasons why Walt didn't take me out of the game. But I was really beat. It was the most uncomfortable I've ever felt in a game. The smog was just hanging in the park, it was hot, and I was thinking how happy I was going to be when this thing was over." The end was nearly in sight; the Dodgers were only three outs away from the National League pennant.

A somber silence permeated the Giants' dugout. After a seemingly interminable pause, Alvin Dark stood up. There would be no pep talks, no references to 1951. The time for such rhetoric was past. With pitcher Don Larsen due to lead off, Alvin looked down his bench, stared Matty Alou in the eye, and simply said, "Matty, grab a bat."

All season long, the younger Alou had been limited to part-time duty while big brother Felipe ascended to all-star status. But this was Matty's moment. He drilled Roebuck's second pitch to right field for a base hit, and the moribund Giants had life.

"You can't imagine the pressure I was feeling by now," admitted Roebuck. "My salary back then was $14,000. If we get into the Series, we make at least another $10,000, but nothing if we lose." Wills, perhaps sensing the pitcher's distress, went to the mound and told him, "Forget all this b.s. and just get 'em to hit a grounder to me. We'll get the double play, and the game'll be over."

"Now Harvey Kuenn comes to the plate and he hits a perfect double play ball, a one-hop to Wills," recalled Fairly. "But unfortunately somebody had moved Larry Burright, our second baseman. They moved him over toward first base. If he's playing a normal second base, we turn the double play and Kuenn is thrown out by ten feet."

Roebuck had a ringside seat for the action. "The ball is hit to Maury, but he has to wait for Burright to get to the bag. The throw finally got there and Larry made a hell of a pivot, but too much time had elapsed and Kuenn beat the relay at first."

Watching from the bench, Daryl Spencer was dumbfounded. "Normally, Kuenn was a great right-field hitter, but against Roebuck's sinker, it's almost impossible for him to hit it that way. Now, if Gilliam had been playing second, he'd have moved a couple of steps toward first, then gone right back as the pitch was thrown. But Burright, being a rookie, stayed where he was told to, so he was out of position to make the double play."

In Vero Beach the following spring, a running gag at camp was the sarcastic question, "Who moved Burright?" Years after the incident, Ron Fairly still wasn't sure. Others, like Spencer, believed it was Alston. John Roseboro put the blame on Lee Walls. "Some players who aren't playing feel like they have to become cheerleaders on the bench," Roseboro wrote later. "Walls was always providing pep talks. He didn't know what to do with himself. Burright was young and needed help from the managers and coaches on where to play. It wasn't Walls' job to give it."

Roebuck proceeded to dig the Dodgers into a deeper hole by walking McCovey and Felipe Alou, loading the bases with one out for Willie Mays. "Alston came out to the mound and asked me if I felt okay," said Roebuck, "and I just said that I wanted to finish this thing one way or the other.

"That particular year, I'd had pretty good luck against Willie. So now I'm thinking I just want to get a groundball and hope he hits it at somebody. Somehow, he hit my inside pitch back up the middle, which is a very tough thing to do. This white blur was coming right at me. I had one of these huge gloves on, a model I think they called 'The Claw.' The ball hit in the web and if it had been a smaller glove, it probably would've stuck there and I could've gotten as many outs as I wanted. But it rolled out on the grass and was sitting there spinning while a run scored. I knew we were in big trouble then. So Walter took me out and brought in Stan Williams, and to be truthful, I was surprised to see Stanley coming in."

Others shared Roebuck's opinion. "Stan Williams!" roared Durocher. "He'll walk the park." Andy Carey agreed: "For my money, you've gotta go with a Drysdale in that spot. He was the key to our surviving the season without Koufax. And Drysdale was not a wild man—but Williams, on occasion, had trouble throwing strikes."

The Giants were also confounded. "Alston was a great manager over the years," observed Billy O'Dell, "but if he ever made a mistake, it was when he brought in Williams. No Koufax? No Drysdale? I couldn't believe it. He must have been saving them to pitch in the Series." Dark's view was similiar: "In a situation like that, I've always believed there is no tomorrow—you can only think about the situation that's happening right now. Stan Williams was a good pitcher, but if I had a Drysdale down there, I'm thinking pretty seriously about seeing if he can't finish the ballgame."

Williams believed there were additional factors that influenced Alston's decision: "I'd pitched pretty well to get the win the day before—and here's something most people don't know—I'm the only guy who ever won two playoff games, because I also beat the Braves in '59. Maybe that was part of his thinking."

Orlando Cepeda was scheduled to bat, so the percentages called for Alston to bring in a righthander. His only other reasonable option, Larry Sherry, could not get his arm loose, so Williams had to be his choice. With the left-handed Ed Bailey hitting afterwards, Walter could then make another change. "As Stan was getting ready to leave the bullpen," recalled Ron Perranoski, "I patted him on the back and told him, 'You get Cepeda—and I'll get Bailey.' At least that's what I thought was going to happen."

"I tried to jam Cepeda with the fastball, but I only got the job done halfway," Williams remembered. "He hit a short fly to right field and Fairly, who had a pretty decent arm, got off a good throw, but not good enough." The sacrifice fly scored pinch-runner Ernie Bowman and sent Felipe Alou to third. "To me, that was one of the biggest RBIs I ever had in my career, because it tied that game," Cepeda admitted later.

"So now there's two outs," continued Williams, "it's 4-4 and the only right-handed hitter they've got left is John Orsino, a kid who they weren't going to use in that situation. So that means Bailey, a left-hander, is next. I figure that's it for me—Ronnie will be pitching to him—so I started walking to the dugout, then looked up and saw Alston wasn't coming."

That was fine with Bailey. "I never had much luck against Perranoski, although Williams was tough too," Ed confessed. After getting ahead in the count, Stan uncorked a wild pitch that allowed Mays to move up to second while Alou remained at third.

"Now I'm ordered to put Bailey on," said Williams. "Roseboro came to the mound and I told him I'd rather pitch to Bailey than Davenport. Let's just throw carefully because we still have an open base. So we figured we'd call Walter out to talk to him about it, but we couldn't find him. He might've been up the runway to have a cigarette or something. Well, we couldn't go against the manager's decision, so we had to walk him.

"Up next is Davenport— a guy with a small strike zone and a .320 or so lifetime average against me. My first two pitches are low and away, but just missing. I'm thinking, there's no more room—it's time to throw a strike. I got one over, but I lost him on the next two pitches." Davenport strolled to first, forcing Alou home, and the once all-but-dead Giants took a 5-4 lead.

Only then did Alston signal for Perranoski, but San Francisco nicked him for an insurance run when Burright booted Jose Pagan's grounder, sending Mays home. Pinch-hitter Bob Nieman finally struck out to end the inning, but there were no cheers from the stunned Chavez Ravine crowd. The damage was done—and the fans could feel their pennant slipping away.

Before the Giants' ninth inning rally had begun, Dark asked Billy Pierce, "If I need you, can you pitch?" Even though Pierce had thrown a complete game two days earlier, he answered affirmatively, then went down to warm up in the bullpen.

"Just before the Dodgers batted in the bottom of the ninth," Pierce remembered, "a little bat boy came out to get my jacket and was all excited. He couldn't understand how I could be so calm at a moment like this. I told him to relax, that everything was going to be all right. When you're going into a spot like that, you tell yourself you feel great whether it's true or not.

"Wills was their first hitter, and he's the guy that makes their offense go, but I got him on a grounder. Then I got Gilliam to fly out and I knew we were in pretty good shape."

The Dodgers were down to their last out. If any miracles were going to happen, they probably wouldn't be coming from the next hitter, Burright, with his puny .205 average. Praying for lightning to strike twice, Alston picked Tuesday's hero Lee Walls to pinch-hit. This time, there was no magic in his bat. Walls lifted a soft fly to center, and Mays, for one of the few times in his career, disdained his trademark basket catch, gloving the ball in conventional fashion. Asked later why he had switched, Mays replied, "Are you crazy? That was $15,000 a man!"

Just before the ball came down, Willie reminded himself to save it as a souvenir for Pierce. But after recording the out, Mays changed his mind and heaved it into the center-field bleachers in a cathartic act of pure, unadulterated ecstasy.

It was 1951 all over again. The Giants had come from behind in the ninth inning of the playoffs to beat the Dodgers and win the National League pennant.

* * *

The seesaw affair made for a hectic afternoon down in the lower depths of Dodger Stadium. Three different times park maintenance workers had been forced to wheel cases of victory champagne from one clubhouse to the other. Only minutes before the final out, NBC's postgame TV crew hastily transported its bulky cameras, cables, and lights out of the Dodger clubhouse, then just barely squeezed into the Giants' locker room in time for the postgame celebration. "The visitors' facilities at Dodger Stadium in those days was just not that big," remembered Mike McCormick, "and it was wall-to-wall people in there."

Reporters and radio interviewers aggressively pushed their way towards the ebullient victors. One grabbed McCovey, who shouted into his microphone, "This is the greatest moment of my life!" NBC's floor director suggested that Cepeda, Pagan, and Marichal dance the cha-cha before the cameras, and the obliging trio enthusiastically formed a conga line. "Hey Skip, drink this," chortled Bailey as he handed a glass of champagne to Dark. The teetotaling manager declined, but was smiling as he did so. Then Bailey added, "If we drink all this stuff, we'd be sick for a week. And if we had blown that game today, we'd have been sick for a year."

One clubhouse visitor who'd managed to work his way through the crowd was Richard Nixon, former vice president and current candidate in the '62 California gubernatorial race. After congratulating Dark, Nixon told him, "Your players have heart. You'll beat the Yankees."

The Giants had just beaten one former New York rival; in less than 24 hours, they would oppose the other. But at that moment, next day's World Series opener seemed terribly unimportant. "This was it—this was the pressure," said the relieved Mays. "We've got no time to worry about the Yankees now. We'll take them as they come." "Winning those playoffs was better than the Series," Felipe Alou disclosed some years later. "Because of the rivalry, the animosity between the Dodgers and Giants, the way we came from behind. This was the biggest thing that ever happened to me in baseball—even more than the day I played in the same outfield with my two brothers."

* * *

Outside the Dodger clubhouse doors the reporters were rapidly losing patience. "We've got deadlines!" moaned more than one writer. It was team policy to always allow the press into the locker room immediately after the game. Today was different. The Los Angeles Dodgers had just blown a pennant they should have clinched the week before. Nobody felt like talking.

Nearly 20 minutes after the game ended, a solemn Duke Snider finally emerged from the clubhouse. The Dodger captain recognized nearly every writer standing in the corridor. Some he had known from his Brooklyn days. These men understood Duke's pain. First Bobby

Thomson's home run in '51 and now this. Two crushing playoff losses to the Giants. It seemed unfair for one ballplayer to suffer the identical fate twice in a lifetime.

Snider stood in the doorway as he spoke to the mob of reporters. "Let's wait a few minutes before you come in. It's pretty grim in there. The guys are kind of in a daze." A chorus of objections quickly followed, but the Duke was undeterred. "I know you've got deadlines, but it's not a pretty scene right now." The press couldn't see anything. But they could hear the anguish inside of voices choked with anger. Shattering beer bottles. The whimpers of grown men crying. The sounds of defeat were heard only for an instant. Snider quickly retreated inside and closed the door.

Outfielder Wally Moon appeared a few minutes later. "How the hell would you feel if you'd just lost $12,000? Give the boys a little time to cool off." It was a full hour before the writers finally got into the Dodger clubhouse, and by then, many of the players had already left. Some were drunk. Others were simply found staring off into space with nothing to say.

A great deal had been said already, fueled by what was supposed to be bottles of victory champagne. Moments earlier, an angry Buzzie Bavasi had called down from his office. The champagne was not to be touched. "If anybody opens a bottle of champagne they won't be in Vero Beach next year," warned the general manager. The order was ignored. Equipment manager John "Senator" Griffin upped the ante by bringing out his private stock of whiskey. It was guzzled rapidly, and the more the players drank, the nastier they became.

The most obvious target of derision was Walter Alston. The manager had locked his office door, sitting alone, still numb from what had happened. More than a few in the clubhouse were quick to lay the blame at Alston's feet.

"Come on out here, you gutless sonofabitch!" bellowed one veteran. "Tell us about your strategy, skipper. How we gonna play the World Series, you bastard?" Tommy Davis was even more direct. "Walt, you stole my money. $12,000. You stole it." Johnny Podres, his eyes red from weeping, moaned, "Smokey lost it, boys. Old Smokey lost the pennant for us." Still another vet wandered the room, telling anyone who cared to listen, "We should have won. We could have won, too, if Durocher was managing this club." At last, someone had said it loud enough for Alston to hear.

The scene was deteriorating rapidly. Broken glass was all over the floor. Some players had ripped their uniforms to shreds, scattering the torn cloth around the lockers. Several were dead drunk. Three of them passed out in the shower, including Daryl Spencer. "I'm not a drinker, but I drank about a fifth of VO in 30 minutes. I still don't even remember how I got back to my hotel room." Senator Griffin, loaded on his own whiskey, collapsed into a locker, wedged in so tightly that it took three men to pry him loose. "I don't like to be around drunks, so I got dressed and left," recalled John Roseboro. "It was the worst scene I ever saw with the Dodgers. It was the one time we did not conduct ourselves with class."

Others followed Roseboro's lead. An exhausted Ed Roebuck showered and quickly departed, meeting his wife in the parking lot. "She's an old pro. She knew not to say anything. We drove home in silence. It was like a death in the family."

Stan Williams and his wife dealt with the loss differently. "I was just stunned. I felt like I'd let the whole team down, that it was my fault. We couldn't go home. We just couldn't. We spent the rest of the evening playing putt-putt golf. I had to take my mind off what happened. Believe me, we weren't there because of my great love for miniature golf."

"A lot of the guys who lived in the San Fernando Valley drove over to Don Drysdale's restaurant," recalled Ron Perranoski. "When we cleaned him out, we went to [local TV personality] Johnny Grant's house. It lasted all night long, and it was pretty rough."

Andy Carey's anger cost him more than just a Series share. "I was so upset that when I got home I took five to eight hundred dollars worth of World Series tickets and said, 'these are no good any more,' and I burned them in the fireplace. I didn't know the club had already deducted the cost of the tickets from my salary, so I couldn't get my money back."

The cruelest ordeal was reserved for Alston. Walt had just suffered through the worst game of his managerial career, and now he would be held accountable for his actions by a press corps still pondering his ninth-inning strategy and still furious over being barred from the Dodger clubhouse.

Displaying the calm and candor that was his trademark, Alston proceeded to answer every question, explaining the ill-fated moves made in the disastrous ninth. No, he wasn't going to pinch-hit for Roebuck because he was his best reliever at holding leads. Yes, it had to be Williams out of the bullpen because Larry Sherry's shoulder was stiff. No, he'd do everything exactly the same if they played the game over again.

Walt's voice was measured throughout, never strident, never self-pitying. Yet his hands nervously picked apart the foil from a tightly gripped pack of cigarettes. As the Dodger manager meted out his answers, his fingers rolled the pieces of foil into tiny silver balls. When the foil finally wore out, Alston let the tiny pellets drop to the floor while reaching next for his cigarette lighter. With his thumb, Alston flicked the lighter cap open, then shut, open, then shut as he relived the most painful defeat in Los Angeles Dodgers history. When the reporters had finished, Walt thanked them and walked back to the dressing room, still clicking the cap open and shut. He opened the clubhouse door and shut it behind him.

Alston's outward calm contrasted sharply with the seething rage of Buzzie Bavasi. The Dodgers' general manager locked himself in his office, grabbed a blanket, switched off the lights, and lay on his couch. Physically ill from the day's events and too angry to speak to anyone for fear he would say something he might later regret, Bavasi neither took nor made phone calls. Even his wife was excluded. Reclined in silence, Bavasi replayed the final week of the season over and over again in his head. "Just one more win that week and there wouldn't have been a playoff," he muttered to himself. The loss had torn him apart. Years later, Bavasi admitted, "Of all the games we ever played, this was the one we should have won.

"I was mad. I was mad at Walter. First time in my life I ever got mad at Walter Alston. He shoulda brought in Koufax, he shoulda brought in Drysdale. You've gotta go with your best."

Bavasi remained in his darkened office for more than seven hours. At 12:30 in the morning, he finally left Dodger Stadium. Down in the clubhouse, there were still ballplayers who had never gone home.

Earlier that evening, what was originally planned as a victory celebration at the Grenadier Restaurant (owned by stadium club caterer Tom Arthur) became the setting for the next Dodger bombshell. No players were present, but several club employees were, including Leo Durocher. The liquor flowed freely, as did a continuous stream of second-guesses. One unnamed Dodger official bellowed, "Leo, if you were the manager, we'd have won." Durocher softly replied, "Maybe."

The Leo loyalist continued. "We would have won with you. You know it as well as I do. We all know it. Every person in this room knows it."

Durocher was quiet for a moment, then finally said, "I know one thing. I'd have liked to go into the ninth inning with a 4-2 lead. I'd take my chances with a two-run lead."

Leo always contended that he said nothing more that night at the Grenadier. "It wasn't exactly a call to mutiny and it wasn't the most revolutionary idea since the movies discovered sound. Who wouldn't like to go into the ninth with a two-run lead? A man asked me a question and I answered."

Another question was resolved the following morning when Bavasi met with Alston at the stadium. Earlier, O'Malley told Buzzie that he was thinking of canning Alston and hiring Leo to replace him. Bavasi, in no uncertain terms, replied, "If you fire Alston, then I go out the door with him."

The last thing O'Malley wanted was to lose the shrewd Bavasi to another ballclub. The owner backed off, telling Buzzie it was his call and that he'd support him, whatever his decision. Alston's job was safe for another season, although the *Los Angeles Times* erroneously reported that Walt would be fired, with hitting coach Pete Reiser taking his place.

Bavasi met with Alston later that morning. The Dodger skipper was still remorseful. "I wouldn't blame you if you fired me right now," said Alston. Instead, Buzzie consoled his manager by saying, "Everyone's entitled to a bad game, a bad year." The two men shook hands and Alston departed. Bavasi was beginning to feel better.

Then the phone rang. On the line was Chicago White Sox president Hank Greenberg, who'd attended the party the night before at the Grenadier. Leo had been popping off, said Greenberg, publicly second-guessing and humiliating Walter Alston. Eventually the afternoon papers printed a similar story. Bavasi was livid.

Durocher and Buzzie met face-to-face soon after, just before a Friars' Club roast for Maury Wills. "I was coming down the stairs with Vin Scully when Leo showed up," remembered Bavasi. "I stopped Leo and called him an ungrateful sonofabitch. Vinnie turned white. He must have thought I was gonna hit Leo. Leo denied everything but I said, 'Don't tell me that. I know what you said. You're fired.' I fired him, right by the stairs at the Friars' Club. 'Don't come around anymore, you're through. I gave you a job when you needed one, and this is what you do to me?'"

According to Durocher's version, Bavasi conducted an investigation, then called him later to apologize, apparently convinced that Leo was telling the truth after all. Bavasi remembered the episode differently. "After I'd fired Leo, I phoned Alston. I told him, 'Walter, you're going to need a new third base coach. I fired Leo last night.'"

Alston seemed genuinely surprised. As Bavasi explained why Durocher had been dismissed, Alston interrupted. "Buzzie, I'd really like to have Leo around. Let me have him back."

It was an astonishing gesture by the Dodger manager. After enduring a season of Leo's flamboyance, stubbornness, and outright disobedience, it surely would have been understandable if Alston had been delighted to be rid of Durocher. Instead, The Organization Man moved quickly to heal a serious rift within the team ranks. He knew that behind Leo's bluster and vanity was a brilliant baseball mind, capable of helping the Dodgers win a pennant. In time, Alston would be proven right.

* * *

The grizzled cabbie craned his neck out of the taxi window to survey the madhouse on Market Street. San Francisco's busiest downtown boulevard, even on normal days, was teeming with thousands of jubilant Giant followers. Car horns were honking. Orange and black confetti was fluttering from windows above. Strangers were shaking hands, then embracing. More than a few pedestrians were already drunk or headed in that general vicinity. The driver shook his head and proclaimed, "There hasn't been anything like this since V-J Day."

From the time Lee Walls' pop fly landed in Willie Mays' glove, the city of San Francisco had gone absolutely crazy. At a matinee of the musical *Oliver*, transistor-toting patrons of the arts cheered during the middle of a vocalist's solo. A gleeful lounge owner broke open a bottle of Paul Masson and sprayed it on the sidewalk. And an overenthusiastic verger at Grace Cathedral rushed to the church organ and tapped out an inspired stanza of Handel's "Hallelujah Chorus."

The celebration continued well into the evening, but not without incident. Street fighting and property damage were reported throughout the city, and virtually the entire police force was pressed into service. Cable cars were tilted and trolleys were yanked from their wires. Nearly a dozen arrests were made and several roads sealed off, but by midnight, relative calm had been restored. Even the most zealous fans needed their rest; the World Series opener was only 12 hours away.

The weariest San Franciscans—the Giants themselves—were still airborne hours after the game had ended. As their flight from

L.A. approached San Francisco International, pilot Orv Schmidt announced, "There's a little disturbance down below. We're told there are at least 25-75,000 people down there. They've overrun the entrance ways. We don't know if we can land there or not. We may have to land in Oakland."

The Giants groaned at that possibility, and one anonymous wiseacre on board shouted, "What a way to end a day. First we win the pennant, then we go up in flames."

For more than an hour, the Giants' jet circled overhead. The runways were as clogged as the entrances surrounding the airport itself. Thousands of well-wishers flocking to greet the team simply abandoned their cars, bringing automobile traffic in and out of the airport to a virtual standstill.

A few minutes after nine, the DC-7 was finally given clearance to land at United Air Lines' maintenance base, a fenced-in area adjacent to the primary runways. A small crowd of mechanics and the Giants' bus driver politely applauded as the National League champions descended from the aircraft.

Several players left the UAL area and headed toward the Bayshore Freeway, looking for a ride home. Orlando Cepeda recalled that "a lot of us ended up hitchhiking—Matty and Felipe Alou, Pierce, Marichal. People we'd never met in our lives pulled up, offered us rides, and we jumped in."

The rest of the team boarded the bus and headed to the main concourse, where wives and families were anxiously awaiting their arrival. But the tenacious throng of fans discovered their whereabouts, broke through police barricades, and converged on the vehicle like a human tidal wave.

"Those folks meant well," insisted Dark, "but they really shook us up." The mob began rocking the bus, pounding on its sides, and shattering the windows. "I really thought they were going to turn the thing over and crush some of the people," said Billy O'Dell. "They just went absolutely crazy," shuddered Ed Bailey. "That was about as scared as I've ever been." Almost miraculously, no one was killed or injured.

A chant began echoing through the crowd: *We want Mays! We want Mays!* They didn't know that Willie had already commandeered the only cab available back at the United maintenance center, and was safely on his way home. Suddenly a light bulb clicked on in Bob Nieman's brain. He cast a conspiratorial glance over at Willie's identical twin and chuckled, "Let's throw 'em Boles and get the hell outta here!" Boles later noted, "I think Bob was kidding, but at the time, in that kind of crowd, I couldn't be too sure."

"In all my born years, I have never seen anything like this," stated astonished general manager Chub Feeney. "It certainly wasn't this way when we won in 1951."

"But that was back in hysterical New York, not sedate San Francisco," cracked the *Chronicle*'s Art Rosenbaum.

The bus eventually was able to navigate its way out of the airport. Then Feeney ordered the driver to stop near a roadside motel called the International Inn. "The bus was heading into town, but a lot of us lived down the peninsula and needed to get there. I knew this was a place where you could rent cars.

"So it's late at night, there's about eight of us, including Alvin. We're walking along the highway, across this empty field, in total darkness. I thought to myself: Here we are. Here come the champions of the National League."

14
OF SERIES RINGS AND BRIDESMAIDS' DREAMS

After the playoffs, many of the Giants, including Orlando Cepeda, felt a bit cheated. "You win the pennant, then you have to go out the very next day and play the Yankees. That didn't give us much time to savor our win against the Dodgers." Billy O'Dell agreed. "The way the season ended, and the way the playoffs went, it took away a lot of the excitement of the World Series. We never really got the thrill of the Series that I believe everybody else gets."

It certainly wasn't for lack of opportunity. Four rainouts, coast-to-coast travel, and the prolonged National League playoffs helped extend the October classic to 13 days—the most time-consuming Series since the Giants played the Athletics in 1911.

As anticipated, the battle-fatigued Giants dropped the opener to the Yankees, but bounced back in the second game. With only two days rest, a still-sniffling Jack Sanford, on sheer guts and antihistamines, pitched a surprising three-hit, complete game shutout.

Back home in New York, the Yanks took game three, but the Giants evened the Series the next day with another unexpected feat of heroism. No National Leaguer in history had ever homered with the bases loaded in a World Series until game four of 1962. The blast, though, did not come from such likely candidates as Mays, McCovey, Alou, or Cepeda. After slugging only three home runs during the regular season, it was Chuck Hiller, borrowing Billy Pierce's lighter bat, who belted the seventh-inning grand slam. It proved to be the decisive blow in San Francisco's 7-3 victory.

A heavy downpour postponed the fifth game, which the Yankees then won the following afternoon. Trailing three games to two, the Giants would have to sweep the remaining pair at Candlestick if they hoped to win the Series. But Mother Nature was conspiring to prevent those games from even being played.

As the Giants and Yankees flew west, a massive storm battered the northern California coast. Winds of hurricane force caused five deaths, knocked out power lines, and ravaged property as far as Oregon. In less than a day, nearly two inches of rain fell on San Francisco alone. The commissioner postponed the Series, prompting Dodgers executive Fresco Thompson to crack, "Why call off the game? When we play here it's wetter than this."

Such irony was not lost on baseball pundits who watched with amusement as Matty Schwab's grounds crew worked feverishly to prevent the Candlestick Park turf from washing away. The rain fell steadily for two more days, then finally abated, but still the Series could not be continued. Another Candlestick architectural blunder—poor drainage—halted action for an additional 24 hours.

To expedite the cleanup, Horace Stoneham hired three helicopters to buzz the field in hopes of hastening the dryout process. The grass, particularly in the outfield, remained soft and slippery, but finally, baseball's hierarchy could wait no longer. Despite what Commissioner Ford Frick admitted were "miserable conditions," the Series resumed at last on October 15th.

The delay proved a godsend for the tired arms of the Giants' pitching staff. With four days of inactivity, Dark had been able to reshuffle the rotation to San Francisco's advantage. The game six choice was easy: Billy Pierce and his perfect 12-0 Candlestick Park won-lost record. The rejuvenated Pierce kept his home record unblemished by taming the Yankees, 5-2, sending the Series to a seventh and deciding game.

For the finale, the Yankees started Ralph Terry, the American League's winningest pitcher, while the Giants countered with Jack Sanford. The choice of Terry was especially symbolic. "I was real thankful I had a chance to redeem myself in the seventh game of the World Series," he later told author John Tullius, "because I'd been the loser in the seventh game at Pittsburgh in 1960." That was the year Ralph had served up Bill Mazeroski's Series-winning home run in the bottom of the ninth, a stain Terry hoped to expunge against San Francisco.

Neither team got a run until the fifth when New York scored on a bases-loaded double play. Terry did not even allow a baserunner until the bottom of the sixth when Sanford, of all people, lined a single to right, but was stranded. And in the seventh, Willie McCovey ripped a two-out triple, only to die at third when Cepeda struck out. By the bottom of the ninth, Terry was still clinging precariously to his shutout and slender lead.

Dark needed a pinch-hitter to lead off the inning, virtually the identical situation he'd encountered two weeks earlier against the Dodgers in the third game of the playoffs. His choice once again was Matty Alou, and Alou responded by beating out a drag bunt for a base hit. But Terry battled back to strike out Felipe Alou, then Hiller. Only one more out was required for another Yankee world championship, but it would have to come against Willie Mays.

In Mays' last at-bat of the regular season, he homered to put the Giants in a tie for the pennant. In his last at-bat in the playoffs, he singled to keep the winning rally alive. Now, in his final at-bat in the Series, Willie delivered one more time.

After jamming Mays twice on inside pitches, Terry decided to go "low and away, about knee-high on the corner. I felt like I had real good stuff on it, but Willie opened up and just hit it with his hands. He wristed the ball and just hit a shot into right field." Mays coasted into second with a double, but the fleet-footed Alou was held up at third by coach Whitey Lockman.

A damp playing surface had been a valued home-field asset in 1962, but at this critical moment, the soggy turf actually prevented San Francisco from tying the game. "Roger Maris was playing me to pull," recalled Mays, "and he cut the ball off before it could get to the fence. If that field was dry, the ball rolls to the fence, Matty scores, and I'm on third."

Dozens of reporters later questioned whether Lockman shouldn't have taken the chance of sending Alou home. The coach vehemently stood his ground, insisting "I'd make the same decision 1,000 times out of 1,000." Dark emphatically supported Lockman, as did opposing manager Ralph Houk who said, "Matty would have been out by a mile."

The Yankee lead was still intact, but in serious peril. The next hitter was McCovey, who'd already scorched Terry for a triple in his previous at-bat, as well as a home run in an earlier Series game. First base remained open, but Terry was sure "I could get McCovey out. I felt I had a pretty good line on him...Maybe I was overconfident."

After a brief conference on the mound with Houk and catcher Elston Howard, Terry went to work. "I threw him a slow curveball that was down and away, and he hit it kind of on the end of his bat to right field. Maris was moving in for the ball and, oh boy, this looked like the last out. Then, all of a sudden, that damn wind at Candlestick took the ball and lifted it foul way up over the bullpen."

On the next pitch, McCovey swung mightily, a moment that still burns in the memory of every Giants fan who witnessed it. Willie uncoiled on Terry's hissing fastball, sending it on a straight line toward right-center field. "I hit that ball as hard as I could," McCovey said later. "I wasn't thinking about anything when I connected, but when you hit it good, you assume it's going to be a hit."

It wasn't. The ball headed straight into the webbing of Bobby Richardson's glove, arriving with such force that the impact sent the second baseman staggering almost to his knees. But the stumbling Richardson held on—and the Yankees were world champions for the 20th time in 39 years.

After the game, a reporter speaking to Dark asked, "McCovey hit that ball so hard, if it *had* gone through for a single, could Mays have made it home from second?"

"By the time they got the ball home," Alvin answered, "Mays would have been dressed."

Perhaps the most enduring image of the Series, other than that play itself, was a *Peanuts* cartoon which appeared in the comic strips a few days later. For three panels, Charlie Brown sits quietly in a near-catatonic trance, then bursts into tears, cursing to the heavens: "Why couldn't McCovey have hit the ball just three feet higher?"

* * *

Considering the circumstances, the mood in the Giants' postgame clubhouse was remarkably upbeat. "I'm just as proud of my players as if they had won the Series," proclaimed Dark. "They played just great. When you go down to the last out and the Series is decided by maybe one foot on a line drive, you've battled all the way."

Horace Stoneham agreed, and as an expression of his appreciation, threw a party that night in Candlestick's Stadium Club. Over 400 people attended, including every player on the team. But Horace's gratitude did not end there. "In those days, unless you won the Series, you didn't get rings," recalled Mike McCormick. "So Mr. Stoneham gave each of us solid gold money clips. The engraving read: *San Francisco Giants—1962 National League Champions* over crossed bats and baseballs. Each person's name was then carved on one of the bats. I carried it with me for years, but I don't anymore because I think its value is probably too great. Horace told us the clips would be incentive for us to earn Series rings the next year."

Unfortunately, McCormick would not get the chance. Two months later, he was traded to Baltimore, along with Stu Miller and John Orsino. McCormick's mysterious arm problems and subpar '62 season virtually guaranteed he would be gone. Miller wasn't particularly surprised at his own departure, either. "I did not have a very good outing in a clutch situation during the playoffs," confessed Stu, "and I think that had a lot to do with that trade."

The offseason was equally as unsettling for two of the Giants' Latin players. Juan Marichal was still bristling from comments Dark made during the Series after he had injured his hand on a bunt attempt in game four. Juan hoped for at least one more start against the Yankees, but Alvin shattered that notion when he curtly informed the press, "He won't pitch again in this Series even if it rains for a week."

Dark made the statement because he knew both Pierce and Sanford would have enough rest after the long delay, a situation Juan tacitly understood. Still, as Marichal wrote later in his autobiography: "This left the impression, with [the media]—and with me—that he thought I did not wish to pitch, and that with an attitude like that he didn't want me pitching." It was an unnecessary episode that bothered Marichal over the rest of the winter.

Felipe Alou's offseason was even more troubling. When officials from the Dominican Republic asked him to appear in an exhibition series in Santo Domingo to help quiet political unrest, Alou accepted. Unfortunately, the games were to be played against an all-star team from Havana, just weeks after the tense showdown between the United States and Russia in the 1962 Cuban Missile Crisis.

With American opinion still running fiercely against all matters related to Cuba, Ford Frick announced that any major leaguers who participated in the series would be penalized. Fearing physical reprisals by local rebels if he backed out, Felipe decided he had to play. Without taking into consideration the circumstances that trapped Alou in the first place, Frick fined him and threatened a one-year suspension if the sum was not paid.

After initially refusing to comply, the angry Alou finally sent the money to the commissioner's office. It was a bitter conclusion to what had otherwise been his most satisfying year in baseball. For Alou, this was just another example that Latin ballplayers "were, are, and will always be foreigners in America and we cannot hope that we will ever be totally accepted."

* * *

Shortly after the Series ended, the Dodgers called a press conference to announce the rehiring of Walter Alston for his 10th season as manager. Once the writers were seated, Buzzie Bavasi telephoned

Alston in Darrtown and said, "Smokey, if you haven't got anything better to do next spring, meet me in Vero Beach."

Walter's new contract had actually been expected by the media when he wasn't fired right after the playoffs. But they were taken aback when Bavasi revealed that Leo Durocher would also be returning to the coaching staff. From a squawking phone speaker box, Alston explained Leo's surprise resurrection: "I am not convinced he said those things [at the Grenadier]. And I've always gotten along well with him."

Even if Leo was coming back in '63, several Dodgers were not. Alston's rehiring signalled the opening of a hectic offseason for Bavasi, who publicly stated he had been dissatisfied, and even "disgusted" with the behavior of some of the players. A prophetic headline in *The Sporting News* accurately predicted: "Dodger Yelpers to Face Bavasi's Pruning Shears," and within weeks, the team's transaction wire began to hum.

Norm Sherry had already been sold to the Mets during the World Series, and would soon have company. Larry Burright and Tim Harkness were sent packing to New York in December. Duke Snider joined them the following spring. Andy Carey was released and promptly retired. Daryl Spencer lasted only until the following May when he was cut loose. Ed Roebuck was eventually banished to the lowly Senators and Stan Williams was dealt to the Yankees.

"I felt very badly about that trade," Williams admitted later. "I thought I was being used as a whipping boy for the '62 season, for the playoff loss. I resented their making an example of me. Sure, I was part of it, but I'd have liked the chance to redeem myself." On January 26, 1963, the Dodgers learned of a development that would impact their future far more drastically than any offseason deals. The Major League Rules Committee voted to expand the strike zone, restoring it to pre-1950 standards: from the top of the shoulders to the base of the knees. With this modification, the dominating Los Angeles pitching staff would become nearly invincible. It was a vital factor in the Dodgers winning the '63 pennant and World Series, but it was not the only one.

"The disappointment in '62 was definitely a springboard for the success we had in '63," claimed Ron Fairly. "We were just about the same ballclub, but we had greater resolve during the course of the '63 season. We swore we wouldn't let 1962 happen again."

"Nineteen-sixty-two was a crucible year for a lot of the players," observed Vin Scully. "Then they added a healthy Sandy Koufax and that '63 team was off and running. To win the pennant and then sweep the lordly Yankees in four straight—that's probably the greatest moment in the history of the Dodger organization."

Under Alston, the Dodgers won another World Series in 1965, and two more pennants in '66 and '74. In five other seasons, his teams finished second. When Walter retired after the 1976 season, he had 2,040 victories, the fifth most of any manager in the history of major league baseball. He died in 1984, a year after being voted into the Baseball Hall of Fame.

A few years before his passing, Alston confessed to Duke Snider, "Out of my whole managerial career, I'd like to have back the last week of the '62 season, and the playoffs." Given that Walter Alston was a man who rarely second-guessed himself, this was an astonishingly candid admission. It was the only time he ever allowed himself the luxury of regret.

Alston's *bete noire*, Durocher, stayed on as a coach with the Dodgers through 1964. During those two years in Los Angeles, there were virtually no flareups between the two—at least none that became known to the public. However, despite such outward calm, O'Malley and Bavasi decided not to renew Leo's contract in 1965.

In 1966, Durocher returned to managing with Chicago—and promptly finished last. But the Cubs steadily improved, and by 1969, Durocher fielded a team good enough to stay in first place for 155 days. Unfortunately for Leo, none of those days came during the final two weeks of the season. Many still believe it was Durocher who cost the Cubs the '69 title by overusing his everyday players. Following two more second-place finishes, Leo was let go during the middle of the '72 season.

Surprisingly, the 68-year-old Durocher was hired by Houston a month later, and he piloted the Astros through the end of 1973. But the years had finally caught up with the aging lion, who often fell asleep in the dugout, forcing others to assume his responsibilites. It was to be The Lip's last stop in the major leagues.

Only five managers in the Hall of Fame won more games than Durocher, yet there never seemed to be quite enough votes for his induction. Embittered, Leo finally told his friends to reject any Hall entry if he made it posthumously. Durocher died in 1991 at the age of 86, still waiting to be enshrined in Cooperstown. Three years later, the Veterans Committee finally voted Leo in.

* * *

Alvin Dark lasted two more seasons with the Giants, slipping to third in 1963 and fourth in '64. Both years were blighted by controversy, beginning with increased flareups between Alvin and Orlando Cepeda. Dark also became entangled with personal problems in his marriage. It was a situation that deeply disturbed Stoneham, causing him to question his manager's ethical code. Then, in July 1964, a story was published in *New York Newsday* that probably sealed Alvin's fate in San Francisco.

In a column written by Stan Isaacs, Dark was quoted as saying: "We have trouble because we have so many Negro and Spanish-speaking players on this team. They are just not able to perform up to the white ballplayer when it comes to mental alertness. You can't make most Negro and Spanish players have the pride in their team that you can get from white players."

Dark issued an immediate denial, reasoning that, "If you're going to make such statements, you are either stupid or ready to quit baseball." Isaacs admitted he had not made notes during the interview but insisted, "Dark knows he made the remarks and they must stand as written." Another sportswriter, Leonard Schecter, confirmed he had heard similiar thoughts from Alvin in the past.

Several prominent figures, including columnist Red Smith and former playing adversary Jackie Robinson, rushed to Alvin's defense. "I have known Dark for many years," said Robinson, "and my relationships with him have always been exceptional. I have found him to be a gentleman and, above all, unbiased." *Sports Illustrated, Newsweek,* and *Time* each recounted episodes that portrayed Dark as a manager who "has treated [Latins and Negroes] as individuals, not stereotypes."

The testimonials may have helped Dark keep his job for the moment, but were not enough to overcome the Giants' also-ran finish. At the end of the season, Alvin was fired. He coached briefly with the Cubs, then managed in Kansas City and Cleveland before returning to the Bay Area as skipper of the Oakland Athletics. He guided the A's to a world championship in 1974 and a division crown in '75, then completed his managerial career with San Diego in 1977.

"When I was with the Giants, I didn't like playing for Alvin, but I feel much differently today," Cepeda revealed many years later. "I was 24, 25 years old and he said certain things to me that got me very upset. Now, I wish I had paid more attention, because he'd been through it, he was a good ballplayer, he knew the game. Instead of fighting him, I should have listened to him and learned from him.

"Back then, he did some things that were hard to figure out. Sometimes, I believe he had it out for me personally. But I wasn't always easy to live with, either. It worked both ways—my fault, his fault.

"I think it was around 1988 when he came up to me at an old-timer's game and apologized. He said he was sorry for some of the things he had done. It takes a lot for a man do that. Alvin really is a fine person, and we are good friends now."

* * *

After Dark's departure, the Giants became little more than perennial bridesmaids. From 1965 through '69, they finished in second place every season, with teams never quite good enough to win the pennant. In 1971, they eked out a western division title, but lost to Pittsburgh in the playoffs. Afterwards, the Giants wallowed through 15 mediocre seasons until 1987, when they finally recaptured the division crown. In 1989, San Francisco made it back to the World Series for the first time in 27 years.

Because of their struggles, both on the field and at the turnstiles, the Giants lagged far behind their wealthier, more successful adversaries in Los Angeles. Even after Walter O'Malley's death in 1979, the Dodgers continued as baseball's top-drawing team, while the Giants battled simply to survive in San Francisco. Twice between 1976 and '92, the Giants were on the verge of leaving the Bay Area completely, a move *The New York Times* decreed would have "put the Giant-Dodger rivalry on its deathbed." When a transfer to Tampa-St. Petersburg appeared imminent during the fall of 1992, *Times* columnist Dave Anderson lamented, "west coast fans can add [the rivalry] to a list of endangered species."

A last-minute rescue by Peter Magowan's local business consortium kept the Giants in San Francisco, allowing their regional war with the Dodgers to continue. It is a rivalry worth preserving, even if the financial realities of the modern game have muted its intensity. As Giants manager Roger Craig lamented before the critical season-ending series of 1991, "Can you imagine Brooklyn and New York players standing around the batting cage, telling stories? We've got [L.A. outfielder] Brett Butler coming into our clubhouse. What would Sal Maglie have said if Jackie Robinson walked into the Giants' clubhouse? This is what happens with free agency. Everyone's friends."

Since 1962, there have been other memorable Dodger-Giant confrontations: the frightening Marichal-Roseboro brawl during the heat of the '65 campaign…The Dodgers' hot pursuit of the tattered but resourceful '71 Giants…Joe Morgan's ninth-inning home run to prevent Los Angeles from clinching a first-place tie on the last day of the '82 campaign…the 1991 ambush, when the Giants ruined L.A.'s hopes for a division flag during the final weekend…San Francisco's "Black Sunday of '93," when a fusillade of Dodger home runs in the last game of the season finished off the Giants' run at the western title.

Each of these seasons are storied chapters in baseball's longest-running rivalry. But none will ever surpass the drama of 1962. As Alvin Dark observed, "You never forget a year like '62. Even with all the Dodger-Giant battles I've been a part of, I still have to rank that season right at the top."

*   *   *

Beneath the looming shadows of South Mountain and Tovrea Castle, the traffic crept sluggishly along Van Buren Street, emptying into the dusty parking lot of Phoenix Municipal Stadium. The gathering crowd of Arizona fans was about to witness a distinctively different baseball matinee.

Down on the field, the two teams stretched their tired, aging muscles with half-hearted pepper games and languid warmup tosses. Even with their bellies sloping south and hairlines receding north, the names and faces were still recognizable. The date was February 8, 1987, a quarter-century removed from the most epic of West Coast pennant races. The '62 Dodgers and Giants were ready to have at it again, perhaps for the last time.

The six-inning rematch was being held to raise funds for Phoenix Memorial Hospital's child development center, a worthy cause that lured most of the players back into uniform, if only for a day. While the atmosphere around the batting cage remained congenial, there was no mistaking the sentiments in either dugout. "We're out here to win," declared Tommy Davis. "I'm not coming out here to lose 25 years later."

One by one, each player was introduced to the fans, many who weren't even alive in 1962. "As they were announcing the San Francisco lineup," recalled Johnny Podres, "they were calling out the names—Mays, Cepeda, McCovey, Felipe Alou, Marichal. I said to myself, how did we ever even make it to the playoffs against guys like that?"

The Giants touched Podres for two quick runs in the first inning, but L.A. cut the lead in half in the second. In the top of the third, the

Dodgers exacted revenge against playoff nemesis Billy Pierce when the still-wiry Willie Davis crashed a three-run homer over the right-field wall. As the grinning Davis circled the bases, his pleasure was obvious. Still beaming after the blast, Three-Dog declared, "I knew I could do it. I can do anything I want to. Man, I'm in shape to play [in the big leagues] right now!"

Some things remained unchanged after 25 years. Willie Mays pulled in outfield flies with his basket catch. Stu Miller's junk continued to fool Frank Howard, who struck out as the Giants' bench roared with laughter. "That's dirty pool, there's not an ounce of compassion in you," Hondo whined in mock anger to Alvin Dark. And Harvey Kuenn proved he could still hit, lining a single down the right-field line. Only one slight concession was made —because of Kuenn's artificial leg, a pinch-runner was permitted to jog the basepaths in his stead.

Perhaps the eeriest similarity was the score. By the fifth inning, the Dodgers led, 4-2, just as they had going into the ninth inning of the third playoff game. It was a circumstance not lost on Stan Williams. "What was really ironic was that after all those years, I come into the ballgame to relieve and it's the same score." After yielding a leadoff single to Ernie Bowman, Williams retired the next two hitters. With Mays at the plate, Stan's erratic ways resurfaced as he uncorked a wild pitch, moving Bowman to second. This time, however, The Big Hurt was determined not to let history repeat itself. After two long fouls, Mays struck out to end the inning. "It took 25 years, but I finally got even," gloated Williams.

In the top of the final inning, the Dodgers decided they didn't like the karma of 4-2. Observed Tommy Davis: "We all realized it was the same score as it was from '62, so we squeezed in another [run] just to make sure." After Willie Davis doubled and went to third on a groundout, Ron Fairly laid down a bunt single that sent Davis home with the fifth and final run of the afternoon.

"The Dodgers really wanted this game bad," noted Willie McCovey afterwards. "They were drag-bunting and everything. If they wanted it that bad, they deserve it."

Joe Moeller quickly dispatched the Giants in their last at-bat, ending the game with Tom Haller's sinking fly that was speared by the backpedalling Willie Davis. As the rest of the '62 Dodgers embraced the hero of the day, Willie pumped his fist and cried, "We couldn't let that happen again…we reversed the tide. They beat us then, but the victory today means just as much."

The Dodger-Giant battles continue today, even as the game of baseball confronts inevitable changes. Like the ebb and flow that characterizes all great rivalries, baseball itself struggles with a push towards the future and a sentimental pull from the past. The legacy of the rivalry is inherited from one generation to the next, challenged by its predecessors to equal, even surmount past glories of October.

AFTERWORD

Here's what became of the players on the 1962 Giants and Dodgers:

SAN FRANCISCO GIANTS

Felipe Alou stayed one more year in San Francisco, then was traded to the Braves in 1964. He later played with the Athletics, Yankees, and Brewers before retiring at the end of the '74 season. He finished with 206 career home runs and a lifetime batting average of .286. He coached for four different seasons with the Expos before being named their manager in 1992.

Matty Alou lasted with the Giants until 1965, when he was traded to the Pirates. His .342 average won him the league batting title in 1966. In 1971 he joined the Cardinals, and Alou also played with the Athletics and Padres. He retired in 1974 with 31 home runs and a lifetime batting average of .307.

Ed Bailey made the All-Star team as a Giant in 1963, then was traded to the Braves the following year. He came back to San Francisco in '65, then completed his career with the Cubs and Angels. He retired after the '66 season with 155 career home runs and a lifetime average of .256.

Carl Boles never played another season in the major leagues. After three more years in the minors, he went to Japan in 1966 and starred for six seasons. He retired from the Japanese leagues in 1971 with 117 career home runs and a .265 lifetime average.

Bob Bolin remained with San Francisco until 1969, then finished with the Brewers and Red Sox. His career ended after the '73 season. He posted a lifetime record of 88-75, with 50 saves and a 3.40 ERA.

Ernie Bowman played one more season with the Giants before his major league career concluded at the end of the 1963 season. His lifetime statistics include one home run and a batting average of .190.

Orlando Cepeda was traded to the Cardinals during the 1966 season. In '67 he won National League MVP honors and led St. Louis to a world championship. The Cards won another pennant the following season. Cepeda later played for the Braves, Athletics, Red Sox, and Royals before retiring at the end of '74. Cepeda completed his career with 379 home runs and an average of .297, and coached for the White Sox in 1980.

Jim Davenport played his entire career in San Francisco, retiring after the 1970 season with 77 home runs and a .258 lifetime average. He coached with the Padres and Giants for parts of 10 seasons, and returned to Candlestick as field manager in 1985. Davenport also coached later with the Phillies and Indians.

Tom Haller remained in San Francisco through 1967, then became one of the few Giants in history ever to be traded to the Dodgers. He played four seasons in Los Angeles before finishing his career with the Tigers in 1972. Haller hit 134 career home runs with an average of .257. He coached with San Francisco from 1977-79, then served as Giants vice president of baseball operations from 1981-86.

Chuck Hiller was traded to the Mets in 1965, and later played for the Phillies and Pirates. He retired in 1968 with 20 career home runs and a .243 average. He later coached in the majors with the Rangers, Royals, Cardinals, Giants, and Mets.

Harvey Kuenn played with the Giants until the middle of 1965 when he was traded to the Cubs. He finished his career with the Phillies, retiring at the end of the '66 season with 87 career home runs and a .303 lifetime average. From 1971-82 he was a coach with the Brewers. During the middle of the '82 season he became Milwaukee's manager and led a group of sluggers known as "Harvey's Wallbangers" to the World Series. He left the Brewers at the end of the folllowing season. Kuenn died in 1988 at the age of 57.

Don Larsen was traded to Houston in 1964, then finished his career with the Orioles and Cubs. He retired in 1967 with a lifetime record of 81-91, 23 saves, and an ERA of 3.78.

Juan Marichal was the ace of the Giants' pitching staff through the rest of the '60s, winning 20 or more games six times. He was sent to the Red Sox in 1974 and finished his career in a Dodger uniform in 1975. Marichal retired with a lifetime record of 243-142 with an ERA of 2.89. He was elected to the Baseball Hall of Fame in 1983.

Willie Mays remained a Giant for another 10 years, winning the league MVP award in 1965. During the summer of 1972 he returned to New York to finish his playing career with the Mets. He retired at the end of the '73 season with 660 career home runs and an average of .302. Mays served six years as a coach with the Mets beginning in 1974, and was elected to the Baseball Hall of Fame in 1979.

Mike McCormick struggled after being swapped to the Orioles, and was sent to the Senators in 1965. He returned to the Giants in '67 and won the Cy Young Award with a 22-win season. He stayed in San Francisco until mid-1970, then closed out his career with the Yankees and Royals in 1971. McCormick's lifetime record was 134-128 with an ERA of 3.73.

Willie McCovey became a full-time player with the Giants beginning in 1963, won three home run crowns, and was named league MVP in '69. He joined the Padres in '74 and played for two and a half years before he was dealt to the Athletics. McCovey returned for a final tour with the Giants from 1977 until his retirement in '80. McCovey hit 521 career home runs with an average of .270. He was elected to the Baseball Hall of Fame in 1986.

Stu Miller pitched five more seasons in the majors with the Orioles, then ended his career in 1968 with the Braves. He finished with a lifetime record of 105-103, with 154 saves and an ERA of 3.24.

Manny Mota was sent to Houston at year's end, and then was traded to the Pirates in 1963. He played in Pittsburgh until joining the expansion Expos in '69. That same season, he was dealt to the Dodgers, where he remained until the end of his career in 1982. He retired with 150 pinch-hits, the most in the history of the major leagues. Mota hit 31 career home runs with an average of .304. From 1980-89, he served as batting coach with the Dodgers.

Billy O'Dell continued to pitch for the Giants through 1964, then was traded to the Braves. In mid-1966 he was sent to the Pirates, then retired at the end of the '67 season. He finished with a career record of 105-100, with 48 saves and a 3.29 ERA.

Jose Pagan was traded to the Pirates during the 1965 season and remained in Pittsburgh through '72. He played his final season with the Phillies a year later. Pagan finished his career with 52 home runs and a .250 average. He returned to the Pirates as a coach from 1974-78.

Gaylord Perry pitched with the Giants for nine more years, twice posting 20-win seasons. He joined the Indians in 1972, then went to the Rangers in '75. He also spent parts of his later years with the Padres, Yankees, Braves, Mariners, and Royals. He won the Cy Young Award in 1972 and '78. Perry retired in 1983, finishing with a career record of 314-265 and an ERA of 3.10. He was elected to the Baseball Hall of Fame in 1991.

Billy Pierce pitched two more years with the Giants until his retirement at the end of the 1964 season. He finished with a career record of 211-169 and an ERA of 3.27.

Jack Sanford remained with the Giants until the middle of 1965 when he was dealt to the Angels. He completed his career in '67 with the Athletics, posting a lifetime record of 137-101 with an ERA of 3.69. From 1968-69, he served as pitching coach with the Indians.

LOS ANGELES DODGERS

Larry Burright played parts of the next two seasons with the Mets before his major league career ended in 1964. He hit four lifetime home runs with an average of .205.

Doug Camilli continued to catch with the Dodgers through the 1964 season, then was traded to the Senators, where he remained until his final year in '69. He hit 18 career home runs with an average of .199. He coached with Washington during his last two years as an active player, then was a Red Sox coach from 1970-73.

Andy Carey retired after his release at the end of the '62 season, finishing his career with 64 home runs and a lifetime .260 batting average.

Tommy Davis won his second straight league batting title in 1963, then remained with the Dodgers through '66, when he was dealt to the Mets. He later played for the White Sox, Pilots, Astros, Athletics, Cubs, Orioles, Angels, and Royals. He retired at the end of the '76 season with 153 career home runs and an average of .294. In 1981 he served as hitting coach with the Mariners.

Willie Davis continued his career with the Dodgers until the end of the 1973 season, when he was traded to the Expos. In '75, he split time with the Rangers and Cardinals, then joined the Padres in '76. After two years in the Japanese leagues, Davis played his final major league season with the Angels in 1979. He hit 182 career home runs, with 398 stolen bases and a lifetime average of .279.

Don Drysdale spent the rest of his career with the Dodgers, adding another 20-win season in 1965. In '68, he set a major league record (since broken) by pitching 58 2/3 scoreless innings. He retired in the middle of the '69 season with a lifetime record of 209-166, with 2,486 strikeouts and an ERA of 2.95. Drysdale later became a broadcaster with the Dodgers. He was voted into the Baseball Hall of Fame in 1984. He died in 1993 at the age of 56.

Ron Fairly played with the Dodgers until 1969, when he was traded to the Expos. He was shipped to the Cardinals in '75, then closed out his career with the Athletics, Blue Jays, and Angels. He retired in 1978 with 215 career home runs and an average of .266. He later broadcast for the Angels and Giants before joining the Mariners announcing crew in 1993.

Jim Gilliam played through 1964 before retiring to join the Dodgers' coaching staff. He was then reactivated to help out during the pennant-winning '65 and '66 seasons. He remained with the team as a coach through 1978, when he died of a brain hemorrhage shortly before the start of the World Series. He was 49 years old. Gilliam finished his career with 65 home runs, 203 stolen bases, and an average of .265.

Frank Howard was traded to the Senators at the end of 1964, and remained in Washington for seven seasons, winning two American League home run crowns. In 1968, he hit a record 10 home runs during one week. He moved with the club to Texas in '72, then finished his career with the Tigers in 1973. He hit 382 lifetime home runs, with a .273 average. A career in Japan lasted only one game because of a back injury. Howard managed the Padres in 1981 and the Mets in '83. He also coached for the Brewers and Mariners, along with two separate coaching stints for both the Yankees and Mets.

Sandy Koufax earned league MVP honors in 1963, and the Cy Young award in '63, '65 and '66. He won ERA titles in every season from 1962-66, posted three 20-win seasons, and set the seasonal record (since broken) of 382 strikeouts. Concern over future arm problems caused him to retire at the end of the 1966 season. Koufax' lifetime record was 165-87, with 2,396 strikeouts and an ERA of 2.76. In 1972, he became the youngest man (36) ever voted into the Baseball Hall of Fame.

Rene Lachemann ended his fourth and final season as Dodgers batboy after 1962, then enrolled at the University of Southern California. He later signed as a catcher with the Athletics, playing parts of three major league seasons. He managed the Mariners from 1981-83 and the Brewers in 1984. He also coached with the Red Sox and Athletics until he was named manager of the Florida Marlins in 1992.

Joe Moeller pitched parts of seven more seasons with the Dodgers until departing the majors at the end of the 1971 season. He finished his career with a record of 26-36 and an ERA of 4.02.

Wally Moon lasted as a part-timer with the Dodgers through the 1965 season, then retired, with 142 lifetime home runs and an average of .289. He coached with the Padres in 1969, then spent the next two decades coaching and managing in college and the minor leagues.

Ron Perranoski won Fireman of the Year honors in 1963, and remained ace of the Dodger bullpen through 1967, when he was traded to the Twins. He was dealt to the Tigers in '71, then pitched briefly for the Dodgers again in '72. After one more season with the Angels, Perranoski retired in 1973. His lifetime record was 79-74, with 179 saves and an ERA of 2.79. He became the Dodgers' pitching coach in 1981.

Johnny Podres continued in Los Angeles until the middle of 1966 when he was sent to the Tigers. He remained with Detroit through the end of '67, then was out of baseball for a year before joining the Padres in 1969. He retired that same year with a career record of 148-116 and an ERA of 3.67. Podres later coached with the Padres, Red Sox, and Twins before joining the Phillies as their pitching coach in 1991.

Pete Richert was traded to the Senators at the end of the 1964 season, then was swapped to the Orioles in '67. He starred in relief for three pennant-winners in Baltimore before coming back to the Dodgers in '72. He closed out his career in '74 with the Cardinals and Phillies. Richert's lifetime record was 80-73, with 51 saves and an ERA of 3.19.

Ed Roebuck was traded to the Senators during the middle of the 1963 season, then went to the Phillies the following year. He finished his major league career in 1966 with a lifetime record of 52-31, with 62 saves and an ERA of 3.35.

John Roseboro continued to catch for the Dodgers through the 1967 season, when he was dealt to the Twins. After two seasons in Minnesota, he completed his playing career with the Senators in 1970. He retired with 104 career home runs and a lifetime average of .249. He coached in Washington in 1971, then with the Angels from 1972-74.

Larry Sherry was dealt to the Tigers after the 1963 season, and continued to pitch in Detroit for four more years. In '67, he was sent to the Astros, then finished his career the following season with the Angels. His lifetime record was 53-44, with 82 saves and an ERA of 3.67. He served as pitching coach for both the Pirates and Angels during the late '70s.

Norm Sherry played one more season in the major leagues with the Mets before retiring at the end of 1963. He hit 18 career home runs with a batting average of .215. He managed the Angels from 1976-77, and later was pitching coach with the Expos, Padres, and Giants.

Duke Snider returned to New York as a Met in 1963, then finished his career with the Giants a year later. He retired with 407 career home runs and a batting average of .295. He eventually became a broadcaster with the Dodgers. Snider was elected to the Baseball Hall of Fame in 1980.

Daryl Spencer was released by the Dodgers during the '63 season, then finished his major league career with the Reds. He totalled 105 home runs with a .244 batting average. Spencer then played eight more seasons in the Far East, becoming renowned as the man who first brought the art of aggressive sliding to the Japanese leagues. In Japan, he hit 152 home runs with a career average of .275.

Lee Walls stuck with the Dodgers as a bench player through the end of the 1964 season, completing his big league career with 66 lifetime home runs and an average of .262. He played two more years in Japan, then returned to the majors as a coach with the Athletics from 1979-82, and the Yankees in '83. He died in 1993 at the age of 60.

Stan Williams pitched two years with the Yankees after being traded to New York in 1963. He was sent to the Indians in 1965, remaining in their organization till '70, when the Twins acquired him. Williams also pitched briefly with the Cardinals and Red Sox before his retirement in 1972. His lifetime record was 109-94 with an ERA of 3.48. Afterwards, he was pitching coach with the Red Sox, White Sox, Yankees, and Reds.

Maury Wills was the Dodgers' regular shortstop until the end of 1966, when he was dealt to the Pirates. He joined the Expos in '69, then was traded back to the Dodgers that same summer. Wills remained in Los Angeles through his final playing season in 1972. He hit 20 career home runs, with 586 stolen bases and a batting average of .281. He later served as manager of the Mariners during the 1980 and '81 seasons.

1962 CHRONOLOGY

APRIL

10th   52,564 attend opening day at Dodger Stadium, but Cincinnati spoils Dodgers' debut, 6-3. Giants win their season opener in Candlestick, beating Braves, 6-0, behind Juan Marichal's shutout. Willie Mays belts HR on his first pitch of the season.

11th   Dodgers win first-ever game in their new park as Sandy Koufax tames Reds, 6-2.

12th   L.A. southpaw Pete Richert ties major league rookie record by striking out the first six batters he faces as Dodgers club Cincinnati, 11-7.

16th   Giants reach season-high run-scoring output by crushing Dodgers, 19-8, in their first meeting of '62. Willie Mays, Felipe Alou, and Jim Davenport hit HR.

17th   Strong pitching from fireman Larry Sherry helps Dodgers edge Giants, 8-7, at Candlestick, their first win in San Francisco since May 21, 1961.

24th   At Wrigley Field, Sandy Koufax becomes first pitcher ever to strike out 18 batters twice in a game, beating Cubs, 10-2.

25th   Knockdown pitch, then near-brawl with Pirates pitcher Bob Friend inspires Ed Bailey to swat dramatic sixth-inning HR, as Giants win in Pittsburgh, 8-3, launching team's best winning streak of season.

29th   Giants notch doubleheader shutout at Candlestick as Jack Sanford and Billy Pierce whitewash Cubs, 7-0 and 6-0.

MAY

4th   Aircraft problems force emergency landing in Salt Lake City and Giants don't arrive in Chicago until 6:00 A.M., but still thrash Cubs that afternoon, 11-6, for 10th victory in a row, San Francisco's longest streak of 1962.

21st   In first Dodger-Giant game ever played at Chavez Ravine, L.A. wins, 8-1 on three RBI from Tommy Davis and 10 strikeouts by Sandy Koufax.

27th   Giants sweep Mets at Candlestick, 7-1 and 6-5, while Willie Mays gets into first fight of his big league career, a brief brawl with New York's Elio Chacon.

30th   Dodgers' first appearance in New York since leaving Brooklyn five years earlier is a rousing success as L.A. sweeps Mets in Polo Grounds doubleheader, 13-6 and 6-5. Maury Wills becomes the seventh man in history to hit HR from each side of the plate in a single game.

JUNE

1st   Giants return to Polo Grounds for the first time since 1957 and defeat Mets, 9-6, behind two Willie McCovey HRs and solo shot from former New York idol Willie Mays. In Philadelphia, Dodgers sweep doubleheader against Phillies, 11-4 and 8-5, to run winning streak to 13 games, longest of N.L. season.

8th   Dodgers edge Colts in Houston, 4-3, in 13 innings to go into first place for first time in 1962.

10th   Another Bay Area "June Swoon" as Cardinals crush San Francisco, 13-3, in St. Louis, Giants' sixth consecutive loss. Giants hit skids with only four wins in 16 games during latter part of June.

12th   Giants end six-game losing streak by sweeping doubleheader in Cincinnati, 2-1 and 7-5.

17th   Tom Haller's three-run HR in bottom of ninth breaks tie in 6-3 win over St. Louis at Candlestick. Victory goes to Jack Sanford, beginning his personal string of 16 straight wins.

18th   Sandy Koufax and Cardinals' Bob Gibson lock up in scoreless pitchers' duel, finally settled by Tommy Davis' HR in bottom of ninth. Dodgers edge St. Louis, 1-0.

29th   Billy O'Dell pitches all 12 innings and fans a dozen Phillies as Giants prevail, 4-3, at Candlestick. Ed Bailey delivers winning hit, a solo HR to break extra-inning tie.

30th   In Los Angeles, Sandy Koufax fires first of his four career no-hitters, striking out 13 Mets in 5-0 triumph.

JULY

2nd   Dodgers sweep doubleheader vs. Phillies in L.A., 5-1 and 4-0. Pitcher Johnny Podres retires first 20 hitters he faces and sets major league record (since broken) by striking out eight consecutive batters.

4th   Independence Day holiday finds both Chavez Ravine tenants (Dodgers and Angels) atop the standings in their respective leagues.

6th   Juan Marichal strikes out 13 as Giants wallop Dodgers, 12-3, in San Francisco.

8th   Sandy Koufax and Don Drysdale combine to shut out Giants at Candlestick, 2-0, giving Dodgers half-game lead over San Francisco at first All-Star break, a lead L.A. holds until final day of regular season.

10th   Maury Wills singles, steals a base, and scores twice in his hometown of Washington, D.C., as N.L. beats A.L. in All-Star Game, 3-1. Giants' Juan Marichal is N.L.'s winning pitcher.

17th   Sandy Koufax leaves game in Cincinnati after only one inning with circulatory ailment in finger that sidelines him for two months. Dodgers lose to Reds, 7-5.

29th   Dodgers crush Giants in Los Angeles, 11-1, to sweep three-game series and lead San Francisco by four games at second All-Star break. Frank Howard's hot hitting continues, collecting his 47th RBI since June 28.

AUGUST

3rd   Don Drysdale beats Cubs, 8-3, in L.A. to become N.L.'s earliest 20-game winner since Chicago's Jim (Hippo) Vaughn in 1918.

9th   In L.A., Dodgers beat Phillies, 8-3, to extend first-place lead over Giants to five and a half games, biggest margin of season.

10th   Dodgers are stymied by Candlestick's watered-down infield, and Giants go on to thump L.A., 11-2. Willie Mays socks HR, drives in four runs.

11th   Willie McCovey's three-run pinch-hit HR in sixth powers Giants to 5-4 win over Dodgers, snapping Don Drysdale's 11-game winning streak, while giving Billy Pierce his 200th career victory.

12th   Giants sweep water-soaked Candlestick series as Juan Marichal four-hits Dodgers, 5-1.

19th   Braves smash Giants, 13-8, in Milwaukee, punctuated by shouting match between manager Alvin Dark and benched Orlando Cepeda.

23rd   Giants end slump of six losses in seven games, as reserve infielder Ernie Bowman hits HR, singles in winning RBI for 2-1 win over Mets in New York.

24th   Lowly Mets beat Dodgers, 6-3, and coach Leo Durocher nearly dies at Polo Grounds from violent reaction to penicillin.

SEPTEMBER

3rd   Angry L.A. fans blow duck calls in response to Giants' August water antics, but San Francisco's Jack Sanford stops Dodgers, 7-3, for 20th win of the season.

4th   Daring baserunning highlighted by John Roseboro's steal of home propels Dodgers to 5-4 win over Giants.

5th   Giants bounce back to shut out Dodgers, 3-0, with Bob Bolin pitching solid relief after Juan Marichal leaves game with foot injury.

6th   Harvey Kuenn's three-run, ninth-inning double lifts Giants to 9-6 win over Dodgers at Chavez Ravine, moving San Francisco to within game and a half of first. Evening's crowd allows Dodgers to set new major league attendance mark (previously held by the '48 Indians) of 2,287,772. L.A.'s final attendance is 2,755,184.

7th   Maury Wills steals four bases (reaching number 82) to break Bob Bescher's N.L. single-season record (set in 1911). Pirates still beat Dodgers, 10-1, in Los Angeles.

11th   Jack Sanford shuts out Pirates, 2-0, at Candlestick for his 16th consecutive victory of the season.

12th   Willie Mays collapses in dugout at Cincinnati and is hospitalized, missing four games. Reds win, 4-1, setting off six-game Giants losing streak.

16th   In Chicago, Bob Buhl pitches shutout and rookie outfielder Nelson Mathews belts HR as Cubs beat Dodgers, 5-0, ending L.A.'s seven-game winning streak.

19th   Giants halt losing skid in St. Louis as Tom Haller swats two home runs in 7-4 victory over Cardinals.

21st   Recently recalled rookie pitcher Gaylord Perry beats Colts in Houston, 11-5, to keep Giants within three games of L.A. In St. Louis, Sandy Koufax makes first appearance since injury and fails to last one inning as Cardinals drub Dodgers, 11-2.

23rd   Giants overwhelm Colts, 10-3, as Billy O'Dell wins 19th. In St. Louis, Maury Wills breaks Ty Cobb's major league record for stolen bases, stealing two (96 and 97). Cardinals blast L.A., 12-2, but Dodgers return for final homestand leading Giants by three with six to play.

26th   Giants beat Cardinals, 6-3, as Billy Pierce wins 11th Candlestick decision without a loss. Back home, Dodgers clobber Colts, 13-1, as Maury Wills swipes 100th stolen base.

27th   Gene Oliver's three-run HR provides winning margin as Cardinals outlast Giants, 7-4, at Candlestick. In Los Angeles, Sandy Koufax struggles through five innings and bullpen fails to hold lead, as Dodgers miss chance to clinch a tie for pennant, losing to Houston, 8-6.

28th   At Chavez Ravine, Cardinals edge Dodgers in 10, 3-2, while Giants are rained out against Colts in San Francisco.

29th   Giants wallop Colts, 11-5, in twin bill opener, but lose nightcap, 4-2. In Los Angeles, Cardinals' Ernie Broglio shuts out Dodgers, 2-0. L.A.'s lead holds at one entering season's final day.

30th   Willie Mays' eighth-inning HR gives Giants 2-1 victory. Later in Los Angeles, solo home run by Cardinals' Gene Oliver off Johnny Podres is enough for pitcher Curt Simmons to beat Dodgers, 1-0. Result creates season-ending first-place tie and forces best-of-three playoff between L.A. and San Francisco.

OCTOBER

1st   Two HRs from Willie Mays, plus solo shots by Orlando Cepeda and Jim Davenport back up Billy Pierce's strong pitching as Giants crush Dodgers, 8-0, in playoff opener at Candlestick.

2nd   Giants blow 5-0 lead at Chavez Ravine as Dodgers rally for seven runs in sixth, and go on to beat San Francisco, 8-7, in longest nine-inning game ever played in the major leagues (4:18).

3rd   Dodgers take a 4-2 lead into ninth, but San Francisco rallies for four runs on strength of only one infield hit and numerous Los Angeles mistakes. Giants win their first-ever West Coast pennant, 6-4.

4th   Yankees topple Giants, 6-2, in World Series opener at Candlestick, behind pitching of Whitey Ford and Clete Boyer HR.

5th   Jack Sanford blanks Yankees, 2-0, getting support from HR by Willie McCovey to knot Series at one game apiece.

7th   In New York, Yankees' Bill Stafford shuts out Giants until ninth but still prevails, 3-2. Yanks lead Series, two games to one.

8th   Chuck Hiller hits first-ever World Series grand slam HR by a National Leaguer as Giants even Series at two with 7-3 victory.

10th   Tom Tresh's three-run HR in eighth breaks tie and propels New York to 5-2 win, giving Yanks three-games-to-two advantage over Giants.

15th   Bay Area rain halts Series for four days, but Giants return from break to win, 5-2, behind hitting of Orlando Cepeda and Billy Pierce's strong pitching. Series is tied at three games apiece.

16th   New York's Bobby Richardson nabs Willie McCovey's searing line drive in bottom of the ninth to preserve Ralph Terry's 1-0 shutout. It is Yankees' 20th Series triumph in past 39 years.

STATISTICS

1962 SAN FRANCISCO GIANTS (103-62)

No.	Batting	AVG.	AB	R	H	2B	3B	HR	RBI	SB
14	Carl Boles	.375	24	4	9	0	0	0	1	0
23	Felipe Alou	.316	561	96	177	30	3	25	98	10
30	Orlando Cepeda	.306	625	105	191	26	1	35	114	10
24	Willie Mays	.304	621	130	189	36	5	49	141	18
7	Harvey Kuenn	.304	487	73	148	23	5	10	68	3
20	Bob Nieman	.300	30	1	9	2	0	1	3	0
12	Jim Davenport	.297	485	83	144	25	5	14	58	2
44	Willie McCovey	.293	229	41	67	6	1	20	54	3
41	Matty Alou	.292	195	28	57	8	1	3	14	3
26	Chuck Hiller	.276	602	94	166	22	2	3	48	5
34	John Orsino	.271	48	4	13	2	0	0	4	0
5	Tom Haller	.261	272	53	71	13	1	18	55	1
15	Jose Pagan	.259	580	73	150	25	6	7	57	13
6	Ed Bailey	.232	254	32	59	9	1	17	45	1
2	Joe Pignatano	.200	5	2	1	0	0	0	0	0
21	Ernie Bowman	.190	42	9	8	1	0	1	4	0
38	Manny Mota	.176	74	9	13	1	0	0	9	3
17	Cap Peterson	.167	6	1	1	0	0	0	0	0
14	Dick Phillips	.000	3	1	0	0	0	0	1	0
		.278	5588	878	1552	235	32	204	807	73

No.	Pitching	ERA	G	W	L	IP	GS	CG	SV	BB	SO
27	Juan Marichal	3.32	37	18	11	263	36	18	1	90	153
33	Jack Sanford	3.43	39	24	7	265	38	13	0	92	147
19	Billy Pierce	3.48	30	16	6	162	23	7	1	35	76
31	Billy O'Dell	3.53	43	19	14	281	39	20	0	66	195
42	Bobby Bolin	3.62	41	7	3	92	5	2	5	35	74
45	Jim Duffalo	3.64	24	1	2	42	2	0	0	23	29
37	Stu Miller	4.12	59	5	8	107	0	0	19	42	78
18	Don Larsen	4.38	49	5	4	86	0	0	11	47	58
28	Gaylord Perry	5.23	13	3	1	43	7	1	0	14	20
28	Bob Garibaldi	5.25	9	0	0	12	0	0	1	5	9
40	Mike McCormick	5.36	28	5	5	99	15	1	0	45	42
39	Dick LeMay	8.00	9	0	1	9	0	0	1	9	5
		3.79	165	103	62	1462	165	62	39	503	886

Mgr. - Alvin Dark (1)
Coaches - Larry Jansen (46), Whitey Lockman (3), Wes Westrum (9)

1962 LOS ANGELES DODGERS (102-63)

No.	Batting	AVG.	AB	R	H	2B	3B	HR	RBI	SB
12	Tommy Davis	.346	665	120	230	27	9	27	153	18
30	Maury Wills	.299	695	130	208	13	10	6	48	104
25	Frank Howard	.296	493	80	146	25	6	31	119	1
3	Willie Davis	.285	600	103	171	18	10	21	85	32
35	Doug Camilli	.284	88	16	25	4	1	4	22	0
6	Ron Fairly	.278	460	80	128	15	7	14	71	1
4	Duke Snider	.278	158	28	44	11	3	5	30	2
14	Ken McMullen	.273	11	0	3	0	0	0	0	0
19	Jim Gilliam	.270	588	83	159	24	1	4	43	17
7	Lee Walls	.266	109	9	29	3	1	0	17	1
15	Tim Harkness	.258	62	9	16	2	0	2	7	1
8	John Roseboro	.249	389	45	97	16	7	7	55	12
9	Wally Moon	.242	244	36	59	9	1	4	31	5
20	Daryl Spencer	.236	157	24	37	5	1	2	12	0
21	Andy Carey	.234	111	12	26	5	1	2	13	0
11	Larry Burright	.205	249	35	51	6	5	4	30	4
34	Norm Sherry	.182	88	7	16	2	0	3	16	0
44	Dick Tracewski	.000	2	3	0	0	0	0	0	0
		.268	5628	842	1510	192	65	140	781	198

No.	Pitching	ERA	G	W	L	IP	GS	CG	SV	BB	SO
32	Sandy Koufax	2.54	28	14	7	184	26	11	1	57	216
53	Don Drysdale	2.84	43	25	9	314	41	19	1	78	232
16	Ron Perranoski	2.86	70	6	6	107	0	0	20	36	68
37	Ed Roebuck	3.10	64	10	2	119	0	0	9	54	72
51	Larry Sherry	3.20	58	7	3	90	0	0	11	44	71
22	Johnny Podres	3.81	40	15	13	255	40	8	0	71	178
45	Pete Richert	3.89	19	5	4	81	12	1	0	45	75
40	Stan Williams	4.45	40	14	12	186	28	4	1	98	108
41	Jack Smith	4.50	8	0	0	10	0	0	1	4	7
38	Joe Moeller	5.23	19	6	5	86	15	1	1	58	46
17	Phil Ortega	6.83	24	0	2	54	3	0	1	39	30
23	Willard Hunter	40.50	1	0	0	2	0	0	0	4	1
		3.61	165	102	63	1489	165	44	46	588	1104

Mgr. - Walter Alston (24)

Coaches - Joe Becker (33), Leo Durocher (2), Greg Mulleavy (31), Pete Reiser (27)

1962 SEASON SERIES—DODGERS VS. GIANTS

Date	Result	Winner	Loser
Regular Season			
4/16	@SF 19, LA 8	O'Dell	Williams
4/17	LA 8, @SF 7	Drysdale	McCormick
5/21	@LA 8, SF 1	Koufax	O'Dell
5/22	@LA 5, SF 1	Williams	Sanford
7/5	LA 11, @SF 3	Drysdale	McCormick
7/6	@SF 12, LA 3	Marichal	Williams
7/7	@SF 10, LA 3	Sanford	Podres
7/8	LA 2, @SF 0	Koufax	O'Dell
7/27	@LA 3, SF 1	Podres	Marichal
7/28	@LA 8, SF 6	Roebuck	Bolin
7/29	@LA 11, SF 1	Drysdale	O'Dell
8/10	@SF 11, LA 2	O'Dell	Podres
8/11	@SF 5, LA 4	Pierce	Drysdale
8/12	@SF 5, LA 1	Marichal	Williams
9/3	SF 7, @LA 3	Sanford	Williams
9/4	@LA 5, SF 4	Perranoski	Pierce
9/5	SF 3, @LA 0	Marichal	Podres
9/6	SF 9, @LA 6	Bolin	Perranoski
Playoffs			
10/1	@SF 8, LA 0	Pierce	Koufax
10/2	@LA 8, SF 7	Williams	Bolin
10/3	SF 6, @LA 4	Larsen	Roebuck

SF—11 WINS   LA—10 WINS

BIBLIOGRAPHY

BOOKS

Allen, Lee, *The Giants and the Dodgers: The Fabulous Story of Baseball's Fiercest Feud* (New York: G.P. Putnam's Sons), 1964.

Allen, Maury, *Baseball: The Lives Behind the Seams* (New York: Macmillan), 1990.

Alou, Felipe with Herman Weiskopf, *Felipe Alou: My Life and Baseball* (Waco, TX: Word), 1967.

Alston, Walter and Si Burick, *Alston and the Dodgers* (Garden City, New York: Doubleday), 1966.

_____ and Jack Tobin, *Walter Alston: A Year at a Time* (Waco, TX: Word), 1976.

Angell, Roger, *The Summer Game* (New York: Popular Library), 1972.

Astor, Gerald, *The Baseball Hall of Fame 50th Anniversary Book* (New York: Prentice-Hall), 1988.

Bankes, James, *The Pittsburgh Crawfords* (Dubuque, IA: William C. Brown), 1991.

Bavasi, Buzzie with John Strege, *Off the Record* (Chicago: Contemporary), 1987.

Bjarkman, Peter C., *Baseball's Greatest Dynasties: The Dodgers* (New York: Gallery), 1990.

Bragan, Bobby as told to Jeff Guinn, *You Can't Hit the Ball with the Bat on Your Shoulder*, (Ft. Worth, TX: The Summit Group), 1992.

Broeg, Bob and William J. Miller, Jr., *Baseball From a Different Angle* (South Bend, IN: Diamond Communications), 1988.

Bronson, Fred, *The Billboard Book of Number One Hits* (New York: Billboard), 1985.

Bryson, Michael G., *The Twenty-Four Inch Home Run*, (Chicago: Contemporary), 1990.

Burt, Rob, *Surf City Drag City* (Poole, England: Blandford), 1986.

Cairns, Bob, *Pen Men*, (New York: St. Martin's), 1992.

Castleman, Harry and Walter J. Podrazik, *Watching TV* (New York: McGraw-Hill), 1982.

Cepeda, Orlando with Charles Einstein, *My Ups and Downs in Baseball* (New York: G. P. Putnam's Sons), 1968.

_____ with Bob Markus, *High and Inside: The Orlando Cepeda Story* (South Bend, IN: Icarus Press), 1983.

Charlton, James, ed., *The Baseball Chronology* (New York: Macmillan), 1991.

Coberly, Rich, *The No-Hit Hall of Fame* (Newport Beach, CA: Triple Play Publications), 1985.

Cohen, Stanley, *Dodgers! The First 100 Years*, (New York: Birch Lane), 1990.

Colton, Larry, *Goat Brothers*, (New York: Doubleday), 1993.

Daniel, Clifton, ed., *Chronicle of the 20th Century* (Mt. Kisco, NY: Chronicle Publications), 1987.

Dark, Alvin and John Underwood, *When in Doubt, Fire the Manager* (New York: E. P. Dutton), 1980.

Deutsch, Jordan A. with Richard M. Cohen, Roland T. Johnson, and David S. Neft, *The Scrapbook History of Baseball*, (Indianapolis: Bobbs-Merrill), 1975.

Devaney, John, *Where Are They Today?* (New York: Crown), 1985.

Drysdale, Don with Bob Verdi, *Once a Bum, Always a Dodger* (New York: St. Martin's), 1990.

Durocher, Leo with Ed Linn, *Nice Guys Finish Last* (New York: Simon and Schuster), 1975.

Duxbury, John, ed., *1969 Baseball Register* (St. Louis: The Sporting News), 1969.

Einstein, Charles, *A Flag for San Francisco* (New York: Simon and Schuster), 1962.

_____, *Willie Mays: Coast to Coast Giant* (New York: G.P. Putnam's Sons), 1963.

_____, *Willie's Time* (New York: Berkeley), 1979.

Eskenazi, Gerald, *The Lip: A Biography of Leo Durocher*, (New York: William Morrow), 1993.

Fiffer, Steve, *Speed*, (Alexandria, VA: Redefinition), 1990.

Finch, Frank, *The Los Angeles Dodgers: The First 25 Years* (Virginia Beach, VA: Jordan and Company), 1977.

Fisher, Roy M., ed., *The World Book Yearbook 1963* (Chicago: Field Enterprises Educational Corporation), 1963.

Fox, Larry, *Little Men in Sports* (New York: Tempo), 1968.

Gewecke, Cliff, *Day by Day in Dodgers History* (New York: Leisure Press), 1984.

Gilbert, Bob and Gary Theroux, *The Top Ten* (New York: Fireside), 1982.

Hano, Arnold, *Willie Mays* (New York: Tempo), 1970.

Hirshberg, Al, *Frank Howard: The Gentle Giant* (New York: G.P. Putnam's Sons), 1973.

Hodges, Russ and Al Hirshberg, *My Giants* (New York: Doubleday), 1963.

Holmes, Tommy, *Baseball's Greatest Teams: The Dodgers* (New York: Rutledge), 1975.

Honig, Donald, *The All-Star Game*, (St. Louis: The Sporting News), 1987.

_____, *The Man in the Dugout*, (Chicago: Follett), 1977.

_____, *1961: The Year That Was*, (New York: Bantam), 1989.

Hynd, Noel, *The Giants of the Polo Grounds*, (New York: Doubleday), 1988.

James, Bill, *The Baseball Book 1990* (New York: Villard), 1990.

Kaplan, Jim, *The Fielders*, (Alexandria, VA: Redefinition), 1989.

_____, *Baseball's Greatest Dynasties: The Giants* (New York: Gallery), 1991.

Kiersh, Edwin, *Where Have You Gone, Vince DiMaggio?* (New York: Bantam), 1983.

King, Joe, *The San Francisco Giants* (Englewood Cliffs, NJ: Prentice-Hall), 1958.

Koppett, Leonard, *The Man in the Dugout,* (New York: Crown), 1993.

Koufax, Sandy with Ed Linn, *Koufax* (New York: Viking), 1966.

Levine, Peter, *Ellis Island to Ebbets Field* (New York: Oxford University Press), 1992.

Makower, Joel, *Boom! Talkin' About Our Generation* (Chicago: Contemporary), 1985.

Mandel, Mike, *The San Francisco Giants: An Oral History* (Santa Cruz, CA: Clatworthy), 1979.

Marichal, Juan with Charles Einstein, *A Pitcher's Story* (Garden City, NY: Doubleday), 1967.

Marsh, Irving T. and Edward Ehre, eds., *Best Sports Stories 1963: A Panorama of the 1962 Sports Year* (New York: E.P. Dutton), 1963.

Mays, Willie and Charles Einstein, *Willie Mays: My Life In and Out of Baseball* (Greenwich, CT: Fawcett-Crest), 1973.

_____ and Lou Sahadi, *Say Hey* (New York: Pocket Books), 1989.

McDonald, Jack, *Something to Cheer About* (San Diego: Harcourt Brace Jovanovich), 1986.

Mead, William, *The Explosive Sixties,* (Alexandria, VA: Redefinition), 1989.

Miller, Richard, *Bohemia: The Protoculture Then and Now* (Chicago: Nelson-Hall), 1977.

Mitchell, Jerry, *The Amazing Mets* (New York: Grosset and Dunlap), 1965.

Mote, James, *Everything Baseball* (New York: Prentice-Hall), 1989.

Murray, Jim, *The Best of Jim Murray*, (Garden City, NY: Doubleday), 1965.

_____, *Jim Murray: The Autobiography of the Pulitzer Prize Winning Sports Columnist*, (New York: Macmillan), 1993.

Neft, David S. and Richard M. Cohen, *The Sports Encyclopedia: Baseball* (New York: St. Martin's), 1990.

_____, *The World Series*, (New York: St. Martin's), 1990.

Newhan, Ross, *The California Angels* (New York: Simon and Schuster), 1982.

Oiseth, Ed, *Giant Orange and Dodger Blue: Where Were You in '62?* (Magalia, CA: Dungeon Printing), 1989.

Oleksak, Michael M. and Mary Adams Oleksak, *Beisbol: Latin Americans and the Grand Old Game* (Grand Rapids, MI: Masters Press), 1991.

Parrott, Harold, *The Lords of Baseball* (New York: Praeger), 1976.

Pepe, Phil, *No-Hitter* (New York: Four Winds Press), 1968.

Perry, Gaylord and Bob Sudyk, *Me and the Spitter* (New York: Signet), 1974.

Peters, Nick, *San Francisco Giants Almanac* (Berkeley, CA: North Atlantic), 1988.

Reichler, Joseph and Jack Clary, *Baseball's Great Moments* (New York: Galahad), 1990.

Reidenbaugh, Lowell, *Take Me Out to the Ballpark* (St. Louis: The Sporting News), 1983.

_____, *Baseball's 25 Greatest Pennant Races* (St. Louis: The Sporting News), 1987.

Rieff, David, *Los Angeles: Capital of the Third World* (New York: Touchstone), 1992.

Robinson, Ray, ed., *Baseball Stars of 1962* (New York: Pyramid), 1962.

_____, *The Home Run Heard 'Round the World* (New York: Harper Collins), 1991.

Rogosin, Donn, *Invisible Men* (New York: Atheneum), 1983.

Roseboro, John and Bill Libby, *Glory Days with the Dodgers and Other Days with Others* (New York: Atheneum), 1978.

Rosenbaum, Art and Bob Stevens, *The Giants of San Francisco* (New York: Coward-McCann), 1963.

Russell, Patrick, *The Tommy Davis Story* (Garden City, NY: Doubleday), 1969.

Sackett, Susan, *The Hollywood Reporter Book of Box Office Hits* (New York: Billboard), 1990.

Schiffer, Don, *1963 Major League Baseball Handbook* (New York: Pocket Books), 1963.

Schlesinger, Arthur, *A Thousand Days* (New York: Greenwich House), 1983.

Schoor, Gene, *Pictorial History of the Dodgers* (New York: Leisure Press), 1984.

Shatzkin, Mike, ed., *The Ballplayers* (New York: Arbor House), 1990.

Shore, Michael and the Editors of Rolling Stone, *Rolling Stone Rock and Roll Almanac* (New York: Collier), 1983.

Smith, Myron J. Jr., *Baseball: A Comprehensive Bibliography* (Jefferson, NC: McFarland), 1986.

_____, *The Dodgers Bibliography* (Westport, CT: Meckler), 1988.

Snider, Duke with Bill Gilbert, *The Duke of Flatbush* (New York: Zebra), 1988.

Spink, C.C.Johnson with Paul A. Rickhart, and Clifford Kachline, *Official Baseball Guide for 1963* (St. Louis: Spink), 1963.

Steinberg, Cobbett, *TV Facts* (New York: Facts on File), 1980.

Stern, Jane and Michael Stern, *Sixties People* (New York: Alfred A. Knopf), 1990.

Sullivan, Neil, *The Dodgers Move West* (New York: Oxford University Press), 1987.

_____, *The Diamond Revolution* (New York: St. Martin's), 1992.

Thorn, John and Peter Palmer, *Total Baseball* (New York: Warner), 1991.

Tullius, John, *I'd Rather Be a Yankee,* (New York: Macmillan), 1986.

Whitburn, Joel, *The Billboard Book of Top 40 Hits* (New York: Billboard), 1985.

Whittingham, Richard, *The Los Angeles Dodgers: An Illustrated History* (New York: Harper and Row), 1982.

Wills, Maury with Steve Gardner, *It Pays to Steal* (Englewood Cliffs, NJ: Prentice-Hall), 1963.

_____with Don Freeman, *How to Steal a Pennant* (New York: G.P. Putnam's Sons), 1976.

_____ and Mike Celizic, *On the Run* (New York: Carroll and Graf), 1991.

Winokur, Jon, *The Portable Curmudgeon,* (New York: New American Library), 1987.

Wise, Bill, *1963 Baseball Almanac* (New York: Golden Press), 1963.

_____, *1964 Baseball Almanac* (New York: Golden Press), 1964.

Wolff, Rick, ed., *The Baseball Encyclopedia Eighth Edition* (New York: Macmillan), 1990.

MAGAZINES AND PERIODICALS

Anderson, Dave, "The Dodgers' Tommy Gun," *Baseball Digest,* (January, 1963), pp. 31-34.

_____, "A Giant Issue," *Newsweek,* (August 17, 1964), p. 54.

Bavasi, Buzzie with Jack Olsen, "Money Makes the Player Go," *Sports Illustrated,* (May 22, 1967), pp. 45-55.

_____, "They May Have Been a Headache but They Never Were a Bore," *Sports Illustrated,* (May 29, 1967), pp. 30-44.

Bingham, Walter, "Dodgers in Mufti," *Sports Illustrated,* (July 15, 1960), pp. 69-71.

_____, "Boom! Goes Baseball," *Sports Illustrated*, (April 23, 1962), pp. 18-24.

_____, "The Race is in the West," *Sports Illustrated*, (June 4, 1962), pp. 12-17.

Boyle, Robert H., "Time of Trial for Alvin Dark," *Sports Illustrated*, (July 6, 1964), pp. 26-31.

_____, "The Latins Storm Las Grandes Ligas," *Sports Illustrated*, (August 9, 1965), pp. 24-30.

Brody, Tom C., "A Miller-Hiller-Haller-Holler-lujah Twist," *Sports Illustrated*, (September 17, 1962), pp. 24-25.

_____, "Snake-Sliding Dodger Tries to Steal the Pennant," *Sports Illustrated*, (October 1, 1962), pp. 22-23.

_____, "A Giant Shot That Forced a Playoff," *Sports Illustrated*, (October 8, 1962), p. 19.

Brown, Joe David, "The San Francisco Myth," *Sports Illustrated*, (January 15, 1962), pp. 51-58.

Bryson, Bill, "Maury Wills Fooled by 'Frisco Whirl," *Baseball Digest*, (April, 1963), pp. 65-68.

Cantwell, Robert, "Leo: Under the Sunset Sun," *Sports Illustrated*, (February 18, 1963), pp. 20-24.

Cohane, Tim, "Alvin Dark, Manager with a Giant Job," *Look*, (May 8, 1962), pp. 77-82.

_____, "Orlando Cepeda: Can He Slug His Way Out of the Doghouse?", *Look*, (May 21, 1963), pp. 84-88.

Cohen, Haskell, ed., "Clubhouse Unrest...or Why the Dodgers Blew the Pennant," *Willie Mays Baseball*, (April, 1963), pp. 28-33.

Cope, Myron, "Closeup of Orlando Cepeda," *Sport*, (April, 1962), pp. 60-68.

_____, "Dodger Hot Seat," *Sport*, (July, 1962), pp. 26-28.

Creamer, Robert, "An Urgent Matter of One Index Finger," *Sports Illustrated*, (March 4, 1963), pp. 20-25.

_____, "The Trouble with Walter," *Sports Illustrated*, (May 13, 1963), p. 54.

_____, "Big Willie's Private War with Cousin Don," *Sports Illustrated*, (July 1, 1963), pp. 38-39.

_____, "Crossing the Delaware with Alvin Dark," *Sports Illustrated*, (July 16, 1963), pp. 46-48.

_____, "The Night the Dodgers Got the Monkey Off Their Back," *Sports Illustrated*, (September 9, 1963), pp. 70-72.

Dexter, Charles, "The Series' Biggest Thrill," *Baseball Digest*, (October-November, 1962), pp. 17-22.

Durocher, Leo with Ed Linn, "Candid Memories," *Saturday Evening Post*, (May 11, 1963), pp. 27-28.

Durslag, Melvin, "Baseball at Chavez Ravine," *TV Guide*, (August 18, 1962), pp. 4-5.

_____, "Frank Howard: Monster in Right Field," *Baseball Digest*, (October-November, 1962), pp. 75-77.

_____, "Koufax and the Reynaud Phenomenon," *Baseball Digest*, (April, 1963), pp. 39-41.

_____, "Walter Alston: Manager With a Hair Shirt," *Look*, (July 30, 1963), pp. 64-70.

Einstein, Charles, "The Stu Miller Mystery," *Sport*, (December, 1961), pp. 58-59.

_____, "Alou, Alou," *Sport*, (September, 1962), pp. 24-25.

_____, "The Willie Mays I Know," *Sport*, (October, 1962), pp. 18-21.

_____, "The Juan Marichal Mystery," *Sport*, (June, 1963), pp. 48-51.

Fimrite, Ron, "The Heart of a Giant," *Sports Illustrated Classic*, (Fall, 1991), pp. 59-64.

Furlong, Bill, "Behind the Scenes in the Maury Wills Record Race," *Sport*, (October, 1962), pp. 59-61.

Gelman, Steve, "Don Drysdale's Inner War," *Sport*, (September, 1962), pp. 56-71.

_____, "Giant-Sized Trouble," *Time*, (August 14, 1964), pp. 44-45.

Grieve, Curley, "Stu Miller: Muscles for a Killer Moth," *Baseball Digest*, (May, 1962), pp. 71-73.

Hano, Arnold, "Tommy Davis: Clutch Hitter," *Sport*, (November, 1962), pp. 55-59.

_____, "The High-Octane Confidence of Willie Davis," *Sport*, (December, 1962), pp. 18-19.

_____, "World Series Confidential: The Loser's Tension and Torment," *Sport*, (January, 1963), pp. 10-11.

_____, "Will Dissension Destroy the Dodgers?," *Sport*, (March, 1963), pp. 33-35.

_____, "Willie Mays: His Loneliness and Fulfillment," *Sport*, (August, 1963), pp. 12-15.

Herskowitz, Mickey, "The Unheralded Dodger," *Sport*, (September, 1964), pp. 44-45.

Holtzman, Jerome, "What Yanks, Giants Did Wrong — and Right," *Baseball Digest*, (January, 1963), pp. 15-28.

Horn, Huston, "Ex-Bad Boy's Big Year," *Sports Illustrated*, (August 30, 1962), pp. 24-26.

_____, "It's the Yankees vs. the West," *Sports Illustrated*, (October 1, 1962), pp. 20-23.

Jupiter, Harry, "Shortstop with the Greatest Range," *Baseball Digest*, (June, 1963), pp. 23-27.

_____, "Even His Catcher Doesn't Know What's Coming!," *Baseball Digest*, (August, 1963), pp. 21-26.

Katz, Fred, "Jim Davenport's Desire," *Sport*, (November, 1962), pp. 32-34.

Kiersh, Edward, "The Boys of October," *San Francisco Magazine*, (August, 1982), pp. 100-106.

Koppett, Leonard, "How the Managers Figure," *Baseball Digest*, (January, 1963), pp. 55-56.

Leggett, William, "L.A.'s Swift Set Sprints to the Top," *Sports Illustrated*, (June 25, 1962), pp. 26-27.

Libby, Bill, "Jack Sanford's Grim World," *Sport*, (March, 1963), pp. 26-28.

_____, "The Ten Years of Johnny Podres," *Sport*, (August, 1963), pp. 38-41.

_____, "The Sophistication of Sandy Koufax," *Sport*, (September, 1963), pp. 60-75.

Mann, Jack, "Gilliam Brings Three Gloves and Waits Around," *Sport*, (January, 1963), pp. 34-36.

_____, "The King of the Jungle," *Sports Illustrated*, (July 18, 1966), pp. 115-134.

Maule, Tex, "The Return of Durocher," *Sports Illustrated*, (March 6, 1961), pp. 16-19.

_____, "The Giants Get Happy," *Sports Illustrated*, (May 22, 1961), pp. 22-25.

Mays, Willie as told to Charles Einstein, "How We Stole the Pennant," *Sport*, (February, 1963), pp. 18-20.

McGee, James K., "Willie Mays," *San Francisco Giants Silver Anniversary Yearbook 1958-82*, (1982), pp. 18-21.

Moss, Morton, "Dodger Flair for Flingers Remains, But Power?," *Baseball Digest*, (July, 1962), pp. 28-29.

Olsen, Jack, "The Very Best Act in Town," *Sports Illustrated*, (July 29, 1963), pp. 20-22.

Schumacher, Garry, ed., *San Francisco Giants 1963 Yearbook*, (1963), pp. 6-44.

Seeberg, Tom, ed., *Los Angeles Dodgers 1963 Souvenir Yearbook*, (1963), pp. 6-43.

Stainback, Berry and Fred Katz, "The New Breed: Larry Sherry, Career Reliever," *Sport*, (May, 1962), pp. 44-45.

Stevens, Bob, "The 1962 Giants," *San Francisco Giants Silver Anniversary Yearbook 1958-82*, (1982), pp. 11-13.

Stump, Al, "Juan Marichal: Behind His Success," *Sport*, (September, 1964), pp. 65-70.

Terrell, Roy, "The Pitchers Stand and Fight," *Sports Illustrated*, (October 15, 1962), pp. 16-20.

Veeck, Bill with Ed Linn, "For He's a Jolly Good Fellow," *Sports Illustrated*, (May 31, 1965), pp. 51-62.

Walker, Eric, "The Giants-Dodgers Rivalry," *San Francisco Giants Silver Anniversary Yearbook 1958-82*, (1982), pp. 36-37.

Walter, Bucky, "The Move West," *San Francisco Giants Silver Anniversary Yearbook 1958-82*, (1982), pp. 4-5.

Westcott, Rich, "Do You Remember Alvin Dark?," *Baseball Hobby News*, (July, 1991), pp. 89-91.

Wills, Maury, "The Great Stealer Tells Some Secrets." *Life*, (September 28, 1962), pp. 50-52.

_____, as told to Al Hirshberg, "How I Made Myself a Ballplayer," *Sport*, (June, 1963), pp. 12-13.

Young, Dick, "San Francisco Loves Cepeda," *Sport*, (November, 1959), pp. 28-29.

NEWSPAPERS

Arizona Republic (1987)
Los Angeles Times (1962)
New York Times (1962)
Phoenix Gazette (1987)
San Francisco Chronicle (1962)
The Sporting News (1962)

FILMS ON VIDEO

Bodziner, Bob and Jeff Kuiper, producers, *A Giants History: The Tale of Two Cities*, Major League Baseball Productions, 1987.

Edwards, Blake, director, *Experiment in Terror*, Columbia Pictures, 1962.

Fonseca, Lew, director, *1962 World Series: New York Yankees vs. San Francisco Giants*, The National and American Leagues of Professional Baseball, 1963.

Mooney, Sean and Helen Ruddick, producers, *Dodger Stadium: The First 25 Years*, Major League Baseball Productions, 1987.

Roy, George, producer, *A Team For All Time—The Dodgers*, Black Canyon Productions, 1990.

Wolfson, Mark, producer, *The Blue of '62*, KTTV-Channel 11, Fox Television, Los Angeles, 1987.

INDEX